Life after Ruin

Following the 1948 War, the landscape of Israel-Palestine was radically transformed. Breaking from conventional focus on explicit sites of violence and devastation, Noam Leshem turns critical attention to 'ordinary' spaces and places where the intricate and often intimate engagements between Jews and myriad Arab spaces take place to this day. Leshem builds on interdisciplinary studies of space, memory, architecture and history and exposes a rich archive of ideology, culture, political projects of state-building and identity formation. The result is a fresh look at the conflicted history of Israel-Palestine: a spatial history in which the Arab past isn't in fact separate, but is inextricably linked to the Israeli present.

NOAM LESHEM is a Lecturer in the Department of Geography at Durham University. He has previously taught at Royal Holloway and Birkbeck, University of London. His research is primarily concerned with the intersection of spatial, political and cultural history.

Cambridge Middle East Studies

Editorial Board

Charles Tripp (general editor)
Julia Clancy-Smith
F. Gregory Gause
Yezid Sayigh
Avi Shlaim
Judith E. Tucker

Cambridge Middle East Studies has been established to publish books on the nineteenth to twenty-first-century Middle East and North Africa. The series offers new and original interpretations of aspects of Middle Eastern societies and their histories. To achieve disciplinary diversity, books are solicited from authors writing in a wide range of fields including history, sociology, anthropology, political science and political economy. The emphasis is on producing books affording an original approach along theoretical and empirical lines. The series is intended for students and academics, but the more accessible and wide-ranging studies will also appeal to the interested general reader.

A list of books in the series can be found after the index.

Life After Ruin

The Struggles Over Israel's Depopulated Arab Spaces

Noam Leshem

CAMBRIDGE
UNIVERSITY PRESS

CAMBRIDGE
UNIVERSITY PRESS

University Printing House, Cambridge CB2 8BS, United Kingdom

Cambridge University Press is part of the University of Cambridge.

It furthers the University's mission by disseminating knowledge in the pursuit of education, learning and research at the highest international levels of excellence.

www.cambridge.org
Information on this title: www.cambridge.org/9781107149472

© Noam Leshem 2017

First published 2017

Printed in the United States of America by Sheridan Books, Inc.

A catalogue record for this publication is available from the British Library

Library of Congress Cataloging-in-Publication data
Names: Leshem, Noam, author.
Title: Life after ruin : the struggles over Israel's depopulated Arab spaces / Noam Leshem.
Description: Cambridge; New York : Cambridge University Press, [2017] | Series: Cambridge Middle East studies; volume 48 | Includes bibliographical references and index.
Identifiers: LCCN 2016026757 | ISBN 9781107149472 (hardback)
Subjects: LCSH: Kefar Shalem (Tel Aviv, Israel)–History. | Urban renewal–Israel–Tel Aviv–History–20th century. | Palestinian Arabs–Israel–Tel Aviv–History–20th century. | Tel Aviv (Israel)–Ethnic relations. | Israel-Arab War, 1948–1949–Social aspects.
Classification: LCC DS110.T36 K465 2016 | DDC 956.94/8–dc23
LC record available at https://lccn.loc.gov/2016026757

ISBN 978-1-107-14947-2 Hardback

Contents

Figures

Acknowledgements

This book evolved over the years through numerous conversations, arguments and correspondences. I have learnt a great deal from all those who were generous enough to share thoughts, ask questions and suggest possibilities. They all helped shape this project, directly or indirectly.

I am deeply indebted to Anthony Julius for his uncompromising intellectual sincerity, critical judgement and unwavering support and encouragement. I am also thankful to Louise Bethlehem for years of open and challenging dialogue, for her intellectual hospitality and long-lasting belief in this project. I am fortunate to be their student.

I am grateful for the loving support and encouragement of my family and friends, and to Aramit Lotem for her empathy and wisdom. This project has greatly benefitted from the support and assistance of the London Consortium. The intellectual community of my colleagues and the challenges posed by faculty members have contributed significantly to the development of my thinking. I have had the privilege to work with great colleagues at Royal Holloway University of London and Durham University – I admire their dedication and friendship. Hannan Hever and Ilana Pardes posed crucial questions many years ago, which actually launched this project, and for that I am very grateful.

Special thanks goes to Adi Ophir, Ariella Azoulay, Alon Confino, Jay Winter, Susan Slyomovics and Joachim Schloer, who have asked challenging questions and contributed their views at various stages of this project. Ayala Ronel has generously shared her practical experience and knowledge of planning in Israel, a perspective that has added a crucial element of sober reality to my reflections. I will never forget that I owe her my very first visit to Salama. A special thank you goes to Matthew Gandy for his enthusiasm and generosity, and to Charles Tripp for his kind encouragement.

My editor Maria Marsh at Cambridge University Press, and the entire editorial team have helped realise this project into a book – their help and expertise were invaluable. The comments and helpful suggestions of Cambridge's anonymous reviewers did much to improve the manuscript and help sharpen my argument.

Lauren Wright provided me with endless support, patience and wisdom. I cherish our ongoing conversation about words and worlds – I couldn't have wished for a better companion on this journey.

This project would not have been possible without the generosity, kindness and cooperation of the women and men of Kfar Shalem, who opened their homes and shared their stories. Their tenacity and resolve reminded me time and again that there is indeed life after ruin.

Research for the book was generously supported by the London Consortium, the Wingate Foundation, the Anglo-Jewish Association, the British Society for Middle East Research, the Council for British Research in the Levant and the University of London Central Research Fund.

Introduction: Tracing Ruination

There is no single moment from which a history of ruination in the Arab-Palestinian village of Salama can commence. Rather, it begins with a trickle, shortly after the United Nations General Assembly approved the partition of Mandatory Palestine on 29 November 1947. Violent incidents were recorded during the first days of December in Haifa, Jerusalem and in the neighbourhoods dividing Jaffa and Tel Aviv. Salama,[1] the largest non-urban Arab settlement in Palestine, became a frontier almost overnight: only a few hundred metres divide the western houses of the village from the eastern perimeter of Shekhunat Hatikva, a Jewish neighbourhood situated between Salama and the city of Tel Aviv. Arab irregulars used Salama, as well as other villages, to initiate assaults on Jewish neighbourhoods or vehicles, mostly in the form of sniper attacks.[2] At the same time, Jewish forces formed a line of military outposts in the outskirts of Jewish neighbourhoods throughout the country. These lines of partition, which were to separate the Arab and Jewish communities, would become the zones of violent friction that left a persistent mark of destruction long after the last gun-shots were fired.

However, the eruption of violence did not occur in spite of the international community's formula for territorial division, but rather because of it. The Partition Plan, which was officially outlined in UN General Assembly Resolution 181, divided Palestine into what was described in the resolution as "Independent Arab and Jewish States". A brief look at the map of the plan reveals, however, quite a different spatial reality: the partition was not between two contiguous territories, but between concentrations of Arab and Jewish populations. This logic meant that Mandatory Palestine was to be dissected and segmented into seven sub-regions – three were to form the Jewish state, three designated for the

---

[1] In Arabic: سلمة, and pronounced Salameh. There are several transcriptions of the name in English, and the transcription used here follows the one used by the Beir Zeit University's Village Archive.
[2] Morris, *Righteous Victims*, 194.

1

Arab state and Jerusalem was to remain an international zone. However, if the division of the entire territory formed a fragmented collection of ethnically differentiated sub-regions, in itself an ambitious endeavour with highly uncertain prospects, the assignment of Jaffa as an Arab enclave at the heart of the Jewish territory required the plan's designers to chart the borders of this area according to the smallest of scales:

The area of the Arab enclave of Jaffa consists of that part of the town-planning area of Jaffa which lies to the west of the Jewish quarters lying south of Tel Aviv, to the west of the continuation of Herzl street up to its junction with the Jaffa-Jerusalem road, to the south-west of the section of the Jaffa-Jerusalem road lying south-east of that junction, to the west of Miqve Yisrael lands, to the northwest of Holon local council area, to the north of the line linking up the north-west corner of Holon with the northeast corner of Bat Yam local council area and to the north of Bat Yam local council area.[3]

With street corners and city junctions becoming border zones almost overnight, the deterioration that followed was hardly surprising. From the first days of December 1947, Salama became part of the south-east frontier of the Tel Aviv and Jaffa region: on 4 December, a Haganah force was sent to take over an abandoned house on the outskirts of Salama, from which they could establish an observation point over a new road that bypassed the village. The force came under gunfire from Salama, which drew in response heavy fire from the 53rd Haganah Battalion and a local Jewish police force that were positioned in Shekhunat Hatikva.[4] The following day events continued to escalate, with heavy fire exchanged across the narrow strip of orchards that separated the warring parties. On 7 December, the Haganah ordered a "retaliation act" and several houses were blown up.[5] This act provided the incentive for what historian Benny Morris describes as "the first, armed attack on a Jewish urban neighbourhood" in the 1948 War:

The following day [8 December] hundreds of Arab irregulars, led by Hassan Salama, launched a frontal assault in an attempt to conquer [Shekhunat] Hatikva. A few of the quarter's peripheral houses fell as British troops looked on without interfering. The Arabs began looting and torching houses. Haganah reinforcements arrived … The attackers were pushed back to Salame. About 60 Arabs and 2 Jews were killed, and after the battle, a British officer returned a baby the Arabs had found and abducted.[6]

It is hard to read through this violent chronology and see beyond mutual bloodletting. But what these events signify is a unique focus, banal as it

---

[3] United Nations, *Resolution 181*, 145–6.
[4] Milshtain, *The War of Independence*, vol. 2: 56; Elon, *The Givati Brigade*, 79–80.
[5] Milshtain, *The War of Independence*, vol. 2: 59; Elon, *The Givati Brigade*, 81–2.
[6] Morris, *Righteous Victims*, 194.

may seem: both Arab and Jewish forces aim their military efforts not only at the other's body but at the other's house. While this proved to be a significant element, at least in the first stages of the war, it did not result in the wholesale destruction of neighbourhoods and villages. Instead, these acts constituted "spatial statements" that would address an unspoken warning. The destruction of Arab houses and buildings was formulated by the Haganah General Staff in a detailed fashion in "Plan Gimel" of May 1946, which specified that retaliatory action will be taken

against villages, neighbourhoods and farms, serving as bases for Arab armed forces ... by arson or explosion. If the aim was general punishment – the torching of everything possible and the demolition of the houses of inciters or accomplices [was to be carried out].[7]

The houses that were blown up or torched in December 1947 were not the last. Far more explicitly "didactic" orders were issued ahead of "Operation Joshua", a retaliation operation planned to take place in Salama on New Year's Eve of 1948:

The villagers do not express opposition to the actions of the gangs and many of the youth even provide [the irregulars with] active cooperation ... the aim is to attack the northern part of the village ... to cause deaths, to blow up houses and to burn everything possible.[8]

These statements of destruction were clearly heard. Only two days after the violence between Salama and Shekhunat Hatikva began, on 6 December 1947, women and children from the Arab village were evacuated to the towns of Lydda and Ramlah, at the same time as residents from the Jewish neighbourhood sought refuge in Tel Aviv. Indeed, most of the residents of the friction zones in the Jaffa and Tel Aviv area fled their homes in the first two months of the fighting: on the Arab side, residents from El Manshiya, Jabaliya, Abu Kabir and Tel a-Rish fled to Jaffa[9]; Jewish residents from Kerem Hateymanim and Neve Tsedek left their homes and moved away from the frontlines, mostly remaining in Tel Aviv. During the first two months of the war, it is estimated that 15,000–20,000 Arab-Palestinians fled the city and approximately 7,000 Jewish residents left their homes by mid-January 1948.[10] Beyond the growing human cost, the fighting began to make an apparent mark on the face of the city. Although in most cases fighting in the first period

---

[7] Morris, *Birth of the Palestinian Refugee Problem Revisited*, 343.

[8] Quoted ibid.

[9] The situation in the Arab-Palestinian villages in north-west Tel Aviv (Jammasin, Summeil and Sheik Muanis) was somewhat different, as they were relatively small enclaves in the midst of a large Jewish population. Summeil and Jammasin began evacuating in early December after attacks initiated by Jewish paramilitary organisations. Golan, *Wartime Spatial Changes*, 76; 79; 80–3.

[10] Ibid., 78.

of the war (December 1947–June 1948) did not result in widespread damage to the urban environment, a "destruction strip" that outlined the boundary between Jewish and Arab neighbourhoods was gradually created. Buildings on both sides functioned as an urban trench-line and bore the clearest signs of damage; beyond this strip, however, most houses and buildings remained unharmed.[11] Destruction strips of this sort marked the boundaries between Jebalya and Bat Yam, Tel a-Rish and Holon, Manshiya and the south-western neighbourhoods of Tel Aviv, as well as between Salama and Shekhunat Hatikva.

The static warfare characteristic of the first months of the war reached its decisive moments in April 1948, as the final days of the British mandate were drawing near. The city of Jaffa, at this point already besieged by Jewish forces and in a state of almost total disarray, was not to be included in "Plan Dalet", a broad operation drafted by the Haganah on 10 March to secure solid military control over territory designated to be part of the future Jewish state.[12] Salama, however, along with the rest of the Arab periphery of Tel Aviv, gained primary strategic importance in ensuring the complete isolation of Jaffa, and consequently, its downfall. The operation was carried out by the Alexandroni Brigade as part of the *Hametz*[13] military operation on 28–30 April.[14] According to the offensive plan, Salama was the last target of the operation and was therefore entered by the 32nd Battalion on 29 April; by that time, the village was completely deserted as the last of its Arab inhabitants – approximately 4,000 out of more than 7,000 before the fighting commenced[15] – fled[16] on 25 April. When

[11] David Tal's analysis of the fighting in the urban regions during what he describes as the Communal War that lasted from December 1947 to June 1948, clarifies that this was characteristic of all urban regions in Palestine. Tal, *War in Palestine, 1948*, 64.

[12] Dinur, Slutsky and Avigur, *History of the Haganah*, vol. 3: 1955.

[13] The name of the operation, *Hametz*, is borrowed from the traditional Jewish term designating the foods containing flour that are prohibited during the Passover period. These foods are traditionally gathered, removed from the house and, at times, a ceremonial burning of the *Hametz* takes place, symbolising the purification of the house. The Alexandroni Brigade's website states that the name for the operation was chosen to exemplify its directives: symbolically "burning the *Hametz* before Passover 1948" ("Operation 'Hametz'").

[14] Gelber, *Palestine, 1948*, 94; Morris, *Birth of the Palestinian Refugee Problem Revisited*, 217.

[15] Golan, *Wartime Spatial Changes*, 87.

[16] It is unclear what led to the desertion of the village. As Morris explains, the divisions between flight that occurred as a result of the influence of a nearby town's fall, fear of being caught up in fighting, or a direct military assault on a settlement, "are somewhat blurred" (2004, xvi). On 25 April the IZL began its assault on Jaffa's northern Manshiya quarter (Gelber, *Palestine, 1948*, 94; Morris, *Birth of the Palestinian Refugee Problem Revisited*, 212–14). This operation must have had an effect on the remaining residents of Salama, as did the harsh conditions in Jaffa itself, on which Salama was dependent politically, economically and socially (Ibid., 591).

David Ben-Gurion visited Salama on the eve of 30 April, he encountered "only one old blind woman".[17]

Despite Salama's complete depopulation, it was hard to ignore all
that remained: apart from the damage caused to some of the houses,
most stood unharmed; the mosque that formed the heart of the village
– Masjid Salama – remained intact, as did the village's two cemeteries;
the schools, cafés and shops that were located along the main roads
were there, just as they were left.

The houses of Salama stood empty for 18 days, but emptiness did
not equal indifference or disappearance from sight. Only one day after
the completion of the military activity in the village, on 1 May, a Jewish
group from Shekhunat Hatikva looted houses in Salama and then set
them on fire. Without their inhabitants, these houses were an accessible target, penetrable and easily damaged. However, torching the Arab
houses after looting them meant that in the eyes of the perpetrators,
these were not merely neutral objects, but sites that still retained the
potential of an Arab return. Emptiness was not enough to alleviate fear
or defuse animosity; ruination was needed for this emptiness to become
permanent. Furthermore, this violence relied on the identification of
these houses as conspicuously Arab signs, which were not erased or
made insignificant by the absence of their owners; as Kathleen Stewart
has noted in another context, signs of local life are "written tentatively
yet persistently onto the landscape".[18] This lingering of meaning in
space will motivate recurring efforts of ruination in Salama, though
the justification for their execution will change to suit the political and
ideological conventions of the times.

However, vengeance and hostility were almost simultaneously
accompanied by curiosity, drawing dozens of residents from Shekhunat
Hatikva to walk the short distance to the neighbouring village. A photograph taken shortly after the conquest of Salama (Figure 0.1) captures
people strolling between the Jewish neighbourhood – seen on the horizon – and the depopulated Arab village. What was described in the
Jewish papers of the time as a "murderers' village" was suddenly an
intriguing place, safe enough so that on the lower-right corner a woman
is seen pushing a white baby pram accompanied by a man carrying a
young child in his arms, while another family walks closely behind. At
the centre of the photograph, two men are leisurely walking their bicy-
cles. At the same time, first signs of the administration and management of space also begin to appear: houses that have been examined by

[17] Ben-Gurion, *The War Diary*.
[18] Stewart, *A Space on the Side of the Road*, 17.

Figure 0.1 Salama, shortly after the Israeli occupation, probably early May 1948.
Photographer: Zoltan Kruger, Israel National Archive.

bomb-defusion squads are marked as safe; the words "Jewish home" appear on houses that will be allocated by the authorities to Jewish war refugees and immigrants shortly thereafter. Literally and symbolically, the writing on the wall anticipated the filling of the physical voids left by the Arab population, but it would take more than graffiti to transform Salama into Kfar Shalem, the Jewish neighbourhood established in the village after the war.

In the years that followed, vast and diverse efforts were invested in completing this transformation from Arab to Jewish space. The settling of Jews in the empty Arab houses was followed by new construction, new histories and new routines that piled up on top of the Arab village, ostensibly leaving the events of 1948 behind.

Yet more than 50 years later, on the night of 9 October 2000, in the first days of the second Palestinian Intifada (uprising) – which sparked violent incidents throughout Israel, the West Bank and the Gaza Strip – the Arab history of Salama reappeared. Armed with metal bars and hammers, a group of residents from Kfar Shalem and adjacent neighbourhoods began tearing down one of the walls of the empty building of Salama Mosque. Despite the fact the mosque had not been used for

Muslim religious purposes since the village's seizure, and although it had served as a community youth club until the early 1980s, the building continued to bear the troubling past of its Arab existence. For those who set out to bring down the mosque, the Arab village of Salama was neither erased nor forgotten.

The unsettled presence of an empty building that attracts such fierce and violent emotions illustrates the fractious and fractured flow of spatial history, in Salama/Kfar Shalem and throughout Israel-Palestine. In the time that passed from the torching of empty houses in May 1948 to the battering of the walls of the Salama Mosque in October 2000, a web of intricate relations between people and space was formed and transformed: alienation made way for intimacy, ruins were rebuilt and demolished again, one antagonism was replaced by others. Yet all took place, as it were, through spatial forms and imaginations, which added their marks to create an unsettled heterogeneity of relations and existences, one that always walks the thin line between the mundane and the explosive.

Emptiness and ruination play a central role in shaping Salama's transformation into the Jewish neighbourhood of Kfar Shalem from the very first days of the 1948 War to the present. This ongoing reshaping of the physical landscape and the re-inscription of its cultural and historical meaning indicates that spatial transformation never takes place uninterruptedly, but constantly encounters forces that seek to conserve and uphold. This tension – at times implicit and at times bluntly evident – resulted in the exceptional perseverance of Salama as a unique space in the midst Tel Aviv's sprawling suburbs. Closely following its evolution redirects our attention from piles of debris and ruined landscapes to all that is still there, to its challenging meaning, and to the significance it has for the people who call it their home.

1   Toward a Spatial History in Israel

"Erasure" and "spatial annihilation" are common tropes used to describe the radical transformation of the Arab landscapes seized by Israel in the 1948 War. The Israeli space is indeed strewn with ruins, ancient and more recent, outcomes of ethnic and national antagonism, mutual exclusion and trenchant sectarianism. Despite the prevalence of rubble and debris, this book breaks from conventional focus on explicit sites of violence and devastation. Instead, it begins with a question: why is so much still there? This question resonates throughout this research, which forms an exploration of spatial transformation and resilience in Israel. It centres on the spatial history of Salama, an Arab village in the eastern outskirts of Jaffa, which was depopulated and transformed into a Jewish neighbourhood yet continues to retain many of its former Arab features. From this humble, working class suburb the book sets out to interrogate the ambivalent negotiation that characterises the intricate and often intimate engagements between Jews and the myriad of Arab spaces they inhabit, move through, and encounter throughout Israel, shedding light on the subtle process through which people, as it were, "take place".

When the question of spatial resilience was first posited to me over a decade ago, I struggled to come up with a convincing answer. Paradoxically, it was easier to chart a history of destruction and erasure than make sense of the presence of the past. The difficulty of the problem lies in its simplicity, in the fact that its referents were blatantly obvious: when referring to my neighbourhood in Jerusalem, I used its common Arab name, "Baq'a", not the Hebrew "Geulim"; some of my friends (those who could afford it, that is) lived in "Arab houses" with high ceilings, arched windows and painted floor tiles; at the entrance to my childhood village in the north of Israel stood a large structure that served as an Arab roadside inn in the pre-state era and was later used as a poultry factory. The examples go on and on. My bewilderment came about not because all this was suddenly revealed, but because it is intimately familiar, implanted in contemporary Hebrew vocabulary and in one's orientation around town, in the memories of school trips and in books that are included in compulsory school curricula. The traces of the Arab past have become an inseparable part of the Israeli present, so much so that their mundane and commonplace presence is discarded as insignificant, a matter of fact.

But this is far from obvious. From the mid-1980s, a growing number of scholars began interrogating the political and ideological forces that shape processes of spatial transformation in Israel. The opening of official Israeli archives in the late 1970s enabled a critical scholarly scrutiny of the dominant narratives about the 1948 War and the events that surrounded the establishment of the State of Israel.[1] It exposed the heavy price paid by the Arab-Palestinian population, many of whom were forced to flee their homes and denied the right to return once the hostilities were over; it examined the mechanisms that were put in place by the state to ensure its control over Arab lands seized during the war; and it illustrated how a concentrated effort was made to marginalise the Arab cultural history of the land in favour of a homogenous national space that adhered to clear ideological and political imperatives. Critical attention also turned to internal tensions within the Israeli society, the treatment of ethnic Jewish minorities and the formation of Israeli culture. Inspired by post-structuralist philosophical trends – notably postmodern and postcolonial critiques of culture, society and the modern nation-state – this debate used a broad theoretical prism to view and analyse spatial processes and phenomena.[2] As an object of scholarly inquiry, "space" was no longer confined to the empirical description of physical formations, but viewed as an essential component in the interrogation of socioeconomic, ideological and cultural forces through which human and political environments were produced.[3]

The formation of the "Israeli space" was critically interrogated by historians, sociologists, art and literary critics, though relatively few

[1] Since first emerging in academic debates and gradually entering the public realm, this critical corpus expanded beyond the historiographical debates around the 1948 War, as is indeed reflected in later stages of the book. For a review of post-Zionsit critique, see, for example: Shapira and Penslar, *Israeli Historical Revisionism*; Nimni, *The Challenge of Post-Zionism*; Silberstein, *The Postzionism Debates*.

[2] During the 1980s, this "post-Zionist" discourse moved from a critique of the Zionist historical attitude toward the Palestinian population in and outside Israel, to a theoretical-political critique of social and cultural relations in Israel as a whole. See: Nimni, *The Challenge of Post-Zionism*, chapter 6.

[3] The Marxist spatial critique presented by scholars such as Henri Lefebvre and David Harvey were highly influential in shaping the terms of the debate, mostly from the mid-1990s onward.

geographers, mostly because of the latters' close historical relation to the Zionist establishment.[4] This critical corpus illustrated the contribution of various fields of knowledge to the evolution and preservation of a spatial logic in Israel, which was governed by a strict political and ideological agenda. Architecture and demographic patterns, literature and visual art, even leisure activity like picnics and hiking, were all understood as practices through which Israelis' consensus about space was devised and upheld. This was not an innocent "common sense",[5] but one that served specific interests and a particular relation of power. During the first decades of the state, these were predominantly the formation of a cohesive national territory in which a homogenous national community can be forged. From the late 1970s, Israel's spatial logic underwent a gradual change in correlation with the growing influence of laissez-faire capitalism on the country's political and cultural spheres. Despite its divergence from social-democratic policies that ruled the county's social and economic agenda until then, this capitalist logic was harnessed to operate hand in hand with the existing national Zionist hegemony.[6] Accelerating processes of neoliberalisation from the mid-1980s eagerly adopted the prevailing discourse of development and modernisation that characterised Zionist attitudes to spatial transformation since the late nineteenth and early twentieth century. Such are the ironies of space: the slogan "making the wasteland bloom" could appeal to socialist Zionist ideologues in the 1930s and continues to be trumpeted by present-day real-estate moguls.

As part of this critical assessment of the Israeli space, specific attention was given to the way Zionism cultivated a diametrical opposition between Jews and Arabs as two conflicting identities that cannot – and indeed, must not – meet. Through both physical and symbolic means, space was utilised to reflect this ideological premise and uphold it. Physically, depopulated Arab villages and towns were seized, appropriated and often demolished, to make way for Jewish settlements. In some cases where demolition was not carried out, Jewish immigrants were settled in Arab houses, while in other cases, emptied villages became part of natural reserves, parks and tourist attractions.

[4] Yoram Bar-Gal discusses the ideological and practical bonds between Israeli geographers and the Zionist authorities from the establishment of the Hebrew University in Jerusalem in 1925 to this day. In addition, Bar-Gal points to traditions and conventions within the discipline – from its origins in German traditions to current training methods of geography students – which enforced its conservative and conformist character. Bar-Gal, "On the Tribe-Elders, the Successors and the New Ones".

[5] On the cultural "common sense" and its relation to the concept of Hegemony, see: Lears, "The Concept of Cultural Hegemony".

[6] Ram, *The Globalization of Israel*; Kemp, Ram and Newman, *Israelis in Conflict*.

Palestinian-Arabs who remained in territory held by Israel following the 1948 War were mostly confined to peripheral villages and remained under restrictive military governance until 1966.[7] Physical and social planning mechanisms were harnessed to ensure the separation of the two communities, though as Gil Eyal importantly notes, these policies often resulted in the blurring of boundaries where strict demarcations were supposed to be found.[8] This incomplete operation of power, whether led by the state or the market, is pivotal to this book's argument, and discussed at length in the following chapters.

Physical measures taken to change Arab spaces in Israel were paralleled by an equally powerful cultural project. As critical scholars increasingly argue, the cultural significance of the Arab landscape was subject to a coordinated political transformation which altered names, maps and histories to fit the ideological scheme of a modern, Hebrew, Jewish national space. In this fusion of seemingly contradictory cultural and ideological components, space played a central role, largely because it was perceived as a passive and malleable vehicle that can bind together the fragmented elements of Zionist discourse and bridge deep social and cultural divides. From this spatial logic, we learn, the Arab past was excluded wholesale. It is unsurprising therefore, that "Erasure" and "spatial annihilation" gained such cachet in the transformation of Arab landscapes in Israel, both physically and symbolically.[9] Furthermore, according to some critics, this extensive eradication not only abolished the presence of Arabs from the landscape, but generated a "collective amnesia" among Israelis regarding the Arab-Palestinian past.[10] More than six decades after the establishment of the State of Israel and the Palestinian *Nakba*,[11] the Arab history of Israel has been "erased from space and consciousness", as one recent book title proclaims.[12]

But so much is still there. Arab buildings, flora, place-names and stories are very much present, coded into the everyday space of Israelis,

---

[7] This aspect of Israel's spatial transformation remains at the margins of this book's analytical focus, though it is not at all divorced from the policies designed toward the depopulated Arab villages and their repopulation with Jewish residents. For a discussion of the treatment of the Arab minority in Israel during the first decades of the state see Pappé, "An Uneasy Coexistence"; Cohen, *The Present Absentees*.

[8] Eyal, *The Disenchantment of the Orient*, chapters 5 and 6.

[9] For example: Benvenisti, *Sacred Landscape*; Falah, "The 1948 Israeli-Palestinian War and its Aftermath".

[10] Abu-Sitta, *The Palestinian Nakba 1948*; see also Ram, "Ways of Forgetting".

[11] An Arabic term meaning "catastrophe" or "disaster". It is commonly used to describe the 1948 depopulation of Palestine and the establishment of the State of Israel.

[12] Kadman, *Erased from Space and Consciousness*.

the space they inhabit in body and tongue, its past and present. Though critical scholarship importantly illuminated the political and ideological forces that shape the Israeli space, a fuller, more nuanced account of this persistent Arab presence is still called for. A critical intervention that follows the unsettled and unfinished interaction between people and space is essential if we are to come to terms not only with the heterogeneity of the Israeli landscape but with the immense social, cultural and political repercussions such heterogeneity potentially generates.

From the unresolved gap between absence and presence, between destruction and persistence, this book aims to shed light on patterns of spatial resilience in Israel. This is not a fascination with relics of the past as such, but instead, a shift of the analytical focus to highlight the lingering effects these resilient spaces have on the operation of state mechanisms, cultural systems and representations, and on the lives of those who inhabit these heterogeneous places. It revisits the vast critical corpus that documented and analysed the formation of a Jewish national space in Palestine, and challenges some of the methodological and theoretical prisms through which different aspects of spatiality have been viewed thus far. Taking notice of all that is still there brings to light a prolific and invaluable archive that remains, to a large extent, overlooked. From all that remains, this project sets out to illuminate one case of spatial history in Israel and the life of its present pasts.

Directions: Arriving at Salama/Kfar Shalem

To reach Kfar Shalem one has to travel eastward, away from Tel Aviv. Although the neighbourhood is included in the municipal boundaries of the Tel Aviv-Jaffa metropolis, it is located at the eastern edges of the dense conurbation that surrounds the city. En route, you cross the main highway that separates Tel Aviv and Jaffa from the hinterland of the eastern suburbs; this "far east" – which for many is not "really" Tel Aviv – features, as one critic put it, an Israeli "anthology of public housing"[13] from the late 1950s to the present, the familiar rows of indistinguishable tenement blocks common to most Israeli cities. Getting closer, the monotonous sprawl is intermittently interrupted by small houses that appear in between the blocks. At one point, the broad double-lane road ends, blocked by houses clustered together and hidden by thick vegetation. To proceed, one needs to turn into a narrow road that gradually winds up a small hill.

---

[13] Rotbard, *White City, Black City*, 198.

Stopping at a little traffic circle, which marks the centre of the neighbourhood, it is clear Tel Aviv has been left behind: on one side, a small synagogue; behind it, a large domed structure surrounded by a thick stone wall; across the street, a row of old-looking buildings – a Yemenite restaurant, the offices of the Tel Aviv Sanitation Department and another synagogue; a little park with large eucalyptus trees is on the right; look closely and you can spot some peacocks walking around the playground. It is surprisingly quiet. Through the park, a small path leads into narrow streets that wind between densely built, single story buildings, often hidden behind makeshift fences. Small empty lots are planted with olive trees and accompanied by municipal signs bearing the peculiar statement "Temporary Grove". Along the small road that leads west from the traffic circle, all the buildings appear to be either synagogues or religious seminaries, though all are situated in rather humble, flat-roofed structures. Circling the clusters of houses, the imposing flat facades of public tenements mark an unofficial, yet highly discernible boundary.

The serenity of the place partly clarifies why residents often refer to it as "*hakfar*", Hebrew for "the village". There is another explanation of course: Kfar Shalem was formally the Arab-Palestinian village of Salama. Like many other Arab villages throughout Mandatory Palestine, Salama was depopulated during the 1948 War, but unlike most, it continues to retain many of its past features. While Tel Aviv takes pride in its history as the "First Hebrew City", Kfar Shalem appears to be a rather ambivalent space: it continues to bear the marks of its Arab past even when its Arab inhabitants have never been allowed to return to their village. After nearly seven decades, Kfar Shalem has yet to completely shake off Salama.

And yet, this spatial cohabitation is not the result of a special effort to preserve a heritage that has otherwise been effaced. This is no "living museum", nor a heritage site of sorts. It is an utterly mundane, working-class neighbourhood, tucked away in Tel Aviv's south-eastern poverty belt. Kfar Shalem is of unique importance because the remnants of its past form the space in which practical and daily life takes place. Without commemoration plaques or guided tours, Kfar Shalem conserves the multiplicity of its past. Where ruin and destruction have gained such prevalence, this small place presents a humble, yet remarkable, tale of spatial resilience.

This is not to say that Kfar Shalem is invisible to the public eye. The neighbourhood has often been mentioned in the Israeli media, partly with regard to the inhumane living conditions residents have had to endure, and more recently, with relation to recurring demolition of illegal construction and the eviction of residents who unlawfully "invaded" houses in the neighbourhood. Since the mid-2000s, Kfar Shalem has become a quintessential arena for the high-profile struggle against urban regeneration backed by the Tel Aviv municipality and private entrepreneurs seeking to take advantage of the valuable land reserves still found in the peripheral regions of the city.[14] Residents in Kfar Shalem have been actively lobbying their demands in the Knesset (Israel's unicameral parliament) and succeeded in placing several members on the municipal council during the 2008 local elections. Most of these media reports are understandably preoccupied with the urgencies of the present, or at most, with the crises of recent pasts. In some cases, a laconic mention of the neighbourhood's Arab past is also included. Rarely, and only with regard to Salama Mosque, will this past be identified as part of the neighbourhood's landscape.[15] These portrayals implicitly convey the perception of 1948 as a watershed moment that marks the abrupt end of an Arab village and the beginning of the Jewish-Israeli neighbourhood. But this rigid historical division inevitably collides with a complex spatial reality in which "end" and "beginning" are dubious terms. Calamitous political transformation and large-scale demographic change cannot be overlooked, but they do not simply wipe the spatial slate clean.

In order to account for all that remains, not just as incidental "detritus" from some archaic past or objects of melancholic memorialisation, a new and attentive re-engagement with space is required. Inspired by Paul Carter's formulation,[16] this project traces the "spatial history" of Salama/Kfar Shalem, and following Carter, challenges the conventional historical paradigm, "which reduces space to a stage, that pays attention to events unfolding in time alone".[17] Space, according to this paradigm, is emptied of its active qualities and, in effect, relegated to insignificance. Carter's critique was part of a broader postcolonial effort to explore not only the way power relations construct spatial meaning, but also how social relations, power structures and affective domains are formed and altered through spatial experiences. The analytical prism applied in this book is therefore part of this critical effort to take space seriously, not through some material essentialism but through what geographer Doreen Massey described as a perception of space as "a simultaneity of stories-so-far",[18] stories that accumulate to form an archive of material objects and symbolic practices. This form

---

[14] Rapoport, "Suddenly They Are Called 'Squatters'".
[15] Rapoport, "A Mosque Once Stood Here".
[16] Carter, *The Road to Botany Bay*.
[17] Ibid., xvi.
[18] Massey, *For Space*, 9.

of historical inquiry is not an attempt to override the existing archive, and in many cases deals with objects or phenomena that have been analysed and discussed elsewhere. Rather, it seeks to overcome the stringent logic of cause and effect that often pacifies the role of spatiality in history and ignores the unique qualities of spatial *inter*action. This book therefore traces the encounter between people and place over time, and examines how space becomes an arena for the ongoing negotiation between past and present. Importantly, the "spatial forms and fantasies"[19] that function as the building blocks of spatial history are not archival objects whose relevance is confined to the past. Instead, they redirect "the engagement elsewhere, to the politics animated, to the common sense they disturb, to the critiques considered or disallowed, and to the social relations avidly coalesced or shattered around them".[20]

If space indeed functions as an archive of historical processes, it stores its "artefacts" in a unique fashion that challenges strict periodisation and linear sequentiality. Instead of a vertical accumulation of historical layers – one period on top of the other, one replacing the other – the analysis presented in this book highlights the spatial capacity to simultaneously contain past and present. To reflect the rich historical paths that intersect to form the spatial phenomena of Salama/Kfar Shalem, the analysis is not restricted to a specific historical period but brings together traditions and practices that at times date back hundreds of years. Nevertheless, the book is primarily concerned with the spatial transformation of Salama in the six decades that followed its depopulation in 1948. Instead of chronicling the events that took place since then, it follows the interaction between spatial phenomena and socioeconomic, cultural and political processes. As shown in the course of the analysis, the various spatial components that make up the neighbourhood were found to be deeply rooted in spatial, ideological and political trends whose origins already appear in the first half of the twentieth century and even prior to that. Summoning the diverse historical forces that took part in the transformation of the village is not exhaustive, but demonstrates the ambiguities and complexities of historical transition and the heterogeneous space they produce.

The non-linear, fractured and repetitive patterns identified in the course of this book question existing paradigms of historical transition, which exceed the spatial and historical specificities of the Israeli-Arab conflict. The construction of Somerset House in London in 1549, for example, included the destruction of several buildings around the city

---

[19] Carter, *The Road to Botany Bay*, xxii.
[20] Stoler, "Imperial Debris", 196.

in order to produce materials for the palace. In the case of one cloister, the "demolition gang" removed 1,000 cartloads of bones from an adjacent burial site, which were later dumped in unhallowed ground outside the city; as one witness pointed out, "nothing thereof was left but a bare plot of ground".[21] According to James Simpson, the construction of Somerset House is indicative of deep-set patterns of historical transition, which fall into two basic categories:

> one kind of historical transition aims to destroy and efface the immediate past, while another recognizes historicity. I call the first the revolutionary model and the second the reformist model. The revolutionary model obsessively advertises its own novelty, and operates within strictly defined and contrasted periodic schemata. The second, instead, highlights continuities across historical rupture. Each deals differently with artefacts and buildings of the past: the revolutionary model works by iconoclasm and demolition, while the reformist model operates by accretive *bricolage* ... In rhetorical terms, the characteristic trope of the revolutionary model is antithesis, while the reformist model deploys *translatio* (i.e. metaphor), or simile.[22]

The resilience of Arab space after 1948 in Salama/Kfar Shalem would seem to suggest its association with Simpson's reformist model, a *bricolage* that "posits continuities between the past and its future".[23] In this sense, despite the absence of an identifiable agent that consciously orchestrated this effort, the physical and material presence of Salama provided the basis on which the foundation of a Jewish neighbourhood was made possible. However, the persistence of Salama's Arab space and its existence as part of new national order took place against a predominantly revolutionary approach that governed the production of the "Jewish" or "Hebrew" space. We know, for example, that Arab structures were used by Jewish inhabitants in only 35 out of approximately 418 depopulated Arab villages; only in 13 of these cases – 4 per cent of all new Jewish settlements established between 1949 and 1951 – were settlers expected to make permanent use of Arab structures.[24] Surveys conducted more recently indicate that two-thirds of the depopulated villages were completely razed, with only 15 sites retaining most of the Arab built environment.[25] Demolition policies that were initiated in the first years of the state[26] were followed by a second wave

---

[21] Quoted in Simpson, *The Oxford English Literary History*, vol. 2: 34.
[22] Ibid., 35.
[23] Ibid., 36.
[24] Golan, "The Transformation of Abandoned Arab Rural Areas", 102.
[25] Khalidi, *All That Remains*; Falah, "The 1948 Israeli-Palestinian War and its Aftermath".
[26] Morris, *Birth of the Palestinian Refugee Problem Revisited*, chapter 6; Golan, "The Transformation of Abandoned Arab Rural Areas".

of demolitions in the mid-1960s when the Israel Land Administration initiated the "clearing" of all remaining villages depopulated in 1948.[27] This is clearly not an attitude that seeks to build itself on the past, at least not the Arab one. The resilience of the Arab past in Salama/Kfar Shalem is therefore an example of a spatial *bricolage* that survives *in spite of* official policies that sought its eradication. The anomaly of this resilience constitutes a pivotal analytical axis of this book, prompting a closer scrutiny of the conditions that made it possible and its impact on society, politics, ideology and culture.

Ostensibly, this project is not part of the high-profile events that dominate the mass media coverage of the Middle East. It is not a direct engagement with *The Occupation*; namely, the Israeli seizure and administration of the West Bank and Gaza Strip since 1967. As such, it may be seen as an old skeleton, a *fait accompli* that should perhaps make way to more pressing matters. Salama/Kfar Shalem is indeed a modest place in scale and appearance, which has no claim to historical or political pre-eminence. But like other small places,[28] its idiosyncratic fate allows us a close, even intimate insight into the micro-relations of people and the environments they live in. What does it mean to move into somebody else's house? How does the place of "the enemy" become one's own? Who governs a space that has been officially declared "abandoned"? What populates the emptiness left by recurring demolitions and destruction? These may not be urgent questions at the height of war, but they are central to the experience of post-conflict space, especially because they question the finitude implied by the preface "post". Furthermore, the significance of these questions is not confined to those who call Salama/Kfar Shalem their home. They may also sound familiar in Turkish northern Cyprus, the western regions of the Czech Republic, the Punjab, or the villages of ethnic Azeris and Kurds in Azerbaijan. This is only a partial list of places that have experienced large-scale depopulation and repopulation in the past century, where questions of spatial transformation are woven into wider political, social and ideological processes.

Neither, it should be emphasised, are the questions posed in this book confined to the realm of phenomenological contemplation. The aftershocks of crisis, Ann Laura Stoler reminds us, "reside in the corroded hollows of landscapes, in the gutted infrastructures of segregated cityscapes and in the microecologies of matter and mind".[29] The

---

[27] Shai, "The Fate of Abandoned Arab Villages".
[28] Jamaica Kincaid's *A Small Place* and Jonny Steiberg's *Midlands* are two examples that come to mind.
[29] Stoler, "Imperial Debris", 194.

lingering effects of crisis may not be "headline material", but they are crucial to the understanding of the spectres that haunt social, economic and political realities. This book sets out to engage with big questions through a small place, and point out the new horizons that open from recognising the simultaneity of past and present.

Positions: Spatial Transformation in an Ethno-National Conflict

A growing body of literature challenges the assumption that urban development can be described solely through set models of modernisation, regeneration or even domineering ethnic or national ideologies. Contrary to the ideological pretence to represent the city as a coherent and homogenous whole, urban space is shaped by unexpected and even catastrophic events that leave physical and psychic residues in their wake. Folded into grand master-plans and utopian schemes, founding narratives and prescribed behaviours are often contrasting, mutative and changing dynamics of urban life. In this sense, city-building is always unpredictable, provisional and incomplete, "a ceaseless, Sisyphean task without finality or closure".[30] This open-ended encounter between urban planning and human practice received special attention in the context of colonial and postcolonial analysis of urban space, which documented the hybridisation of power through the specific prism of spatiality.[31] This spatial critique illustrated how space, and urban space in particular, remains an unstable, dynamic and elusive medium, which is at once a microcosm of power and the site of its most creative manipulations and provocative contestations.

With this in mind, it is rather surprising that until recently, urban space in Israel has been critically analysed as an environment dominated and shaped almost entirely by hegemonic apparatuses serving either ethno-national or neoliberal economic agendas. Historically, Israel's urban space was indeed susceptible to the operation of a powerful state-controlled planning mechanism, which championed and supported the nationalising mission.[32] But the prevailing scholarly focus on

---

[30] Murray, *Taming the Disorderly City*, 40.

[31] From the vast corpus of scholarly literature dealing with this issue, the conceptualisation in this book especially benefitted from Perera, "Contesting Visions"; Simone, *For the City Yet to Come*; Robinson, *Ordinary Cities*; Murray, *Taming the Disorderly City*; Yeoh, *Contesting Space*; Appadurai, "Spectral Housing and Urban Cleansing"; Home, *Of Planting and Planning*.

[32] See, for example: Sharon, "Planners, the State, and the Shaping of National Space in the 1950s".

centralised forms of spatial power also determined to a large extent the symbolic meaning and historical sense these environments were seen to convey. Its underlying assumption stipulated that physical governance of the city through regulation, planning, policing and taxation, also offered unlimited control over its meaning. One critique of the contentious historical relation between Tel Aviv and Jaffa exemplifies this conflation of political power and historical meaning:

> Every act you do or do not do in the physical body of a city, is also an act of writing history, a histriographical act. A decision to demolish an old building, to construct a new building or conserve an existing one, determines what is deemed to be forgotten … and what is worthy of remembrance. Therefore, there is a *clear* and *essential* link between the history of a city and its geography. Geography is a matter of historiography. *A city remembers what history tells it to and erases what it tells it to forget.*[33]

As the quintessential Zionist "product", the self-proclaimed "first Hebrew city", Tel Aviv was planned, designed and built to express the ideological pillars of modernism and cosmopolitanism, while binding them to the national mission of Jewish sovereignty and cultural revival.[34] The importance of inserting a sober distrust toward the ideological manipulation of space, which was one of the main contributions of this critical effort, should not be underestimated. Indeed, the recent emergence of a public debate on urban planning and policy in Israel owes much to this critique. However, it also runs the risk of unconsciously duplicating the model it seeks to critique by confining spatial meaning to narrow ideological projections, by contending that the city *is* its representation.

Though space and representation are deeply intertwined, the conflation of the two has a particular history in the course of Jewish national revival in Palestine. The destruction of the Second Temple in Jerusalem by the Romans in 70AD marked the end of Jewish sovereignty in the historical Land of Israel. Although Jewish communities remained in several towns of specific religious significance, the majority of the Jews living in diasporic communities maintained their connection to the land predominantly through religious rite and tradition.[35] This meant that for generations of Jews, *Eretz Yisrael* (the Land of Israel) was more a textual creation than a physical reality.

---

[33] Rotbard, *White City, Black City*, 15, emphasis added.
[34] Several works that have illustrated various aspects of this process include: Azaryahu, *Tel Aviv*; LeVine, *Overthrowing Geography*; Mann, *A Place in History*.
[35] Yerushalmi, *Zakhor*.

This traditional kinship between spatiality and textuality perco-
lated into emerging trends of national Jewish revival in the latter half
of the nineteenth century in eastern and central Europe. The adoption of these textual traditions for the production of space occurred
despite the fact that many of the Zionist movement's founding figures
left religious life and adopted secular, modern lifestyles.[36] However,
writing the land provided the Zionist movement with the building
blocks for the imagination of the national community and the territory in which it would fulfill its aspirations, even when the material,
demographic and economic conditions were unfavourable, to say the
least. As is the case with many other national movements, Zionism
wrote its mythology at the same time as it was forming its ideology,
and long before its territorial visions were realised. It is important
to remember, however, that Zionist mythography was not the sole
responsibility of ideological essayists: the fusion of people and territory was an interdisciplinary effort that brought together historians,
geographers, archaeologists, architects, theologians and linguists.
Revisiting this corpus of "land writing", the critique that emerged
from the 1980s onward sought to expose the ideological interests
that guided the production of the "Israeli Space" as a culmination of
national fantasies and unveil its pretence for neutrality – geography
as a matter of mythography.

Spatial history, by contrast, approaches this relation with caution.
Without essentialising space as the medium through which some form
of social, political or historical "truth" can be revealed,[37] it seeks to
reconsider space as the unfinished sum of all its texts, forms and practices. As a critical engagement, spatial history seeks to highlight the
gradual evolution of power relations as part of an unfinished process
of negotiation in which neither space nor its meaning reach a point of
absolute stasis. In addition to the ways space is utilised as a medium
for the operation of power, the analysis in this book outlines the spatial
tactics and practices through which power is reclaimed and appropriated by individuals and communities, and the way the top-down flow

---

[36] Jewish modernisation began almost a century before the emergence of Zionism, in the
latter half of the eighteenth century. Jewish national trends followed disillusionment
with the promises of Jewish emancipation and integration into the European societies
in which they resided, and as a reaction to the rise of European anti-Semitism in the
latter half of the nineteenth century. This transition from emancipation to nationalism
also had a direct impact on Jewish perspectives of history and historiography. For a
discussion of this historical process, see Myers, *Re-inventing the Jewish Past*; Meyer, *The
Origins of the Modern Jew*; Conforti, *Past Tense*, 61–2; 80–5.

[37] This follows Lefebvre's warning against the double illusion of space when its nature
as a social product is ignored. Lefebvre, *The Production of Space*, 27–9.

of authority is disrupted and fractured at various points of encounter with space. As such, the analysis suspends the assumption that spatial phenomena necessarily reflect prescribed hegemonic meaning. It turns instead to record the multifaceted interaction between people and place, as it shapes and reshapes historical perception, political allegiances and cultural identities. Surely this is not an innocent encounter, but neither does it simply act out a predetermined script of ethnic, national or cultural chauvinism.

This conceptual framework does not emerge out of an analytical vacuum. Carter's conceptualization of "spatial history" in the late 1980s was a sharp critique of conventional historiography, but also signalled a parallel critical turn in historical geography, which increasingly adopted social and cultural theory to its critical toolkit. In this emerging cultural-historical corpus, which quickly exceeded disciplinary boundaries, landscape was increasingly seen as playing an actant role in shaping social relations and normalising hierarchies of power,[38] and inspired more recent engagements with place histories and their political significance.[39]

Yet as Carter wrote more recently,[40] spatial history did more than chart the biased and violent cosmology of colonisation or illuminate the role of landscape as a social and political instrument. It also sought the "poetic logic" involved in the production of space – fantasy, movement, tactility – by first significantly expanding the theoretical and methodological scope of both historiography and geography. Its objects of inquiry most closely resemble what Kathleen Stewart describes as "registering forms", "in which intensities lodged in institutional effects and lived affects, materialities and dreamworlds, differences and energies, reach a point of expressivity and become legible".[41] These elements, she notes, "are thrown together not through the conspiracy of a state power, or a preexisting common ground or ideal, but through events of articulation, histories of use, unintended consequences, and experiments that register".[42] This openness to the radical potentialities of spatial production directly relates to the second shift spatial history argues for in the

---

[38] Stewart, *Space on the Side of the Road*; Mitchell, *The Lie of the Land*; Schein, "The Place of Landscape".

[39] Mills' ethnography of one neighbourhood in Istanbul is a recent and especially relevant example, examining the interconnectedness of national/minority histories and ways through which they are compelled to reconcile with one another through place and landscape. Mills, *Streets of Memory*; see also Navaro-Yashin, *The Make-Believe Space*; Till, *The New Berlin*.

[40] Carter, *Dark Writing*.

[41] Stewart, "Road Registers", 549.

[42] Ibid., 550.

temporal orientation of the historical investigation. Here Carter draws on Husserl's distinction of recollection from retention: recollection signals out something from the past and re-presents it in memory – but does not relive it. By contrast, retention, or primary memory, is "the consciousness of the past as the horizon or background against which the present stands out".[43] And this concern with the past as a transformative component in the present, as an active element and one that can be acted upon, explains spatial history's particular emphasis on the kinesthetic elements of active place making – what he describes as "participatory eventfulness".[44]

This book and the spatial history it documents are inspired by these conceptual reorientations and their political implications. David Carr's invocation of the experience of objects echoes both the grave spatial-political processes charted here, but also their generative, transformative potential:

> To experience an event is to be conscious of something *taking place*, that is, its *taking the place* of something else. What is replaced or displaced recedes into the background but is not lost from view; I am still conscious of it but in a different way.[45]

This is the critical task at hand.

Several works in recent years have made the first steps toward this theorisation of a spatial history of Israel. Tamar Berger was perhaps the first to present a micro-history of urban transformation in Tel Aviv, detailing the evolution of the Nordiyah neighbourhood from a citrus orchard owned by one of Jaffa's Arab families, through the construction of shacks for Jewish residents during the 1920s, the appropriation of the land in 1948 and the eventual demolition of the neighbourhood for the construction of a large shopping mall in the 1970s.[46] Berger's work foregrounds the various histories that intersect in the site of the neighbourhood, giving voice to chapters sidelined by mainstream accounts of Tel Aviv's past. However, aside from their shared location, the relation between these historical chapters remains rather vague. It is unclear, for example, how the annulment of Arab land rights in 1948 affected the undetermined status of Jewish residents living in the neighbourhood in the decades that followed the establishment of the state.[47] Nevertheless,

[43] Carr, *Interpreting Husserl*, 251.
[44] Carter, *Dark Writing*, 90.
[45] Carr, *Interpreting Husserl*, 251.
[46] Berger, *Dionysus at Dizengof Center*.
[47] See also Elgazi, "Between Man and Place. Review of Tamar Berger's 'Dionysus in Dizengof Center'".

the phenomena Berger described in her book paved the way for a broader theorisation of historical spatial politics.

More recently, important scholarly contributions have focused the attention on spatial transformation through the overlap between Jewish and Arab space. In two separate case-studies, Benny Nuriely[48] and Shlomit Benjamin[49] identify the potential threat posed to the homogenous ethno-national aspiration by Jewish communities that settled in the Arab city of Lod and the former Arab village of Qubeiba, respectively. In both cases, the writers illustrate the ways these sites blur the Zionist dichotomy between Arab and Jew and shed light on the incomplete national mission that seeks to distinguish between and separate "Us" from "Them". Against this familiar categorisation through which group identity is formed and maintained, Nuriely and Benjamin suggest that the sites in question expose the hegemonic double negation, first of Arab-Palestinian space and second the negation of Jewish-Arab identity. In addition, they draw attention to cultural and political counter-currents that emerged out of these "third-spaces", referring to Homi Bhabha's theorisation of this term.[50] The identification of ambivalence and heterogeneity during the formation of the Israeli national space enabled these projects to broaden the category of "Arab-Jew" beyond local identity politics, exploring concrete spatial experiences.

It is worth noting that Nuriely and Benjamin's projects are part of a broader analytical effort to move beyond the binary opposition between Arab and Jew, though as Hannan Hever and Yehouda Shenhav note, this was a two-phase process.[51] In the first, Jewish intellectuals and political activists of Arab descent began identifying themselves as "Arab-Jews", insisting on a hyphenated identity that was otherwise considered an oxymoron by the homogenous ethno-national logic of the Jewish state.[52] Contrary to "neutral" hyphenations that stress countries of origin – Moroccan-Jew, Iraqi-Jew and so on –"Arab-Jew" implies identification with a perceived enemy embodied by the Arab.[53] In this first phase, the term acknowledges the discursive dichotomy between Jew and Arab, but seeks to overcome their mutual negation by

---

[48] Nuriely, "Strangers in a National Space".
[49] Benjamin, " 'Present-Absent' ".
[50] Bhabha, *The Location of Culture*; Rutherford, "The Third Space: Interview with Homi Bhabha".
[51] Hever and Shenhav, "Arab Jews – A Genealogy of a Term".
[52] Ballas, *Outcast*; Shohat, "Reflections of an Arab Jew".
[53] The discursive constitution of enmity between the polarised categories of "Arab" and "Jew", which ranges beyond specific geopolitical circumstances and relates directly to the European legacies that forged this formulation, is illuminated in Anidjar, *The Jew, the Arab*.

reinstating a defiant identity that re-presents "a kind of logical paradox, even an ontological subversion".[54] The second, post-structuralist phase of the term begins at this defiant point and takes it further. It posits that the binary opposition between Arab and Jew is produced through discursive practices that take place over time and space. As Hever and Shenhav point out, the hegemonic act of erasure is simultaneously a process of re-inscription, and both "leave numerous traces in the broad margins that surround the separation line" between Arab and Jew.[55] What is exposed here is a "discursive labour" that is never simply a linear transition from one (political or cultural) category to another. As such, critical analysis turns to record hegemonic coercion and the evidence it leaves behind, highlighting the Sisyphean operation of power and meaning.

The post-structuralist phase proved highly useful for the reconsideration of spatial politics and its correlations with ambivalent social and cultural categories. Both Nuriely and Benjamin present powerful illustrations of the coordinated operation of spatial policies and social engineering in the state's attempt to forge the national community, and identify the limited success this operation had. However, both are primarily concerned with the social and cultural politics rather than with their spatiality and materiality. Nuriely, for example, states that "it is the threatening presence of Arab-Jews that prompts the state apparatuses to reorganise space, to demolish it and remove the population from it".[56] At the same time, he notes clear discrepancies between the spatiality of Lod's eastern Arab quarter populated by Arab-Jews, and the new Jewish neighbourhoods built in the city after 1948, from the shape of the streets to the absence of clear ownership of houses.[57] Even so, the effect of these spatial features remains secondary to the socio-ethnic struggle. The rich description of residents' disorientation in the new space – "it was really complicated" says one of the Jewish interviewees about the irregular structure of the Arab house she inhabited – is glossed over too briefly, allowing the writer to focus instead on the subversive identification and cooperation between the Jewish residents and the Arab space.[58] There, in the "third-space", the boundaries between Jews and Arabs temporarily collapse and the separatist ethno-national logic is

---

[54] Shohat, "Reflections of an Arab Jew", 14.
[55] Hever and Shenhav, "Arab Jews – A Genealogy of a Term".
[56] Nuriely, "Strangers in a National Space", 16.
[57] Ibid., 20.
[58] Ibid.

disrupted, until they are reinstated by the coercive intervention of the state and the demolition of the Arab quarter in Lod in 1959.

While this compelling historical chapter elucidates the potential of using the category of Arab-Jew to broaden the analytical investigation of power and space, several questions remain unanswered: what is the status of Arab-Jewish space beyond its function as a receptacle of an Arab-Jewish community? Would it provoke such institutional antagonism if, for example, its Jewish residents were of European descent? Furthermore, one wonders whether the encounter between the Jewish residents and the Arab space was indeed experienced as liberating. Nuriely acknowledges that in retrospect, interviewees express ambivalence toward their relations with the Arabs who still resided in the quarter during the 1950s, but points to no such unease at the time the neighbourhood was still inhabited. Were there none? Was it a rare moment of idealised coexistence? These pivotal questions, which potentially open radical new avenues for historical-political analysis, remain unanswered.

Shlomit Benjamin's work on the Jewish community that settled the Arab village of Qubeiba raises similar questions. Benjamin notes that the village mosque was used as a synagogue, part of the authorities' attempt to deny the "Palestinian memory space" and resignify it as part of the national Jewish space.[59] Within this model, the physical and material practices through which space is transformed and re-inscribed – a fundamental dynamic in this critical paradigm – seem to be taken for granted: is it enough, for example, to change the physical arrangement of a mosque and insert a bible scroll for it to comply with the symbolic standards of a new national order? Benjamin's important interrogation invites a more detailed look at the evolution of the intimate relationship formed between people and the environment they inhabit, and the practices they employ in this process. The repetitive acts of re-inscription and resignification are not just evidence of the limitation of authoritative state power, but also of the unresolved, at times conflicted relationship, between Jewish-Israelis and the Arab spaces in which they live.

A deeper problem exists with regard to the notion of "third-space" often adopted by critical scholars of the Israeli space, and what seems to be a celebration of resistance harboured within it. Using Bhabha's conceptualisation of the term, several scholarly works have championed the "third-space" as the site that blurs clear distinctions between

---

[59] Benjamin, " 'Present-Absent' ", 95.

the colonial rule and its subjects, and provides the conditions for the emergence of hybrid forms of identity and political practice. Within this space, it is asserted, identities are formed and transformed in a manner that exceeds fixed delineations of ethnicity, nationality or any other essentialised discourse that rests on a politics of polarity and cultural binarism. The problem emerges, as Louise Bethlehem importantly reminds us, when hybridity is simplified into yet another form of resistance.[60] All too often, the term's origins in racial-scientific discourse and its strong psychoanalytic foundations in Bhabha's theory are sidelined while the disruptive potential of hybridity becomes the focus of the analysis. The problem becomes even more acute when strictly defined "third-spaces" become the prime loci for the accommodation of these hybrid identities. This confinement loses sight of the subtle nuances that define hybridity as a "zone of psychic relations ... across which an unstable traffic of continuously (re)negotiated (counter-)identifications is conducted".[61] Surely, this entails more than unambiguous opposition between the freedom supposedly found in hybrid third-spaces and the restrictive homogeneity that governs all other spaces of socio-political interaction.

It is worth briefly noting that postcolonial theory, which deeply informed the analysis carried out in this book, has been criticised for its focus on discursive and representational practices, while paying insufficient attention to the "real politics" of actual spaces and material practices in the urban sphere.[62] This is a valid point, but the alternative is not to give up theoretical intricacy for a narrow prism through which the entire spectrum of human relations is viewed solely as a series of socio-political antagonisms. Bhabha himself notes that if our interest in critical scholarship "is limited to a celebration of the fragmentation of the 'grand narratives' of postenlightenment rationalism then, for all its intellectual excitement, it remains a profoundly parochial enterprise".[63]

My second, perhaps more pressing concern with the "thirding" of spaces regards the manner by which it unconsciously duplicates a segregationist logic that often guided state apparatuses in dealing with these sites in the first place. As broadly discussed in the third and fourth chapters, in cases where the destruction of former Arab spaces could not be completed, the authorities often resorted to forms of containment that isolated these sites and the communities who inhabited them. These

---

[60] Bethlehem, "Towards a Different Hybridity".
[61] Moore-Gilbert, "Spivak and Bhabha", 458.
[62] King, "Actually Existing Postcolonialisms".
[63] Bhabha, The Location of Culture, 4.

enclaves, cut off both by physical means and through socio-ethnic stig-matisation, indeed became hospitable environments for communities that contested the prevailing logic of the Zionist hegemony. However, only on very rare occasions were these communities looking to cat-egorically reject Zionism or the emerging Jewish national community. Instead, these groups sought to challenge the normative foundations of the national enterprise as equal participants in the production of civil discourse. Based on this, I would argue that conceptually confin-ing these voices into a "third space/place" works against the notion's fundamental intention "to keep the consciousness *of* and the theorizing *on* spatiality radically open".[64] In numerous cases I encountered while researching this book, individuals and communities strongly protest against the identification of Salama/Kfar Shalem as an "Other" space; time and again, residents try to break through the confines imposed on them and the environment they inhabit, to be recognised as a legitimate and equal part of the national space. In other words, it was an attempt to break a state-initiated separatism that was all too keen to adopt, per-versely perhaps, tactics of "thirding-as-othering" that resonated dec-ades later in critical strands of spatial theory.[65] Partly as a response to this plea and partly as an attempt to shed light on the hidden relation-ships between ostensibly contradicting spaces, the analysis presented throughout the book consciously refrains from placing yet another ring of enclosure around Salama/Kfar Shalem.

Two more works stand out in the corpus that explores the dynamics of Arab spatial transformation in Israel. In *The Object of Memory*, Susan Slyomovics illustrates the transformation of the depopulated Arab village of Ein Houd into a Jewish artists' colony in the early 1950s.[66] Slyomovics work is a detailed illustration of the practices employed by the new Jewish residents in order to come to terms with the Arab space and overcome its inherent foreignness. The book situates the spatial transformation of the village in a broad discursive and ideological con-text, and importantly emphasises the co-dependency of the two spheres. But Slyomovics's analysis presents a rather unique case of a Dadaist artists' community and the way it harnessed a specific aesthetic ideol-ogy in order to realise the transformation of the place into a picturesque artists' village. These were not resources that were commonly available in most cases of repopulation, though some parallels can be found in

---

[64] Soja, "Thirdspace" (2008), 50, emphasis in the original.
[65] Lefebvre, *The Production of Space*; Soja, *Thirdspace* (1996); Ikas and Wagner, *Communicating in the Third Space*.
[66] Slyomovics, *The Object of Memory*.

the village of Ein Karem, near Jerusalem, and parts of urban Jaffa and Safed, which were intentionally transformed into artists' quarters. The transformation of Salama presents a rather more mundane example, and therefore demands attention to a different set of practices and to a significantly different relationship between the Jewish residents and state authorities. In more than one sense, Salama presents a more common form of post-war transformation of Arab space in Israel, drawing critical attention to everyday routines and practices that remain largely overlooked precisely because they do not qualify as "special" or "extreme". *Life after Ruin* fills this analytical gap and accounts for a myriad of "ordinary" places and their extraordinary histories.

The final effort to use spatial transformation in order to tell and retell a history of a place and its people is Yfaat Weiss's historical analysis of Wadi Salib, one of Haifa's Arab neighbourhoods depopulated in 1948.[67] Weiss's book is notable not only for its careful reconfiguration of familiar historical accounts through their concrete spatial manifestations, but for drawing critical attention to the role of Arab spaces repopulated after 1948 as incubators of Jewish social dissent and political opposition. The local history Weiss weaves through the depopulated Palestinian neighbourhood sheds new light on the roots of pivotal moments of social protest in Israel. Rather than unrest caused solely by socioeconomic deprivation and ethnic marginalisation, the violent demonstrations that erupted in Wadi Salib in 1959 are traced back to the neighbourhood's Arab past, situating these events in a radically new context of a diachronic relationship between Arab past and Jewish present. The meticulous research Weiss conducted illuminated these spaces as rich archives for socio-political historians, but nonetheless highlights the need to supplement rigorous historical investigation with broader theoretical reflection on spatial history as a analytical tool, which can be used to explore the multifaceted experience of the past in the present as it inscribes itself into material objects, spatial practices and socio-political processes.

The existing body of research into spatial transformation in Israel emerged from a critical urge to challenge the perception of spatial production as a neutral, matter-of-fact process. As evidence accumulated, the heavy-handed intervention of ideologically motivated bodies became apparent and the traces of its operation themselves became an object of inquiry. Absence was gradually made present. Spatial history as it is developed here brings together these methodological

---

[67] Weiss, *A Confiscated Memory*.

foundations to further explore the spatial archive, not just for new evidence about the past, but for knowledge that can inform our understanding of the Israeli present and future.

War, mass depopulation, the plight of immigration, poverty and cultural marginalisation have all made their mark on the face of Salama/ Kfar Shalem and the Israeli landscape more broadly. As this book shows, the accumulation of these pasts is neither orderly nor disciplined. More often, it is subliminal and easily ignored: a road that ends abruptly or an abundance of banana trees in a city that takes pride in its ficus boulevards. At other times, it returns in violent and explosive ways. But the severity of events that are directly and implicitly dealt with in this book should not obscure the warning sounded by Ann Laura Stoler: "Making connections where they are hard to trace is not designed to settle scores but rather to recognize that these are unfinished histories, not of victimized pasts but consequential histories that open to differential futures."[68] Taking these traces and spatial phenomena as a point of departure we are invited to ask, using Gayatri Spivak's formulation,[69] the question of simple semiosis – what does this mean? – and begin to plot a history.

Materials: Methodologies and Practices of Spatial History

As an analytical methodology, spatial history seeks to avoid two pitfalls. First, a simplistic notion of material essentialism, which assumes that historical truth is somehow stored in the physical properties of space. Second, it rejects the reduction of space to a passive receptacle that is easily manipulated simply through visual or textual representation (in maps, place-names, guidebooks, etc.). The method of spatial history developed here exists therefore in the cleft between physical phenomena and their representation, and illuminates the tense relation between them. It recognises that neither spatial form nor fantasy exists independently of each other, and both derive meaning from an ongoing process of negotiation, which itself overlaps with other parallel processes of social, economic and cultural production.

Compared with other works on the historical corpus on the 1948 War and its political and physical aftermath, archival work conducted for this spatial history was rather more "strategic" in its goals, reviewing familiar materials from a unique perspective. If, as Carter suggests,

---

[68] Stoler, "Imperial Debris", 195.
[69] See: Spivak, "Can the Subaltern Speak?", 297.

spatial history presents an alternative to history as the sequence of events unfolding in time alone, then its return to the archive takes place in search of the often easily overlooked discrepancies of narrative, repetitions and ironies that characterise the encounter with and negotiation of spatial forms and fantasies. The paradigmatic shift in the practices through which archival material is reviewed is not limited to official state documents. It also applies to the canonical corpus of Zionist thought, which, as several important works have shown, established the ideological foundations for Israel's territorial logic.[70] These texts customarily appeared as short articles, pamphlets or polemic essays that, contrary to common perception, portray a complex and ambiguous relation toward the actualisation of national territorial ambitions. In addition to official archival documents and ideological literature, the third and perhaps most problematic type of written material analysed here is Hebrew prose and its representation of space and spatial encounters. Several literary critics have illustrated in recent years the role of Hebrew literary fiction and poetry in the construction of Israeli spatial imagination.[71] However, I use this medium sparingly and cautiously, especially because it easily blurs the fine line between *what is* and *what ought* and runs the risk of defusing the tensions and conflicts that are so crucial for this spatial inquiry. Surely, literary fiction plays an important role in the production of space, delineating the horizons of spatial imagination and its unrealised potentials. Constituting space through writing has now been recognised as the founding practice of exploration and colonisation; it is, as de Certeau posits, a "concrete activity that consists in constructing, on its own, blank space (*un espace propre*) – the page – a text that has the power over the exteriority from which it has first been isolated".[72] Wary of the utopian pitfall of literary resolutions[73] – utopian in the sense of a detachment from concrete spatial actualities – my use of prose in this work is intended, in most cases, to highlight a more intimate dimension of instability and uncertainty that is an inseparable part of people's encounter with the ambiguous physicality and materiality of the land.

---

[70] Shapira, *Land and Power*; Kimmerling, *Zionism and Territory*.

[71] See, for example, Hever, *Producing the Modern Hebrew Canon*; Laor, *Narratives with No Natives*; Peled, "Mizrahiuot, Ashkenaziuot, and Space"; Zakim, *To Build and Be Built*.

[72] de Certeau, *The Practice of Everyday Life*, 136. On the spatialising function of literary fiction, see also Noyes, *Colonial Space*.

[73] Hannan Hever, for example, discusses the role of spatiality in Hebrew literature of the 1950s and 1960s, as a medium through which political and ethical questions can be defused in favour of national-collective or individualistic resolutions. Hever, *Producing the Modern Hebrew Canon*.

While spatial history is primarily an archival endeavour, it is certainly not confined solely to traditional repositories of documents. Throughout this book, material and physical phenomena often pose the initial conundrum from which the analysis begins: a fractured dome of an empty mosque, a street-sign, wildly overgrown hedges or a plaque in Greek on the wall of a small synagogue – all mark subtle traces of a richer sociopolitical history. These "concrete" objects do not, of course, exist in isolation. Spatial history simultaneously seeks to account for the practices and routines through which these sites become meaningful in people's lives. These include multiple registers of social interaction, from home-making and routes of travel to religious rites and violent protest.

Part of a broader postcolonial project that sought to shed critical light on the rhetorical construction of notions of empire and imperialism, Carter insists that knowledge comes into being through language, criticising the tendency to assume that space somehow precedes its cultural assimilation. Furthermore, his conception of spatial history provides an opportunity to interpret "statements as indicative of states of mind, as symbolic representations of intention".[74] However, as Simon Ryan notes, these individual motivations are also already dependent on pre-existing modes of experience, preconstructed by earlier scientific and fantasy discourses of exploration and discovery.[75] The return to spatial objects and practices is not an attempt to circumvent the power of discursive practices, but rather to fully explore the adaptations that discourses of power are forced to make when they are actualised in lived social and material environments.

While spatial phenomena provided the thematic axis for the organisation of the work, it does not imply that the two other components of this methodological triad – i.e. practices and representations of space – are somehow secondary to material objects or physical conditions. Instead, the analysis points to the overlaps and interconnections between these spheres: spatial objects, for example, are shaped by human practice as much as they influence and direct these activities. In a similar manner, representations of space (in visual, oral or textual form) shape the meaning of objects in space and at the same time are altered by spatial practices and tactics.[76] In the long history of imperial exploration, representation has served the (real or imagined) will-to-power of signification over the world of objects that is always already anterior to it.[77] This is true with regard to textual narratives of

---

[74] Carter, *The Road to Botany Bay*, 138.
[75] Ryan, *The Cartographic Eye*.
[76] In the sense famously outlined in de Certeau, *The Practice of Everyday Life*.
[77] Bethlehem, *Skin Tight*, 22; Ryan, "Inscribing the Emptiness", 115.

space and its visual representations, most notably cartography, which shaped the world according to the economic, ideological and cultural desires of European powers.[78] A critical analysis of these representations exposes this fissure between the space of the page and the space of the earth, and interrogates the tropes and conventions which conceal or slyly gloss over the gap between word and world. Behind these discursive conventions, one finds the fingerprint of power and the structures it seeks to create and uphold – though this has become somewhat of a familiar characteristic of critical analysis since Foucault's critique in the latter half of the 1960s.[79] Yet the analysis does not stop there. When these representations are assessed against spatial practices and physical phenomena, a new history begins to emerge, highlighting the incomplete work of spatial production. External orders are not simply projected onto the land, but constantly reproduced and maintained, making adjustments and corrections in response to the dynamic matrix in which they operate.[80] The encounter between space and power is not predetermined, and its uncertain results provide a fertile ground for enquiry of a charged and complex historical process.

Any critical engagement with the history of Israel-Palestine is analogous to walking into an intellectual and ideological minefield. The scholarly discourse on the matter is politically saturated and divided along trenchant lines to such an extent that one is constantly self-conscious of the potential implication one's work may have on grave matters that range well beyond the scope of the specific analysis. This regards not only the subject matter and political applicability of specific scholarly interrogations but the language and terminology used or avoided. Throughout the book I have made an effort to use terms, names and descriptions to provide the highest degree of clarity without losing sight of their specific historical and political context: I use the name Salama, for example, when referring to the period that preceded the 1948 War and until the new name of Kfar Shalem becomes more commonly used in archival material, approximately from the late 1950s. The depopulation of the village, meanwhile, is referred to as the forced flight of the

---

[78] It is beyond the scope of this book to overview the enormous body of work that charted the multifaceted inscription of Western fantasy into representations of space. However, exploring this issue in the specific context of this project, I found the following to be of specific interest: Lestringant, *Mapping the Renaissance World*; Noyes, *Colonial Space*; Carter, *The Road to Botany Bay*; Tiffin and Lawson, *De-scribing Empire*.

[79] Foucault, *The Order of Things*; Foucault, *The Archaeology of Knowledge*.

[80] Amy Mills explores a similar dynamic in her ethnography of an Istanbul neighbourhood, emphasising how residents "inhabit this nationalizing city and make sense of the state's national imaginary". Mills, *Streets of Memory*, 36.

population, in accordance with the specific historical records that do not bear evidence to an organised deportation as was the case in other towns and villages. Despite this, the volatility of the terms and the sensitivities they involve remain present throughout the analysis and become part of the unsettled landscape of the space at hand.

Similarly, a conscious effort has been made to avoid the temptation to resolve the conflicts and tensions that appear here through an alternative envisioning of the future. This first and foremost regards the depopulation of Salama's Arab residents and the settling of Jews in the village shortly after. Stating that the Arab environment continues to exist in and as part of the new Jewish space formed in the village is a political statement insofar as it depicts a state of affairs that results from political action and counteraction on different levels of the social and civil matrix. Furthermore, it illustrates a highly contentious reality that challenges powerful ideological and political apparatuses, which shaped spatial logic in Israel, at times through the use of coercive force and ideological manipulation. However, critically revisiting the historical archive does not turn back the wheels of history; it does not undo the damage, compensate for the loss, or bring about some form of reconciliation. As will be discussed at some length in the Conclusion, it is possible to outline challenging horizons that take place in the present, even when these do not live up to radical visions of political consolidation.

The spatial history presented throughout this book is obviously incomplete, most notably as it offers a history of an Arab space from which the voices of its former Palestinian residents are conspicuously absent. Important scholarly works in recent years have shed new light on the role of social networks, commemorative literature, and constantly evolving online platforms in preserving Arab village history in Palestine. From Walid Khalidi's pioneering encyclopaedic collection of Palestinian village histories, to the more recent work of Rochelle Davis on Palestinian village books and the growing corpus on Palestinian memory work,[81] the experience of Arab-Palestinians who were made refugees in the course of the 1948 War and its aftermath is far from absent or silent. Yet unlike other cases in which the presence of former Arab residents continued to bear directly on villages and urban neighbourhoods, Salama's Arab residents had almost no direct contact with the physical space of the village: one Arab house owner who remained in Jaffa after the war continued to collect rent from a Jewish family living in his house until 1960, when all Arab property was officially

---

[81] Khalidi, *All That Remains*; Davis, *Palestinian Village Histories*; Sa'di and Abu-Lughod, *Nakba*; Slyomovics, *The Object of Memory*; Masalha, *Catastrophe Remembered*.

annexed by the state; interviewees suggested that an Arab-Palestinian man who lives in the nearby city of Lod occasionally cleans the now-deserted mosque. It is almost impossible to measure the direct spatial effect these rare encounters had on the evolution of the neighbourhood after its depopulation in 1948. Instead, this book's focus is placed on the persistence of Arab spatiality and materiality *despite* the absence of the people who created it. Looking beyond the stringent categories of presence and absence, spatial history illuminates a more nuanced, and perhaps more radical potential of acknowledging the lingering effects Arab-Palestinian space has on the Israeli present.

Chapter Outline

This book does not progress linearly, but gradually assembles spatial themes and features that dominate Israel's social and political history. Each chapter surrounds one spatial phenomenon and examines its evolution, transformation and the unique histories it carries, from ruins to roads, fences and sacred spaces. Through the material, symbolic and practical aspects that take part in the construction and transformation of these spaces, the analysis gradually reveals subtle patterns of spatial interaction and negotiation, as well as the tensions and conflicts harboured in these sites. While the book as a whole is not governed by a chronological rationale, the sequence of chapters progressively establishes the historical, political and ideological foundations of Israel's spatial transformation. The argument does, however, begin with a description of broad phenomena and trends, and gradually narrows the focus to the specificities and actualities of places and everyday human routines. The spatial focus of the work also informed the decision not to include a detailed section of historical background, but approach various historical events through their spatial and material manifestations in specific chapters of the book.

Chapter 2, "Repopulating the Emptiness", establishes the critical impetus of spatial history by tracing two formative tropes: emptiness and ruin. Tied together in an intractable relation, the two play a central role in shaping the Zionist spatial imagination from its early days, and continue to feature heavily in Israel's political discourse in the aftermath of the 1948 War. Reading some of the defining texts of Zionism through a fresh spatial prism, the analysis illustrates the crisis of encounter with the physical realities of an old-new land[82] and the fractured dreams

---

[82] The term alludes to the utopian novel, *Altneulanad*, written by Theodor Herzl, the founder of political Zionism, which became one of the movement's seminal texts.

that accompanied the experience of immigration. Further drawing on detailed analysis of particular instances of house demolition, the chapter explores a history of ruination and the production of emptiness as active processes that attain a unique social and political meaning. On the one hand, they document the destruction of Arab land – the production of emptiness through ruination; on the other, they signify the ongoing effort to overcome the physical and symbolic resilience of that space and its significance.

This chapter provides an exposition of the methodological shift that will be exercised throughout the book; namely, a critical interrogation that is concerned with the physical composition and the discursive construction of seemingly insignificant spaces. Empty or ruined spaces are not meaningless vacuums, but sites of interacting histories and conflicting agendas – the outcome of a long and complex encounter between people and places, texts and material realities.

Chapter 3, "Fences and Defences", examines questions of spatial legality and legitimacy. Fences, an otherwise innocuous feature of the urban environment, appear as highly significant markers of the contentious legal status of Arab space. The chapter follows the legal mechanisms and procedures through which Arab space was expropriated and transferred to Israeli control, mostly through the use of emergency legislation. Employing legal and political theory to the specific emergency period that lasted in Israel until the mid-1950s, the chapter examines the spatial logic that governs the state of emergency and the inherent tension it harbours between the letter of the law and actions on the ground. The ongoing legal battle over the rights of Jews who came to reside in Arab property, and the striking phenomenon of fences that function as "urban camouflage", are highlighted as two distinct results of this troubled legal legacy.

The fourth chapter, "On the Road: From Salama to Kfar Shalem and Back", considers the use of urban planning as part of a broader Israeli effort to comprehensively reorganise Arab spaces and their meaning. A whole set of practical and discursive mechanisms were employed in this process – from infrastructural design to the alteration of street names – illustrating the significance of these seemingly mundane spaces in the production of the national space and narrative. However, rather than focus on the power of planning, the analysis turns critical attention to Arab sites that resist the imposition of a new urban order. Moments of planning failure, it argues, provide critical insights into the ambiguity, fear and the impediments of spatial control. This shift of critical attention highlights the political importance of daily practices and routines that rarely feature in analyses of Israeli spatio-politics. Though often overlooked, such places frustrate the formation of a homogeneous space that adheres to strict national, political and cultural conventions and begins to explain the heterogeneous Israeli urban landscape as an archive of power relations, coercive actions and antagonistic counteractions.

The assertion that spatiality provides a unique prism through which the operation of power can be examined and reconsidered is further developed in the fifth chapter, "Housing Complex: Between Arab Houses and Public Tenements". While the formative role of modernism in shaping Zionism's spatial ideology and practice is widely noted, less attention has been given to planners' actual ability to recreate the uto-pian *tabula rasa* on the ground. Focusing on the Israeli housing block, one of the hallmarks of urban modernism, the chapter suggests that large-scale housing projects constructed around the country from the late 1950s did not replace – and certainly did not erase – the Arab built environment. What began as the ideal antithesis to the squalor and degradation associated with the Arab built environment, came to epit-omise socioeconomic plight and cultural marginalisation. Using rich archival material, the chapter exposes the relatively unknown story of Jews who abandoned tenement flats in government housing projects throughout the 1950s and 1960s, only to return to the Arab houses they inhabited after the 1948 War. The chapter presents an original account of the unfinished work of the "modernising machine": the failure of the tenements project exposed deeper social and cultural rifts in Israeli society, and became part of the emergence of radical political dissent in depopulated Arab neighbourhoods that were resettled with Jews after 1948.

Chapter 6, "Sacred: The Making and Unmaking of a Holy Place", fol-lows the role of religious sites in shaping the intimate relations between Jews and the Arab space they came to inhabit. Two sites, which have undergone parallel processes of transformation, form the core of the discussion. The first regards the transformation of an Arab café on Salama's main street to a synagogue that serves a small Greek commu-nity. The analysis reveals how physical and material transformations take place through subtle gestures and symbolic acts, and focuses on the role of social practices and religious rites in mediating the encoun-ter between Jewish residents and the Arab space. It challenges the com-mon assumption that perceives repopulation of Arab sites either as a purely utilitarian process – Arabs move out, Jews move in – or views it as nothing more than a political and ideological effort to assert ethno-national dominance. The case of Salama's Greek synagogue illustrates the difficulties of immersing oneself in an alien environment, even when it is devoid of its previous human inhabitants. Furthermore, it illustrates how "Judeisation" processes resulted in a palimpsest-like space in which new functions often retrace and follow a pre-existing spatial logic.

The chapter continues to follow a similar, yet highly more contentious process of deconsecration of Muslim holy sites. The symbolic meaning of religious sites, which bear cultural, social and emotive significance in addition to their functional use, makes their transformation one of the most controversial aspects of post-conflict environments. The analysis focuses on the transformation of Salama's mosque into a youth club in 1949, and its function as part of the fabric of the neighbourhood until its closure in the early 1980s. The discussion deals directly with one of the most significant questions of this book: does space lose its meaning once its function changes in such a radical manner? Riots that took place around the empty building in October 2000 illustrate the fragility of Salama's spatial resilience and the difficulty of burying the past, erasing it, or ignoring its explosive potential.

The concluding chapter directly engages with the political and ethical potential of spatial history. Considering other methods of spatial intervention that seek to highlight the past in the present, from familiar forms of commemoration to alternative practices of "memory activism", spatial history's unique qualities are assessed. The discussion will illustrate the material and symbolic aspects of contemporary reparations politics, and point to spatial history's ability to overcome the trenchant absolutism that characterises many of these debates.

The Inevitability of Looking Back

An editorial in the *Guardian* a few years ago presented a firm opinion on some of the main geopolitical challenges facing the Middle East. "Nobody is going to get anywhere discussing 1948", it determined. "Matters will only progress if all sides address the here and now."[83] Pragmatism is indeed a rare commodity in "the region", but the assertion that "the here and now" would provide some magical remedy to the ailments of the past illustrates the wishful thinking that past catastrophes are somehow divorced from those created today. The allure of this suggestion lies in its pretension to break away from the spell of the melancholic gaze into the past and from the trenchant insistence to

---

[83] Editorial, "Iran: Lost in Translation".

perceive 1948 as a primal sin from which no man-made redemption is possible.

In a reversal of this paradigmatic imperative, the spatial history of Israel charts the inevitable histories of the "here and now". The case studies analysed and discussed here show that the past continues to resonate loudly in the concrete reality of a Tel Aviv suburb nearly seven decades after the events of 1948. Whether acknowledged explicitly or coded into socioeconomic inequalities, cultural marginalisation and alienation toward official mechanisms of power, Kfar Shalem's present is imprinted with the signs of its pasts – the Arab past of Salama, as well as the histories of those who inhabited it after the war. "1948" is not just a radical slogan that overwhelms the pragmatic political debate by bringing back the spectral fate of Palestinian refugees. It is also a formative moment that impacts the ongoing relationship between people and the space they inhabit, the material conditions in which they live, and the formation of personal identities and collective alliances.

This book posits that overlooking the past, leaving it out of consideration, is only one side of the coin. In its additional sense, overlooking is an act of inspection, regulation and supervision. Ignoring these present pasts also surrenders them to the ongoing process of regulatory power. The assumption that spatial histories can be compartmentalised into the neat order of the museum or the dusty files of an archive emerges out of the expectation that linearity and sequentiality will overcome the often chaotic and intimidating conflation of past and present. Using the metaphor of the city to explain the psychic process, Freud illustrated this perception, suggesting that, "If we want to represent historical sequence in spatial terms we can only do it by juxtaposition in space: the same space cannot have two different contents."[84] And yet Salama/Kfar Shalem is exactly a space that contains a multiplicity of contents, in a manner that does not freeze life into glass cases and without surrendering to the deterministic eradication commonly associated with historical progression.

Spatial history is an inevitable encounter with the pasts that make up our world. It reflects the fractured timeline that is written in spatial forms, norms and fantasies through which we practice and imagine our relation with the physical, social and political environments we inhabit. As such, it is never fully cohesive or wholly unambiguous, often resulting in a cacophony of narratives, allusions and memories. At the same time, it also bears witness to complex and contradictory negotiations

---

[84] Freud, "Civilisation and its Discontents", 70.

of cultural identities and political convictions, which in turn add their own inscription onto this dynamic spatial archive. Spatial history may not provide utopian political horizons, but it nonetheless presents a sensitive intervention in the material and imaginary aspects that form and transform the Israeli space.

2   Repopulating the Emptiness: The Spatiality and Materiality of the Overlooked

Dudi Balasi's house was partly hidden behind thick vegetation, corrugated iron slabs, car tyres and a run down wire fence. Closer up, other buildings were revealed, most of which were in a rather dilapidated condition. "The city council won't even allow me to replace the asbestos roof. Any improvement in the house is automatically seen as a breach of the law and an excuse for them to tear it down", he said when we first met in autumn 2007. The condition of the interior of the house was similarly poor: cracks were apparent in the walls and ceiling, and in one of the rooms the floor began to sink. Balasi explained:

My father-in-law moved into one of Salama's Arab houses after he emigrated from Yemen. We later needed to expand the house and build another room. Outside there was a well, from which people used to get water before there was a permanent water pipe, so we covered the well with sand and built the floor over it. Recently, the floor began to sink. I guess the well is still there.[1]

Balasi is one of several residents of Kfar Shalem whose house was to be demolished after a private landowner had decided to carry out plans for a real-estate development project. As part of a prolonged legal battle, Balasi challenged the developer's plans, presenting an almost indecipherable fax-copy of a mandatory sale agreement that disputed the ownership claims over the land. The court was not convinced and approved the eviction of the tenants and the demolition of the houses. On 25 December 2007, 30 families were driven out by large police forces and the houses on the corner of Moshe Dayan Way and Mahal Street were razed. The slow sinking of Balasi's house into the sandy land of the Tel Aviv costal plain, which would have led to its eventual collapse, was brought to an abrupt halt by the forces of real-estate capital and "development". Put another way, the actions of future development came just before the subterranean force of the past could complete its gradual erosive process.

---

[1] Balasi, Interview with the author.

The recent events of house demolition in the neighbourhood were not novel to old-timers like Balasi. After four decades in Kfar Shalem, Balasi says he can give "guided tours" around the neighbourhood to recount the stories of numerous houses that were razed over the years, from the old Muslim cemetery behind the school to the site of the Iraqi synagogue in the western part of the neighbourhood. In similar fashion, this chapter "tours" in search of empty sites and ruins; it traces recurring acts of ruination, illustrating the physical, cultural and social marks that remain long after the bulldozers have left.

Much is at stake in this repopulation of emptiness. Critical scholarship of spatial transformation in Israel-Palestine is laden with references to the Zionist trope of the empty land, its numerous variations and diverse articulations. Though this trope has been factually discredited, notions of emptiness and erasure continue to linger in critical scholarship revisiting the formation of ethno-national space in Israel-Palestine and the fate of Arab cultural and physical geographies. As violent and extensive as this process may be, the notions of emptiness, erasure and ruination cannot be taken at face value if we wish to better understand the complex ideological and discursive forces that take part in the production of space. Looking beyond the skewed rhetoric of a settler society, this chapter illuminates specific technologies of power that are employed to shore up what is inherently an unstable and contested foundational fantasy. Returning to the paper trails and material archives of this process enables us to trace instances in which the encounter with the land fractures the ideological construct of emptiness. It exposes the ambivalent discourse regarding Arab spaces seized by Israel in the 1948 War, in which the notion of "empty space" appears increasingly unstable, often conveying contradictory meanings and exposing deep ideological and political uncertainties. This critical revision illustrates the paradox of Zionist efforts to eradicate physical presences in a land that was supposed to be empty in the first place. Understanding emptiness as an *ongoing process* and replacing the ruin by the *acts* and *outcomes* of ruination highlights the unfinished effort to produce a homogeneous ethno-national space in Israel/Palestine and consequently illuminates the fractures in this hegemonic power structure.

Living Ruins

Piles of rubble, shattered remains and infrastructural dereliction are some of the most obvious signs of physical ruination. Most often, however, material landscapes and written archives record more subtle appearances that do not fit this conventional typology. Remaining attentive to the full spectrum of ruination – from the most spectacular and violent instances to faded traces and understated recollections – holds critical insights into the lived experience of these spaces, the social resonance they retain, and the forces that intersect in their creation. Later in this chapter I present a contextual analysis of emptiness and ruin, their genealogies and historiography. Yet my concern begins with the very grounded forms of ruins and the unexpected histories we can plot from them.

Salama/Kfar Shalem is dotted with scenes of ruination, past and present. During the 1948 War, destruction to the built environment was rather limited, conducted mostly during sporadic operations by Jewish paramilitary groups during the first months of the hostilities. Once Jews began settling the village changes became more obvious, yet these same alterations in the fabric of the village also set the new residents on a collision course with the authorities. Because all Arab property seized in the war was considered state property, draconian tenancy agreements prevented residents from carrying out any changes to the buildings, which often lacked basic features like a kitchen or lavatory. Lacking better options, people resorted to building improvised structures adjacent to the Arab houses, and were immediately subjected to threats of demolition from a special inspection force operating on behalf of the Custodian for Abandoned Property.[2] These inspectors issued hundreds of demolition orders during the 1950s: one resident, Avraham Garame, was issued an order to immediately halt the construction of a 9m² kitchen and a lavatory, which was followed by a demolition order issued the same day.[3] These demolition operations were relatively limited in scale, and confined mostly to unauthorised additions to existing houses, but nonetheless set in motion a highly volatile dynamic: residents build, the state demolishes.

This pattern was accentuated in the early 1960s when procedures of eviction and demolition were delegated to "Halamish", one of several governmental housing corporations that were established to handle the redevelopment of former Arab regions. With more substantial resources at its disposal, the firm was able to carry out large-scale relocations of residents and to demolish many of the houses in the southern areas of Salama. A landscape of ruins gradually became part

---

[2] The Custodian and the legal-political context in which it was devised, will be further discussed in Chapter 3.

[3] Garame was only one of many residents who encountered the Custodian Police that operated in the village and contributed to the general suspicion between the authorities and the residents. See: Custodian Police, "Injunction to Halt Construction against Avraham Garame"; Custodian Police, "Demolition Order against Avraham Garame".

of the neighbourhood, fracturing the Arab pattern of spatial organisation. As an official report summarising the first years of evictions noted, "clearance actions brought to the deterioration of the situation. The evictions created empty lots between the houses and in several cases caused entire streets to be deserted, aside from 2 or 3 houses that remain [occupied]."[4] To this day, piles of debris that have been left following the demolition of illegally constructed buildings are discernible throughout the neighbourhood, though often tucked away in back streets or surrounded by plastic sheets. Understandably, residents who have been evicted from their homes are not eager to bear the high costs of removing the rubble after the bulldozers leave. According to most urban plans made for the area, many parts of Kfar Shalem are destined to be demolished. However, despite their efforts, the council and the development corporation operating on its behalf have so far been unable to complete the evictions due to ongoing legal disputes and a lack of resources to meet the compensation demands of the residents. Ruination remains a looming potential, though seemingly an unfulfilled one.

And yet, the spatial status quo that renders ruination almost undetectable is extremely deceiving. The traces of ruination are overtly visible, even as they take somewhat unexpected forms. After the houses on the Mahal-Moshe Dayan corner were demolished, the developer fenced off the area and began to plant trees throughout the lot. Shortly after, a sign placed by the Tel Aviv municipality was posted on site, reading "Temporary Grove" and ordering that the place be kept clean (Figure 2.1). This is not a practical joke: throughout Kfar Shalem extensive efforts are made to plant trees on empty lots, in what would seem at first sight to be an attempt to beautify the neighbourhood and provide additional "green areas" for the residents. But the temporariness of these groves implies that their presence is not merely an ecological endeavour. The Local Sustainability Center, an Israeli organisation advocating and coordinating ecological policies,[5] explains that in order to prevent "vacant areas" from turning into an environmental and sanitary nuisance, or a target for "homeless and criminal invaders", the municipality has begun planting groves that will remain until the sites are used "according to their original purpose".[6]

---

[4] Halamish, Municipal-Governmental Company for Housing in Gush Dan, "Kfar Shalem Survey. The Construction and Eviction of Development Areas".

[5] The centre has been operating since 2006 as a joint venture of the Ministry for Environmental Protection, Tel Aviv University and ICLI, an international association of local governments, and is funded by the European Union. It provides local councils with tools, information and training for practitioners at the local and municipal level.

[6] Local Sustainability Center, "The Planting of Temporary Groves in Vacated Areas – Tel Aviv-Jaffa".

Figure 2.1 A "Temporary Grove" planted on the ruined Mahal-Moshe Dayan compound. Photo by the author.

The fact that the largest temporary grove in Tel Aviv is found in Manshiya – formally Jaffa's northern neighbourhood, which was severely damaged during the 1948 War and almost completely razed in the 1960s and 1970s – is indicative of the political and ideological motivations behind this phenomenon. Through ambitious construction projects, the area is destined to physically and symbolically "fuse" Tel Aviv and Jaffa and "connect" Tel Aviv to the sea; in the meantime, the "vacated zone" is "filled" by a large recreational area and parking lots. In Kfar Shalem, Manshiya, and other sites of ruination, there is no vacuum: spaces are reinserted into the practical cycles of the city, whether through a coordinated planning procedure or through the operation of individuals and groups who take advantage of these sites for their own purposes. In this sense, temporary groves are but one relatively cheap and quick methods through which the municipality can claim possession of the land.

Although city officials were, in all probability, operating according to a purely practical agenda, tree-planting is far from a new practice in situations of spatial contestation and conflict. The role of afforestation has become one of the recurring themes of critical research into the

formation of Zionist space.[7] Historically, Zionism shared the prevailing nineteenth-century European views of "the natural", and sought
to import familiar landscapes of pine and cypress forests to Palestine.
Additionally, the act of tree-planting was also perceived as a symbolic
gesture that tied people and land. Cohen recalls Theodore Herzl's first
and only visit to Palestine in 1898, during which Herzl noted how prior
to his trip he imagined Palestine to be covered in forests similar to those
in his native Austria, and called upon Jews to donate money toward a
vast afforestation project in Palestine.[8] The connection between ecology
and ideology became even more overt once the Jewish National Fund
(JNF) began championing the forest as a productive symbol of Jewish
land possession. Zvi Shiloni notes how, "among those dealing with settlement, recognition grew that the forest was of value, both as a sign of
Jewish settlement and as a tool for maintaining possession of Jewish
areas not given to other use". After the establishment of the State of
Israel, the same spatial logic was applied to areas seized in the 1948
War, and specifically to sites of demolished Arab villages.[9] The forest
was an instrument that completed the act of destruction by "naturalis-
ing" the ruined landscape, literally and symbolically "covering up" the
remains of Arab life in these areas.

The harnessing of nature for geopolitical goals is a well-documented
process. Yet I recall this history to highlight its ironic reappearance in
the present, in the temporary groves planted in Kfar Shalem and other
sites throughout Tel Aviv. Though mostly referred to through "green"
terminology of sustainability and environmentalism, these groves are
an instrument of containment and border supervision, much like the
ones planted in border regions after the 1948 War and the planting policies instituted after the 1967 occupation of the West Bank.[10] However,

[7] See Cohen, *The Politics of Planting*.
[8] Ibid., 47.
[9] In *The Ethnic Cleansing of Palestine*, Ilan Pappé presents perhaps the sharpest critique
of afforestation as part of Israel's attempt to obfuscate the traces of Palestinian villages
in the landscape, though others have previously pointed this out. In his 1963 novella
Facing the Forests (Yehoshua, *The Continuing Silence of a Poet*.), the Israeli author A.B
Yehoshua illustrates the tale of a Jewish student who becomes a forest watchman,
gradually discovering the remains of an Arab village buried under the trees. For critical analyses of Yehoshua's narrative see: Hever, *Producing the Modern Hebrew Canon*,
chapter 6; Zerubavel, "The Forest as a National Icon"; Morahg, "Shading the Truth".
In *The Object of Memory*, Susan Slyomovics examines how forest landscapes provided
Jews with a way to familiarise themselves with the new spaces they had come to
inhabit. Naama Meishar illustrates how forests and national reserves are used to limit
the expansion of Arab villages. Meishar, "Fragile Guardians".
[10] Cohen, *The Politics of Planting*, 66–8; 112–13.

in the case of Salama/Kfar Shalem and other former Arab regions incorporated into Tel Aviv's municipal area, a different set of objectives governs the authorities' agenda. Explicitly at least, Kfar Shalem is no longer an arena of national conflict between Jews and Arabs, where each group seeks to make territorial gains at the expense of the other. The divisions are now drawn along socioeconomic lines, placing under-privileged groups – "homeless and criminal sources"[11] – as the obstacle for development and a threat to private entrepreneurship. Despite their appearance in different historical and ideological contexts, past and present groves are closely intertwined with ruins and the need to "reor-ganise" the traces left by acts of destruction. Viewed as such, groves do not simply erase or cover up the marks of ruination, they quite literally signpost them.

In official discussions, these groves are presented as purely functional devices. Menahem Leiba, Director General of the Tel Aviv Municipality, illustrated this utilitarian logic when he explained to the council forum in 2006 how

you create a grove, it grows, you build what you need to build there, a road, and after that it [the grove] moves somewhere else. And you do another devel-opment and another development, and this machine continues to operate and does not stop for a moment.[12]

Leiba noted the increase in the number of green areas in Tel Aviv, and specifically stressed "the amount of gardens in the Kfar Shalem area, gardens in all sorts of small and hidden places".[13] Not surprisingly, this description remains rather vague about the ruinous process that ena-bled these groves to appear in the first place.

The contentious use of green areas and their relation to (past or planned) ruination has a specific history in Salama/Kfar Shalem. The first comprehensive plan of the neighbourhood, titled Plan 460 and offi-cially presented in 1963, was an attempt by the planning and munici-pal authorities to begin the redesign of Kfar Shalem from a "clean slate", in accordance with a modernist architectural tradition. This, however, required extensive demolition of the entire neighbourhood, apart from the Salama mosque which was intended for preservation.[14] According to the plan, the centre of the neighbourhood was planned as

---

[11] Local Sustainability Center, "The Planting of Temporary Groves in Vacated Areas – Tel Aviv-Jaffa".

[12] Tel Aviv Municipal Council Forum, "Meeting Protocol", 6.

[13] Ibid.

[14] See further discussion of Plan 460 in Chapters 3 and 5. For an extensive analysis of the spatial history of Salama mosque see Chapter 6.

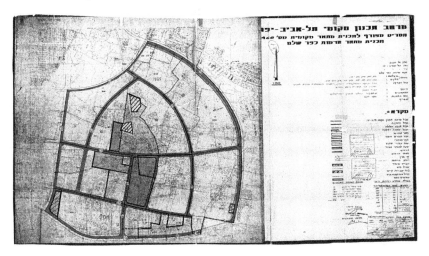

Figure 2.2 Local Master Plan 460, 1963. Tel Aviv Municipal Archive.

an "open public space" and was therefore appropriately painted green (Figure 2.2). The visual quality of the plan exposes the actual price of creating the open, empty spaces that seemed so neutral in the protocols of the Tel Aviv council above. Through the semi-translucent layer of green colour, one can easily observe numerous black marks designating the existing construction, which, according to the plan, was destined to be completely demolished. As I extensively discuss in the following chapter, the plan was never fully implemented. However, it was at this early stage that the intervention of external forces – municipal, national or private – became associated with the "greening" of Salama. Through this historical prism, encountering "gardens in all sorts of small and hidden places" is not a just a pleasant discovery, but a stark reminder of the extensive physical and discursive violence that shaped these spaces.

There are, of course, other emblems of ruination in Kfar Shalem that are perhaps more easily decipherable. Demolition orders are often directed at parts of houses that were built without legal permits or authorisation; once demolished, interior walls are externalised and exposed, revealing previously hidden bathroom tiles or staircases. Similarly, the contours of entrances and doorways that have been blocked up or cemented still mark, for example, the entrance to the Salama boys' school that is now used as a workshop for people with learning disabilities. The Japanese art and architecture collective, Rojo Kansatsu [Roadside Observation], formed in 1986, coined the term "Tomason" to describe "the flashings and detritus of the incessant churn of building, destruction, and redevelopment that characterizes the Japanese city".[15] This phenomenon is of course visible around the world, especially in sites of rapid transition and scarce resources. However, in cases like Salama/Kfar Shalem, taking note of these remnants is not intended just to provide some melancholic pleasure,[16] but rather to expose the political, socioeconomic and cultural conditions of living among and in ruins. Ivan Vladislavic,[17] for example, explored similar sites in Johannesburg during the 1990s, during the decline of Apartheid and the transition of power. As Vladislavic shows, it is possible to use spatial manifestations of this sort to illuminate the effects of broad socio-political trends in time- and site-specific occurrences. Throughout their history – before 1948 and well into the present – Salama's Tomasons are always overlooked in a double sense: discounted and ignored, while constantly subject to inspection, regulation and policing.

Emptiness and ruin in Salama/Kfar Shalem are intimately intertwined. It is often hard to determine where one ends and the other begins. Nonetheless, their appearance in the village is closely tied to a longer history of encounter between people and space, between spatiality as it was culturally imagined and the experience of its material and concrete reality. In what follows, a broader genealogy of these terms illustrates their emergence out of specific historical circumstances of crisis and doubt. Rather than parochial idiosyncrasies, this contextual analysis suggests that temporary groves and Tomasons are in fact part of a broader material and textual archive, which documents a deep, unresolved struggle to fuse people with an old-new land.

Encounter

"Land without a people, for a people without land": this slogan has become a popular target for critical accounts of Zionism's territorial aspirations and its attitude toward the Arab population of Palestine. Yet this slogan has long been a crude political cliché; its circulation in the first decades of the twentieth century among Zionist enthusiasts was part of an attempt to gloss over one of the shaping experiences of Jewish immigration to Palestine; namely, the shattering collision between idealistic pioneering dreams and the mundane actualities that

---

[15] Allan, "On Tomason".
[16] Numerous blogs and online photo-sharing groups are devoted to the visual documentation of ruins and abandoned spaces. See for example the list compiled on the Blue Tea blog entitled, "Aesthetics of decay": www://bluewyverntea.blogspot.com/2006/09/aesthetics-of-decay.html
[17] Vladislavic, *Portrait with Keys*.

make up the experience of colonisation. Indeed, in the writings of those who sought to realise the Zionist settlement dream, the sentiment of the slogan (though rarely the slogan itself) already appears as battered propaganda, scorned for the false impression it helped create. As early as 1914, Moshe Smilansky, a Zionist farm owner, writer, and one of the founders of the agricultural colony of Rehovot, described how "from the first moment of the Zionist idea, the Zionist propaganda described the land to which we were headed as desolate and forsaken, impatiently waiting for its redeemers". Smilansky, who later worked closely with Zionist institutions like the Jewish Agency, noted that this propaganda created a false "feeling that Palestine was a virgin country".[18]

Similar sentiments are also traceable in the writings of more prominent Zionist figures. In a compelling confession-like account, the Jewish writer Yosef Haim Brenner captures a critical moment that has often been marginalised in the accounts of the Jewish immigration to and colonisation of Palestine:

Who can imagine the pain of the unfortunate intelligent Jew who comes here, desirous of a different life, more wholesome, filled with physical labor, the fragrance of the fields – and who, after a few days, realizes that the dream was false, that the land already belongs to Arab Christians, that our farmers are but farmers in the abstract, and that there is no hope here for our people?[19]

With typical candour Brenner describes the awakening from the false dream shared by Zionist idealists who came to Palestine only to realise that the biblical "land of milk and honey" was already owned and farmed by others. What is striking about this passage is not so much the sober awakening but the bleak portrayal of the distance between a collective fantasy and the concrete reality Brenner encounters, the gap between the physical experiences of the land and those "farmers in the abstract".

Brenner was not alone in admitting to this devastating contradiction between ideological fantasy and material reality. As early as 1891, one of the forefathers of the Zionist movement, Asher Zvi Ginsberg – often known by his Hebrew pen-name *Ahad Ha'am* ("a man of the people") – returned from his first journey to Palestine, which inspired the writing of his famous polemic essay, "Truth from Palestine". The essay, which appeared in the St Petersburg Hebrew paper *Ha-Melits*, openly disavowed the imigrationist premises that dominated early mainstream Zionism. The essay was met with fierce rejoinders; some even accused

---

[18] Quoted in Shapira, *Land and Power*, 58.
[19] Brenner, *The Writings of Yosef Haim Brenner*, vol. 4: 153.

Ahad Ha'am of defaming Jewish national efforts in general and the Jewish colonisers in Ottoman Palestine in particular. Indeed, the essay sets off by shattering readers' expectations, contrasting the hope of a dreamt "wonderland" with the despair of settler reality:

After many years spent contemplating and imagining the land of our fathers and the rebirth of our people in it, I have now finally been privileged to see with my own eyes the subject of my dreams, this land of wonders which captivates the hearts of multitudes from all peoples and all lands. I spent about three months there. I saw its ruins, the remnant of its life in the *past*. I observed its miserable condition in the *present*, but I paid particular attention to its *future*, and, everywhere I went, one question was always in the forefront: in the end, what is our hope here?[20]

The moment of encounter between dream and land appears as a moment of crisis in which the powerful prism of biblical Orientalist fantasy famously described by Said,[21] Rabasa,[22] Mitchell[23] and others, is shattered by a place that bears no resemblance to such imaginings. It is not simply a realisation that the dream – the bucolic space waiting to provide the stage for a romantic national play – proved false. What is perhaps more alarming for Ahad Ha'am is the fracturing of a teleological historical course that leads the progression of Jewish life from a biblical nation ("the land of our fathers") to diasporic decline, and finally a revival of Jewish national life in the Land of Israel. The reality of life in "the land" – or more precisely, "its ruins" – undermines the ability to fulfill Zionism's fundamental settler ethos of "returning to history" through the return to a physical territory. As briefly noted above, the return to the historical homeland of the Jewish people was more than a colonial search for productive spaces for the extraction of material resources. The very fundamentals of the Zionist narrative of redemption were at stake: in temporal terms, the promised future is supposed to deliver one from the miseries of the past and the present. As Shai Ginsburg noted in a brilliant reading of Ahad Ha'am's essay, the three temporalities merged into "a continuum marked by ruins and a wretched existence".[24] Furthermore, the spatial antithesis posited between the *here* of Ottoman Palestine and the *there* of exilic lands of Jewish residence – the "negation of exile" – is also fractured. The land that was supposed to resolve "the Jewish problem" of exile eroded the

---

[20] Ahad Ha'am (Asher Zvi Ginsburg), "Truth from Eretz Yisrael", 160; emphasis in the original.
[21] Said, *Orientalism*.
[22] Rabasa, *Inventing America*.
[23] Mitchell, *Landscape and Power*.
[24] Ginsburg, "Politics and Letters", 185.

fundamental binaries (past/future; here/there; exile/sovereignty) that supported Zionism's ideology and political agenda.

As prominent public figures, both Brenner and Ahad Ha'am express concern toward the political future of the Jewish national movement and its ability to "ground" its aspirations. While the fate of the political movement and the imagined community were indeed pressing matters, another description of this moment exposes how the encounter with the land manifested itself in the personal experience of women and men who travelled to Palestine in the first two decades of the twentieth century. In his 1945 novel *Only Yesterday*, S.Y. Agnon illustrates the immigration experience of a young Zionist enthusiast in the Second *Aliyah*.[25] On the day of his arrival in Palestine, the protagonist Isaac Kumer steps for the first time out of his hostel in Jaffa, an experience Agnon depicts in his expressive manner:

As soon as he took one step, both his feet sank in the sand. This is the sand of Jaffa that digs underneath you to swallow you up. As soon as you stand on it, it runs out and turns into holes on top of holes.[26]

The sense that the ground is neither solid nor stable is a moment of crisis that fractures the immense hopes and ideals that were to materialise on and through it. Agnon's illustration captures and individualises the anxiety that Zionist visions of the land are destined to break down at the point of their realisation in space.

The tension of spatial representation – the gap between the word and the world – is essential for understanding the deep unease expressed by these texts. Postcolonial scholarship has often scrutinised the textual construction and sustenance of the colonial *imago mundi*. Edward Said, for example, uses the notion of "textual attitudes" to describe the human tendency to fall back on a text when uncertainties seem to threaten one's equanimity, so much so that the text "acquires a greater authority, and use, even than the actuality it describes".[27] Refining Said's formulation, David Bunn suggests that the colonial encounter with landscape generates "an exaggerated form of *anaclisis*, or 'propping' of one landscape paradigm upon another".[28] Despite the terminological differences, both reflect a broader agreement that writing the land (through cartography, travel journals or landscape painting) asserts a system of control

---

[25] Hebrew for "going up" or "ascent". A term designating Jewish immigration to the Land of Israel.

[26] Agnon, *Only Yesterday*, 40.

[27] Said, *Orientalism*, 93.

[28] Bunn, " 'Our Wattled Cott' ", 144.

long before European colonisers first set foot on the physical ground of "discovered" territories, and continues to perpetuate paradigms of dominance and control long after. Conversely, the writing of Brenner and Ahad Ha'am, I would argue, captures a more complex dynamic in which the authority of the text seems unable to withstand the encounter with the actualities of colonisation. The colonial writing of space appears here not as the exorcism of spatial ambiguities[29] or as the erasure of contesting images, but as yet another site where such ambiguities leave their mark. Attentively reading the spaces of encounter reveals the actuality of colonial experience: the fragmentation of consistent narratives and the penetration of these complexities into seemingly homogeneous forms of representation, the very texts that lie at the heart of the Zionist archive.

In one of the most important critical studies of spatial transformation in Israel/Palestine, Meron Benvenisti coined the term "white patches" to describe a diverse set of mechanisms that prevent the Arab landscape from entering the space of Zionist ethno-national discourse: "Arab communities" he writes, "towns, villages and neighbourhoods had no place in the Jews' perception of the homeland's landscape. They were just a formless, random collection of three-dimensional entities."[30] But at the end of that same paragraph, Benvenisti goes on to claim that, "The attitude of the Jewish population toward the Arab landscape – physical and human alike – was a strange mixture of disregard, anxiety, affection, superiority, humanitarianism, anthropological curiosity, romanticism and above all, European ethnocentricity." The reduction of such a plenitude of interests and diversity of motivations to all-encompassing notions of "white patches" or to the common trope of "empty land", is illustrative of the broader analytical need for a more nuanced approach to the contradictory actualities of colonised space in Israel/Palestine.

A Densely Populated Emptiness

The moment of encounter can hardly be confined to the first waves of Jewish immigration to Palestine and repeatedly appears in the archive long after the establishment of the State of Israel.[31] Yet the gradual

---

[29] de Certeau, *The Practice of Everyday Life*, 134.

[30] Benvenisti, *Sacred Landscape*, 56.

[31] In his first visit to the West Bank after its occupation by Israel in 1967, Yossef Weitz, who served for decades as director of the Jewish National Fund and led its forestation activities, echoed similar sentiments in his diary when he witnessed the achievements of Palestinian farmers: "The more I look closely, the more ashamed and embarrassed I feel

adoption of the ethno-national state as Zionism's dominant frame-work[32] demands particular attention to the role of statist narratives in shaping the cultural perception of national space.

A booklet issued in 1962 by the Israeli Information Administration, an official body that domestically communicated government policies, provides a stark example of a national effort to transform so-called desolate space under the guise of productivity and utilitarian exploitation of resources. In perhaps a less obvious manner, this text exposes the potential threat identified with spatial emptiness. The booklet, which was distributed in the thousands around the country, describes the reality in Israel's northern periphery after the 1948 War. It focuses particularly on the vast tracts seized in the war and the consequent settling of Jewish immigrants in new agricultural settlements. It then continues to argue that after the war,

An important economic factor – land – was suddenly found in relative abundance. On the other hand, wide spaces were now desolate – which enhanced Israel's security problems. The solution was found in agricultural settlement: land was abundant and could be utilized. New settlements will boost agriculture, provide food for the population and prevent the security risks that emerge from empty spaces.[33]

The Israeli critic Yitzhak Laor describes this text as the "imperative of the national narrative",[34] laying down the territorial and discursive conventions on which the Israeli national ethos would be founded – an ethno-national collective of frontier farmer-warriors. On the face of it, the IIA text serves a straightforward purpose of reorganising a chaotic post-war reality into a comprehensible scheme of progress and productive accumulation. This dynamic closely resembles what Deleuze and Guattari describe as capitalist de- and reterritorialization, i.e. the removal of existing significations as a precursor to their redefinition in terms more conducive to capital accumulation.[35] In the case of the IIA text, however, the extraction of resources from the land is not the primary goal of reterritorialization, but a practical solution to

comparing 'our' Jerusalem mountains to their [the Arabs'] Hebron mountains. We, who use steel (large tilling machines), have training, huge budgets, and expensive water, have not achieved anything so flourishing. We are culturally and practically inferior by comparison, and all because they are people who work the land, and that land is their sole livelihood, and we are far from being that." Quoted in Segev, 1967, 426.

[32] As opposed to bi-national or even anti-national visions that emerged in earlier Jewish debates as a response to the rise of Zionism.

[33] Israeli Information Administration, "Pitu'ach ha-karka ve' bitchon ha-medina [Land Development and National Security]", chapter 1.

[34] Laor, *Narratives with No Natives*, 156.

[35] Deleuze and Guattari, *Anti-Oedipus*.

the potential threats empty space poses to territorial control. The emptiness imposed on the Arab landscape links two functions – space as productive resource and its role in an ethno-national political agenda – and seeks to defuse any ability to contest the natural and neutral settler consumption of land. But the process of "inscribing the emptiness", to borrow Simon Ryan's[36] phrase, is not a straightforward erasure or a simple disregard. A closer examination reveals, for example, how the IIA booklet refutes one of the fundamentals of settler colonial logic. In a rather candid manner, the text portrays the Jewish agricultural settlement in Palestine – long celebrated for its doctrine of productivisation and novel social philosophy – as a colonising tool in the formation of a settler project. Although the implication of such agricultural endeavours in the colonising mechanism has been central to scholars exploring the settler-colonial foundations of Zionism like Piterberg[37] and Shafir[38], its matter-of-fact presence in a government propaganda booklet is noteworthy. Instead of a repressive trope in the service of colonial narrative, emptiness invites a wealth of critical readings into the inherent instability and contradictions of the colonial text.

In their study of radical ethno-cultural transitions in Israel, Hannan Hever and Yehouda Shenhav note that the hegemonic act of erasure is simultaneously a process of re-inscription, and both "leave numerous traces in the broad margins that surround the separation line" between Arab and Jewish space.[39] What is exposed in this process is a "discursive labour" that disrupts the seamless transition from one (political or cultural) category to another. Consider, for example, the way the IIA booklet creates a causal relation between "desolate" spaces and a "security threat". While noting that the territory seized in the 1948 War was "empty of human presence", it says nothing about the material presence of more than 400 Arab villages and hamlets that were depopulated during the war. Some were demolished during or shortly after the war, but many, particularly in peripheral regions, were still intact well into the 1960s.[40] The booklet remains intentionally vague on whether these material remnants were enough to instigate such anxiety and sense of threat. Yet these ambiguities in the narration of empty space testify to the challenge of bridging the gap between the neat national imagination and the complex realities on the ground.

---

[36] Ryan, "Inscribing the Emptiness".
[37] Piterberg, *The Returns of Zionism*.
[38] Shafir, *Land, Labor and the Origins of the Israeli-Palestinian Conflict, 1882–1914*.
[39] Hever and Shenhav, "Arab Jews – A Genealogy of a Term", 70.
[40] Shai, "The Fate of Abandoned Arab Villages".

Israeli official discourse in the first years of the state sought to consolidate two seemingly contradictory positions regarding the presence
of Arab physical remains. On the one hand, an encryption of the devastation: the country's first prime minister, David Ben-Gurion, insisted
that the Zionist task was to "resurrect the ruins of a poor and devastated
land ... that stood empty for two thousand years".[41] For Ben-Gurion,
ruins and destruction are meaningful only insofar as they signify the
ancient Jewish kingdom and act as a signifier of teleological return to the
land after two millennia of exile. This is not a *tabula rasa*, but an effort
to dissociate ruins from their cultural, political and historical context.[42]
In other cases, when their Arab origins are acknowledged, the physical
remains of villages are widely deemed a "security threat", which in turn
justifies their demolition. Numerous villages were razed to fight Arab
"infiltrators" – mostly refugees who tried to make their way back into
Palestine from neighbouring countries and found shelter in the abandoned houses. Yehezkel Sahar, the first Chief of the Israel Police, stated
in his memoirs that his request to demolish approximately 50 villages
circa 1952, "considerably eased our war on the infiltrators".[43] The apparent contradiction between Ben-Gurion's "desirable emptiness" and
Sahar's perceptions of emptiness as threat highlights the IIA booklet's
ability to slyly gloss over this tension by trumpeting the national mission of settlement and appropriation. Even so, the recurring sense that
emptiness is never wholly devoid of "things" that continue to carry an
unsettling meaning, illustrates its importance for the critical historiography of colonisation.

So far, we have seen that at its essence, the Zionist production of
space relied primarily on two practices; namely, *erasure* and *writing*.
Both terms allude to a longer colonial history in which the production of space in general, and empty space in particular, was founded
on an inherent subordination of spatial reality to textual representation. Noyes vividly portrays this process when he observes that the
first European explorers of Africa were in fact retracing "the paths

---

[41] Ben-Gurion, *On Settlement*, 73–4.
[42] The selective dissociation of ruins from their historical origins was certainly not a
Zionist "invention": Rashid Khalidi, a historian of Palestinian nationalism, notes the
uproar that followed the 1910 Zionist land purchase in al-Fula, which also included
the ruins of a Crusader castle. Two articles reprinted widely in the Arab press of the
time protested that the sale handed over a "fortress" supposedly built by Saladin, and
as such, a valuable part of the nascent Palestinian national heritage. "The important
thing was not whether the ruin had originally been built by Saladin; it was that these
newspapers' readers believed that part of the heritage of Saladin ... was being sold
off." Khalidi, *Palestinian Identity*, 31.
[43] Sahar, *My Life Story*, 98.

and goals of the natives" and were obliged to follow the native spatial knowledge in order to move from one water hole to the next.[44] However, these movements were defined by different terms, and were to have new meaning:

This is possible because the physical movements of the explorer are only an initial phase, a pretext for a writing which is the true consummation of exploration. Thus the physical goals are always subsumed into a wider system of signification relating to the land (geographical features, mineral deposits etc.) or its inhabitants (as in trade of missionary activities).[45]

The investigation of emptiness is therefore initially concerned with the prominence of writing, a practice that has been conventionally "employed not only to describe the earth, but to actualise its productive potential".[46]

Yet we must not limit ourselves to space as a purely graphic creation. The repetitions, contradictions and tensions within the texts I have been discussing here, expose the potential of investigation of this sort to question not only the ideological mechanisms of national spaces but the philosophical foundation upon which these projects are constructed. Moreover, if we refrain from assuming that physical space "remembers what history tells it to and erases what it tells it to forget",[47] then we gradually begin to see how both spatial and temporal ambivalence are maintained within it:

Where "knowledgeable" discourses attempt to preserve and systematize experience through repetition in the signifying chain, this preservation is necessarily a veiling of reality, since it bears the elision characteristic of signification. Where knowledge and representation aim themselves at a truth situated elsewhere and elsewhen, the truth they specify attains the quality of a lack.[48]

This "lack" should not be confused as yet another manifestation of the emptiness I hope to challenge, but alternatively considered as a versatile and prolific collection of spatial, textual and discursive signs, which are far from being homogenous or predictable. Their appearances provide an insight into the actual negotiations that take place between people – individuals and communities – and the spaces in which they live, work, seek leisure or simply pass by. These are objects that "lack" because they fail to possess the characteristics that will qualify them as

[44] Noyes, *Colonial Space*, 109.
[45] Ibid.
[46] Ibid., 110.
[47] Rotbard, *White City, Black City*, 15.
[48] Noyes, *Colonial Space*, 72.

part of what Noyes calls "knowledgeable" discourse: they are old and decrepit, hidden in the peripheral neighbourhoods of cities; they are encrypted in the contradictions and ambiguity of official documents and texts; they aggravate officials, block policies and frustrate planning authorities. The ambiguity of empty space, the recurring sense that it is never wholly devoid of "things" that continue to carry an unsettling meaning, suggests that there is perhaps more within this emptiness than first considered. The following suggests that the same applies to spaces that have been subjected to "emptying practices" of ruination, destruction and forceful modification.

Unsettled Ruins

Early Israeli official descriptions of Arab landscapes seized in the 1948 War often oscillate uneasily between emptiness and ruination. This conflation of terms established the perception that whilst such spaces were not materially void, they lacked a human quality that would make them historically and culturally significant.[49] Critical scholarship of spatial transformation in Israel often argues that the re-inscription of the land enabled the erasure of indigenous or subaltern presence by a hegemonic national narrative.[50] Yet some of the core examples of the mainstream Zionist narrative illustrate the difficulty of reconciling the ruined post-war landscape with an unambiguous sense of emptiness. A speech by Prime Minister David Ben-Gurion at a conference of the Israel Exploration Society, a Zionist group formed in 1914 to conduct archaeological and historical research in Palestine, offers valuable insights into this tension:

We are not complacent about the fate of our land, even the part in our control. Foreign conquerors have made our land a desert; dilapidation is extensive and vast regions have been deserted. The war of independence expanded the emptiness. And we must know: ... We will not keep hold of the Negev plains, the costal sands and the bare mountains for long. Maintaining our independence forces us to rebuild ruins, to restore wastelands, to settle abandoned areas and populate them in the nearest possible time.[51]

While expressing similar sentiments, this is not an earlier version of the 1962 Israeli Information Administration booklet. Throughout his public

---

[49] This resembles a familiar colonial practice that dehumanises rather than categorically ignores native spaces. See ibid., 196.

[50] Falah, "The 1948 Israeli-Palestinian War and its Aftermath"; Fenster, "Memory, Belonging and Spatial Planning in Israel"; Kadman, *Erased from Space and Consciousness.*

[51] Bulletin of the Israel Exploration Society, "The Sixth Archaeological Conference", 120.

life, Ben-Gurion was never known for apologetic oratory or abstractions, and neither is found here: the new lands gained during the war are not empty spaces, but places that have been subjected to a process of ruination that preceded the war and was extended by it. The emptiness, as Ben-Gurion describes it, is laden with ruins and waste. Two years later, in an essay that appeared in the government's official bulletin, Ben-Gurion reiterated this point while at the same time hinting at the selective nature of this ruination process:

> The war of independence brought ruin and destruction on thousands of settlements, and when the state came into being there stood only the Jewish settlements established in the last seventy years and a few which were not Jewish. The truth is that the state inherited a wasted and deserted land.[52]

Waste and destruction were indeed found mostly in the Arab regions seized by Israel during the war. But it is not precise that ruination was caused primarily by the fighting. As already mentioned, ruination and destruction were also deliberately carried out by army units, police and local municipalities who seized the opportunity to rid themselves of what they portrayed as houses in danger of collapse, or unfit for development and falling short of sanitary requirements. In addition to the presumed security threats they presented, the remnants of Arab habitation were viewed as a source of political unease and even shame. An official in the Israeli Foreign Ministry wrote in 1957 to Yitzhak Eylam, the Director-General of the Ministry of Labor:

> The ruins from Arab villages and Arab neighbourhoods, or intact blocks of houses that have stood deserted since 1948, have difficult associations that cause considerable political damage. During the past nine years many ruins were removed, whether by development projects or by climatic factors; but those that survived protrude even more so in contrast with the new landscape.[53]

According to this memo, special attention should be given to highly visible Arab remnants such as those found in "Jewish settlements, in important centres or along major routes of transportation". The dilapidated state of these sites left, according to the letter, a "very depressing impression". To avoid this, "it would be proper to remove the ruins that cannot be restored, or that do not have archaeological value". In most cases, "removing" meant razing the buildings, though in some cases those responsible for the process showed some concern as to the consequence of their actions. In a 1963 meeting of the Committee for Locating

---

[52] Quoted in Kletter, *Just Past?*, 46.
[53] Dothan, "Letter to Yitzhak Eylam, Director-General of the Ministry of Labour".

and Preserving Sites in Jerusalem, one member offered an alternative to the complete destruction of villages:

I suggest that we perform a survey, and act as they do in Switzerland, where, to preserve old cities, a plan of every old building is made regardless of whether it is destined for destruction or preservation. Photographs or plans of each building are filed. Architectonic parts of Arab houses destined for destruction could be entered into an Arab Museum, to be established in the future, after the houses are destroyed. The photographs will show what existed at the place that is going to be destroyed. Otherwise they will say about us that we have ruined all the antiquities barbarically, without even leaving documentation.[54]

It seems that what separates the "civilised" Swiss from the barbarian is the inclination – perhaps even obligation – to document, chart and archive the process of ruination. It is not the actual act of demolition or destruction that ought to be reprimanded, but the failure to record and provide evidence of what was and is no more. Placing relics in glass cases and archiving architectural charts are the thresholds of so-called civilised ruination, which is inflicted for "progressive" purposes, as opposed to the random, unsophisticated acts of barbaric violence. At least in its programmatic form, the proposition was never endorsed.

"Ruin" was not only a descriptive term for the run down state of buildings and areas. During the renaming process of Arabic toponyms (discussed at length in Chapter 3), the term *Hirbeh* – Arabic for "ruin" – became a colloquial term to signify sites of ruins, mostly the remains of depopulated Arab villages.[55] While the adoption of Hebrew terms for ruin (*Khurva, I'yim, Harisot*) was officially made by the government committee responsible for the renaming of Arab toponyms, the broad dissemination of the term *Hirbeh* was assisted by one of the canonical literary accounts of the 1948 War: S. Yizhar's *The Story of Hirbet Hizah*. The tale follows the expulsion of the inhabitants of an Arab village by an Israeli platoon during the war and was the focus of a heated debate when it was adopted for a television film and screened in 1978.[56] One dialogue between the soldiers is specifically interesting because it points to the fate of those sites that were not, or not yet "removed":

"You listen to what I'll tell you," said Moyshe, and his eyes sought out mine.
   "To Hirbet, what's-its-name, immigrants will be coming. Are you listening? And they'll till it and everything will be fine."[57]

---

[54] The Committee for Locating and Preserving Sites in Jerusalem, "Meeting Protocol", translated in Kletter, *Just Past?*, 64.
[55] Kadman, *Erased from Space and Consciousness*, 57.
[56] For an extensive discussion of the story, its reception and the controversies it aroused, see Shapira, "Hirbet Hizah".
[57] Yizhar, "The Story of Hirbet Hiz'ah", 331.

The protagonist's reaction is sardonic:

Of course, what then? Why Not? Why did I not think of that at first? Our Hirbat Hizah. There will be problems of housing and absorption. Hurrah, we shall build houses and absorb immigrants, and then we shall build a grocer's shop, we shall put up a school, perhaps also a synagogue ... Long live Jewish Hizah![58]

The sarcasm was well founded. In the immediate aftermath of the war, former Arab villages and neighbourhoods were one of the first solutions devised to house the masses of Jewish immigrants that arrived in the country. Many of the "ruins" were made into homes, some by a predetermined government plan and others by "squatters" or "invaders" who sought housing during the severe shortage of those years, as I discuss in Chapter 4. Oftentimes, the decision to invade an Arab house resulted from the lack of better options, as one government minister noted in 1949:

The immigrants who came to Tiberias live in ruins, without windows or doors. It is currently the warm days, but what will we do in the rainy days? For some reason these immigrants were not fortunate enough, and they are called the Moroccan and North-African immigrants ... The government speaks a lot about immigration and its encouragement, but the result is still that people flee the country. They came here and were let down.

One can trace in this statement the echoes of Brenner's disillusioned account quoted earlier. The encounter between people and space – in the 1950s as in the first three decades of the twentieth century – unveiled and exposed the gap between ethos, on the one hand, and social, economic and cultural realities, on the other: if Brenner's description exposed the fallacy of the heroic conquering of the empty land, the quote above illustrates how the ruin became part of the Israeli experience of the new land. Rather than a triumphant sign of conquest and national might, the Arab ruined space exposed the deepest fractures in the national ethos of territorial revival and the end of diasporic Jewish life. In fact, the material degradation and sense of institutional neglect felt by the inhabitants made a return to the diaspora ever more appealing. As such, and rather shortly after the war (the statement above was made in the summer of 1949), the ruin became more than a symbol of Arab past; it was an inseparable aspect of the Israeli spatial present. The fact that the old city of Tiberias was completely razed soon after, does not undermine the critical value of this sort of investigation. Rereading the narratives of colonisation reveals the ruin, even if fleetingly, as site of deep political ambivalence and ideological tension.

[58] Ibid., 331–2.

However, while some Israelis saw the Arab ruins as embarrassing reminders – decrepit objects that stain the image of a progressive modern space or as a security threat – others "discovered" a wholly different kind of ruin. The establishment of Ein Hod, a Jewish artists' colony in the depopulated Arab village of Ein Houd, has been cited as a striking illustration of the way ruins were incorporated into an ideological order that obscured the native script of possession. Marcel Janco's "discovery" of Ein Houd captures the exact moment when the threat of the ruin is replaced by fascination:

In 1953, I worked as an architect for the government. I was assigned to plan national parks, and therefore travelled throughout the country ... One day, as I was trying to locate a site for a park on Mount Carmel ... I suddenly heard loud explosions ... I witnessed the demolition of numerous houses. When I inquired, I was told that the army demolished houses in the abandoned village for security reasons ... I decided to get closer, and since I was a high official, my demand to stop the demolition was obeyed. Being an architect and an artist, I could see that this was not an ordinary Arab village, but an historical one ... And indeed, Roman ruins were discovered there, and probably many other archaeological remains are yet to be found.[59]

Susan Slyomovics suggests that in the eyes of the Dadaist artists who came to live in Ein Houd, decay and destruction were acts of nature, and debris were "both primitive and ancient features of the landscape".[60] Contrary to the ostensibly modernist artistic aspirations of Janco and others who settled the Arab houses of Ein Houd, there is a strong Romantic sentiment behind the valorisation of the ruins and debris left by the army bombers. Janco's "discovery" that this was "not an ordinary Arab village, but an historical one", calls to mind Anne Janowitz's assertion that the ruin constantly threatens to "eradicate temporal difference, swallowing up the present into an unforeseeable yet inevitable repetition of the past".[61] Haim Yacobi rightly notes that the identification of Arab spaces as "primitivist", "folkloristic" or simply "archaeological", helped validate "an atmosphere of certainty and order that lead to the observation of present reality as a linear continuance of the

---

[59] Quoted in Yacobi, "Architecture, Orientalism and Identity", 110.
[60] Slyomovics, *The Object of Memory*, 51.
[61] Janowitz, *England's Ruins*, 10. As one of the most prominent tropes of Romanticism, the Ruin also emerged from the specific historical encounter between European writers and the colonial territories. For a discussion of the relationship between Romanticism and colonialism see Fulford and Kitson, *Romanticism and Colonialism*. Simon Ryan also notes the recurrence of (real or imaginary) ruins in Australian colonial descriptions, providing evidence both to the failure of the Aboriginal people, which in turn creates an "absence [that] demands replenishment" (Ryan, *The Cartographic Eye*, 76–9.).

past".[62] While the ruin was indeed pivotal in creating an ideologically selective anachronism – appropriating Arab landscapes to prove the continuum of Jewish historical presence in Palestine – a closer analysis reveals that this was not a simple case of cultural erasure.

There was no vacuum in Ein Houd in the five years that passed from 1948 to the establishment of Ein Hod in 1953. The artists who followed Janco were not the first Jewish settlers to inhabit the Arab houses and were preceded by two unsuccessful attempts by the Israeli authorities to settle Jewish groups in the place. First, a group of Algerian and Tunisian Jews who were brought to the village were transferred to an alternative site several miles south of Ein Houd, which was more accessible for the transportation of water and the establishment of agriculture.[63] Following this, a group of Jews who survived the attack on Kfar Etzion by the Jordanian army in May 1948 stayed in the village for a short period until the establishment of Nir Etzion village in 1950.[64] These chapters should not be overlooked, because they record the experience of two groups that did not share Janco's discovery of an archaic, Orientalist hamlet in the semi-demolished houses of Ein Houd. Ostensibly, other needs were prioritised by these groups: for the North African immigrants the ability to cultivate the land and develop a means of livelihood took precedence; and one has to assume that for the survivors of Kfar Etzion, who lost many of their friends in the 1948 battles and temporarily lived in the Arab neighbourhood of Jabaliya in Jaffa,[65] resettling in a depopulated Arab village did not hold the same appeal as it did to Janco and his fellow artists.

As Slyomovics illustrates through conversations with the Jews living in Ein Hod, various discursive elements enabled the new residents to overcome the unease of settling in Arab houses when some of their previous Palestinian residents were living only a couple of miles further up the road in the village of Ein Houd el-Jadidh (New Ein Houd). Describing the unease she experienced when moving into one of the Arab houses in the village, one resident of Ein Hod said, "You kind of crawl into somebody else's soul in these houses."[66] It is interesting how this sense of unease, which reappears on various occasions in the literature recording the encounter between Jews and Arab spaces, is defused or at least overcome to the degree that it does not prevent the

---

[62] Yacobi, "Architecture, Orientalism and Identity", 111.
[63] Asaf, *The Workers' Community in Israel*, 177–80; Yacobi, "Architecture, Orientalism and Identity", 110; Slyomovics, *The Object of Memory*, 31.
[64] The Settlement Department, "Monthly Reports for the Haifa Region".
[65] The Israeli Labor Movement, "Nir Etzion – Communal Village".
[66] Slyomovics, *The Object of Memory*, 77.

repopulation of these sites altogether. According to the official narrative that appears in the catalogues and brochures issued by the community in Ein Hod, Janco was successful in amalgamating a potent mix of European cultural avant-garde with Zionist territorial nationalism, which seemingly overcomes the ambiguities and foreignness of the Arab space.

But other factors also contributed to the realisation of Janco's dream, which owed more to material and political privileges than to discursive practices. Janco was working for the Government Planning Authority, one of the most powerful bodies that dealt with the reshaping of Israel in the 1950s, when he came across the ruins of Ein Houd. Using his position Janco was able to halt the military actions that led to the demolition of some of the houses on the site. Here Janco succeeded where others, similarly concerned by the demolition of what they saw to be sites of historical or archaeological significance, failed. Raz Kletter, who researched the archives of the Israeli Department of Antiquities and Museums, recalls several cases where demolitions were carried out despite protests by government archaeologists; although from dissimilar motivations, political figures from the left-wing socialist Mapam and even from the right-wing Herut party also voiced their objections but often could do little to influence the actual results on the ground.[67] Moreover, to gather the group of artists that will establish Ein Hod, Janco was able to broadcast a radio speech in which he invited artists to join the project. Needless to say that access to state-run radio was not open to all.

Janco's recurrent portrayal as a visionary artist-ideologue, and a representative figure of the spatial *zeitgeist* of Israel in the early 1950s, emphasises the orchestrated effort he devised in the unique production of space in Ein Hod. However, this triumphant tale must also invoke the precursors of Janco's "discovery"; namely, the Algerian and Tunisian immigrants and the war refugees of Kfar Etzion, who passed through Ein Houd but in quite dissimilar fashions. The tales of partial or failed transformations are equally important to our understanding of what it means to "take place".

The experiences of groups who were outside, or at the margins of Israeli society in the first years of the state, enable us to reinsert some suspicion and doubt into the role the Arab space played with relation to Israeli Jews who lived in or in proximity to it. For these groups, the Arab space was never reduced to "a neat 'historical collection' that

---

[67] Kletter, *Just Past?*, 60.

served as a controlled instrument for organization of the collective knowledge and memory".[68] The important point here is not to isolate counter-reactions to top-down, state-sanctioned planning. Nor is this process reducible to a postcolonial "third-space" where hybrid identities are formed and where mimicry undermines colonial authority.[69] Rather, critical attention turns to the endemic ideological inconsistencies, political failures and bureaucratic uncertainties found at the heart of the Zionist archive, yet remain largely under-theorised in the ideological and geographical history of Israel/Palestine. Bringing these ambiguities to the fore is a crucial step in articulating a more nuanced critique of cultural hegemony and the landscape of power it produces.

Both emptiness and ruin function as key components in Zionism's relation to space, but neither are reducible to simple national-ideological props. From their appearance in the writings of Jewish thinkers and immigrants in the late nineteenth century, "emptiness" and "ruin" were ambiguous and unstable terms, and remained so in the years that followed the establishment of the State of Israel in 1948. Obviously, the two were closely bound together: to produce empty spaces, a vast process of ruination was required; however, the ruins and debris left behind were not neutral objects in the landscape – often causing embarrassment, unease and fear – which would, in turn, activate both physical and discursive "emptying practices". This paradoxical cycle goes on and on. Although these terms have permeated into more recent works that have sought to interrogate and challenge the presuppositions of the Israeli national project, there is much to gain from preserving the ambiguities and paradoxes that are exposed in an analysis of these terms over time and space. Historicising the process of ruination and the production of emptiness, as well as their manifestations in concrete sites and social-ethnic contexts, enables us to follow a rather more intricate and multifaceted interaction that constitutes processes of spatial transformation and the production of its meanings.

Archaeology of the Surface

Once emptiness is understood as an *ongoing process* and the ruin is replaced by the *acts* and *outcomes* of ruination, one begins to encounter a vast corpus of phenomena that would not otherwise enter the

[68] Yacobi, "Architecture, Orientalism and Identity", 97.
[69] As proposed, for example, in Yacobi, *The Jewish-Arab City*; Benjamin, "'Present-Absent'"; Nuriely, "Strangers in a National Space"; these scholars draw theoretical inspiration from Homi Bhabha's conceptualisation and expand it beyond the confines of the textual-discursive realms. Bhabha, *The Location of Culture*.

analytical purview as artefacts of legitimate historical stature. A col-
league, who drives several times a week from Beersheba to Jerusalem,
told me an anecdotal story that illustrates this point. Part of the way
he travels passes through the Beit Govrin region, where several Arab
villages were depopulated during the 1948 War. Many of the houses
in these villages were demolished by Israeli military forces and later
by park authorities. One evening, while passing through this area, a
friend who accompanied him pointed out: "it's quite remarkable that
the villages have been almost completely wiped out, but the road is still
here, winding in the landscape from one ruined village to another…"[70]
On the face of it, this is inconsequential minutia that presents no real
contribution to the public knowledge about this history of the region,
the events of 1948, or the fate of the villages. Perhaps. But what are the
criteria according to which we select and categorise phenomena and
observations, deeming some worthy and other irrelevant? How do we
measure degrees of presence and absence that direct our attention to
certain objects but not others? This is an epistemological question as
well as a methodological challenge.

It is possible to begin interrogating this problem by taking ruins seriously. Ruin – as an act perpetuated, as the damage one is subjected to, and
as the cause of loss[71] – is a repository of historical processes, of social and
cultural relations, and a site of personal and collective loss. There have
been several noteworthy attempts to illustrate an analytical reconsideration of spatial ruination as an enduring social, material and political process. Arjun Appadurai[72] and AbdouMaliq Simone[73] describe the spectral,
invisible forces that operate on the social and political environments in
cities such as Mumbai/Bombay and Douala, Cameroon, respectively.
Both refer to the spectral as a form of haunting that marks "the space of
speculation and specularities, empty scenes of dissolved industry, fantasies of urban planning, rumors of real-estate transfers, consumption
patterns that violate their spatial preconditions, and bodies that are their
own housing".[74] Neither shies away from the empirical body of facts, but
acknowledges the "sense that there is much more happening than meets
the eye, and that everyday life is a force field of resurgent traces from the
past, something not yet laid to rest".[75] In an exceptional anthropological
account of Appalachia, Kathleen Stewart explores the historical imprint

[70] Feldman, Interview with the author.
[71] Stoler, "Imperial Debris", 195–6.
[72] Appadurai, "Spectral Housing and Urban Cleansing".
[73] Simone, For the City Yet to Come, chapter 3.
[74] Appadurai, "Spectral Housing and Urban Cleansing", 635.
[75] Simone, For the City Yet to Come, 92.

one encounters in ruined sites, invoking what Ann Stoler refers to as the "visible and visceral senses"[76] that are stored and reactivated:

In the ruin that *remembers*, history and place, culture and nature converge in a tactile image that conveys not a picture perfect reenactment of "living pasts" but the allegorical re-presentation of remembered loss itself. The vacancy of a lot in Rhodell *remembers* the fire that burned Johnny Millsap to death while he cried out for help and the others could do nothing but watch; the exposed electrical wire in the hills above Amigo mines #2 *remembers* the image of Buddy Hall, a nine-year-old boy, hanging from it.[77]

This specific concern with ruins constantly moves away from the melancholia of the picturesque ruin, and toward a rediscovery of the "powerful effects that remember things in such a way that 'history' digs itself into the present and people cain't [sic] help but recall it".[78] As such, a critical analysis of ruins is obliged to account for the temporal simultaneity of these sites, at once functioning as objects of the present and as testimonies to past processes of ruination. While highlighting the immense potential of this temporal synchronicity, Stoler cautions against the reduction of these sites into evocative metaphors in a way that obscures their ongoing social and cultural contingency:

The analytic challenge is to work productively, if uneasily, with and across this tension. In so doing, the project is not to fashion a genealogy of catastrophe and redemption. Making connections where they are hard to trace is not designed to settle scores but rather to recognize that these are unfinished histories, not of victimized pasts but consequential histories that open to differential futures.[79]

Stoler's warning seems especially valid with regard to many accounts of spatial transformation of Arab spaces in Israel, a subject that evokes an extremely contentious debate in the public-political sphere as well as in the academic one.

Another problem regards the ability to consolidate the nature of the ruin as part of "the spatial *forms* and *fantasies* through which a society declares its presence".[80] The former regards ruin as tactile objects, from monumental sites to decomposing infrastructures. The latter alludes to the appearance of ruins and ruination as objects of memory, a past remnant sedimented and encoded into language, ritual, body and text. Spatial history is an attempt to account for both forms and fantasies as equally important components. Disciplinary traditions and methodological constraints often require a choice between these

[76] Stoler, "Imperial Debris", 196.
[77] Stewart, *A Space on the Side of the Road*, 90–1, emphasis in the original.
[78] Ibid., 111.
[79] Stoler, "Imperial Debris", 195.
[80] Carter, *The Road to Botany Bay*, xxii.

spheres; in other cases, the boundaries between the two blur, and it is no longer clear when metaphor ends and material object begins. Stoler suggests that the interplay between the two spheres should be the focus of this analytical endeavour: "The point of critical analysis is not to look 'underneath' or 'beyond' that slippage but to understand the work that slippage does and the political traffic it harbors."[81]

Consider, for example, the story of Shekhunat Ha'argazim, roughly translated as the "Boxes Neighbourhood", situated just south of Kfar Shalem. The neighbourhood is considered to be one of the poorest in Tel Aviv and is especially notorious for the recurring flooding of streets and houses almost every winter. Lack of infrastructure is undoubtedly the cause for this ongoing problem. In 2002, the contractor and developer that operated as part of a general regeneration project constructed a rudimentary drainage system that provided a solution to one part of the neighbourhood. Seemingly, this is a local problem with little or no bearing on the issue at hand. But one has to wonder how years of infrastructural neglect by the municipal authorities was tied to other, less apparent histories of the place. Yossi Levi, whose family moved to the neighbourhood after the 1948 War, describes how council officials advised his father "to take over the entire land, all the way to the nearby creek – only for the Arabs not to return".[82] This was the same creek that flooded the neighbourhood the following years. The ideological enthusiasm and practical concerns – which led the state authorities' decision to settle Jewish immigrants in Arab-owned areas without ensuring that these could sustain the influx of new residents – resulted in new ruins being created every winter on top of those which were already there following the war. Similarly, personal memories appear in residents' testimonies as evidence of belonging and possession, against claims of illegal occupancy. Another resident, Meir Sisso, describes how when he moved into the neighbourhood, there was

a house in the middle of a field. They would sow roses and cabbages, and Arab labourers were working for a Jewish landlord. There were no more Arab residents, they all escaped. Ben-Gurion was prime minister at the time and he said that every empty Arab house a Jew enters – he owns. Just occupy a place so the Arab won't have a place to return to.
[...]
We didn't steal this house; we paid for it with money. If anybody invaded, it was the state that invaded the Arabs' land. It's not hers, but theirs.[83]

---

[81] Stoler, "Imperial Debris", 203.
[82] Fishbein, "Eviction-Construction", 29.
[83] Ibid., 34–5.

It is exactly the difficulty of drawing a clear line that would mark the end of one process of ruination and the beginning of another – to separate the ruination of war from that inflicted by real-estate developers – which characterises ruins as an elusive object for spatial, historical and social inquiry. And yet, as these voices attest, ruins are not vacuums of social or historical knowledge. In their material form and articulation in oral histories, official documents or cultural texts, ruins are far from being mute objects. Even when subjected to widespread destruction, ruins and ruination find their way into the archive. At times, there are elaborate debates about and around the ruins: the residents of the Arab-Christian village of Bir'em in the Upper Galilee region, who were ordered to leave their homes in November 1948, became a symbol in their struggle to return to the village, which was turned into a tourist site.[84] For decades, the former residents and their children have repeatedly petitioned the Supreme Court, operated intense parliamentary lobbying, and set up an internet website and summer camps where younger generations learn about the history of their village. Although so far the appeals of the residents to return to their village have been unsuccessful, it is impossible to dismiss the cultural, social and political webs formed through and around the ruins. An anecdotal example of the contestation over ruins once they are exposed to the social and cultural sphere is found in the sign placed by the Israeli Nature and National Parks Authority, which highlights the Jewish history of Bir'em. In the first sentence, which reads "The village of Bar'am was a thriving and prosperous Jewish community", the word "Jewish" was scraped off, perhaps as an act of protest. The sign was then repaired by placing a sticker with the missing word, only for it to be partly scraped off again (Figure 2.3).

There are, of course, more extreme cases of ruination, as in the case of the villages of Yalo, Amwas and Beit Nuba, which were demolished in 1967. After the war, a national park was planted over the ruins. Various signs placed around the park mention the rich history of the site – from Roman and early Jewish periods, to Ottoman rule – remain silent about its Palestinian history. But destruction did not mean that the villages simply vanished. At weekends, whole families of former Arab residents arrive in the park for seemingly innocuous picnics, but ones that nonetheless express a structure of feeling between people and place that has otherwise been severed.[85] Although these are powerful social

---

[84] Kadman, *Erased from Space and Consciousness*.

[85] The only remains of the villages are agricultural terraces and orchards, which have become inauspicious in the national park that was planted there in the following

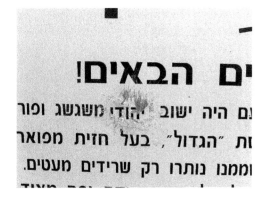

ים הבאים!

:ם היה ישוב יהודי משגשג ופור
ת "הגדול", בעל חזית מפואר
וממנו נותרו רק שרידים מעטים.

Figure 2.3 Visitor information sign at the Bar'am National Park.
Photo by the author.

instruments that maintain a community's relation to its past, it is often easily overlooked. Yet these are precisely the forms of "haunting" that highlight the social and cultural meaning of ruins, explicating "how that which appears not to be there is often a seething presence, acting on and often meddling with taken-for-granted realities".[86]

The inherent ambivalence of the ruin – as a partial presence, a remnant of a whole that is no longer there – is often resolved too easily. The obvious unease evoked by the human and cultural toll exerted in the process of ruination, translates in certain works into an urge to "salvage" the ruin and "refill" the emptiness, usually by summoning an alternative narrative of reparation and reconstruction. Seeking to capture not only "what is" but "what ought", literature and visual art often provide a vehicle through which scenarios of consolidation and reconciliation can be acted out. As the references to several literary works throughout this chapter suggest, prose and poetry are valuable repositories that capture ephemeral moments of shifts in the relation between people and place. The possibility of using fictional narratives to illustrate alternative horizons in which ruins are rebuilt and restored is perhaps as

decades. However, a recent legal appeal made by Zochrot, an Israeli organisation promoting the commemoration of and public debate over the 1948 Palestinian *Nakba* (disaster), demanded that the Israeli authorities acknowledge the Arab history of the site with proper signs. In March 2006, following a two-year legal battle, Israeli authorities conceded Zochrot's request, and placed signs noting the site's Arab history. See Eitan Bronstein's article on Zochrot's efforts to signpost the destroyed villages in the area: "Restless Park: On the Latrun Villages and Zochrot". A discussion of Zochrot's activity in Salama/Kfar Shalem appears in the Conclusion. See also: Leshem, "Memory Activism".

[86] Gordon, *Ghostly Matters*, 8.

important. However, in most of the cases discussed throughout this book, consolidation is rare: even when reconstruction takes place, it remains laden with tensions and conflicts, and never fully compensates for the loss. Furthermore, attempts to reform or rehabilitate ruins often tread a fine line between physical appropriation, financial exploitation and benevolent intentions.

As an alternative to the perception that ruins are in some way flawed spaces, which in turn invite a repairing intervention, this project places its focus on the complex and heterogeneous forces that operate on and around sites of ruination. This endeavour begins, therefore, with ruins and empty spaces as physical entities, sites that possess tactile qualities that attest to their present and their past. Taking the ruin seriously, as was stated earlier, requires one to revisit these sites as archives of historical residues, while at the same time considering the explicit and implicit role the past plays in shaping the present. The latter task is of special significance if we are to avoid the temptation to overlook the function these places serve in and as part of the lives of their more recent inhabitants. In other words, the unique quality of a spatial inquiry into ruins and empty spaces derives from their ability to re-present a multiplicity of pasts in a non-linear way: spatial history of this sort reveals the simultaneity and co-dependency of seemingly unrelated or even conflicting historical strata. In this sense, my concern is as much for the present as it is for the past. More precisely, my emphasis is on the inseparability of these two spheres as it appears in the spatiality of Israel-Palestine since 1948.

Nonetheless, as broadly discussed throughout this chapter, ruins and empty sites are as much a textual creation as they are material loci. Many of the conventions through which these tropes are produced emanate from a textual projection that sets the stage, as it were, for the ruins yet to come. But the reverse process also takes place, when ruination and the attempts to empty space are recorded and documented in official archives. The most valuable information in these archives exposes the forces that motivate ruination and a recurring institutional frustration when this process remains incomplete.

For these reasons, this book may be seen as an "archaeology of the surface", concerned at once with the excavation of the past and its recurring appearance in the space of the present. Like archaeology, the subject matter is often fractured and the evidence about it incomplete, and similar to archaeological sites, it does not intend to recreate the past but illuminate it through fragments, shattered objects and incomplete accounts. However, the present is not sidelined or taken for granted as "simply there". The true challenge lies in the attempt to tie past and present, not as the obvious emergence of the latter from the former, but in spite of apparent incongruities and irreconcilabilities between the two.

There is no direct line that can be drawn to connect the demolition of Dudi Balasi's house in 2008, with the arson of houses shortly after the conquest of Salama in the 1948 War which was noted in the Introduction. Balasi's house was ruined to create emptiness; torching the houses was an act of ruination perpetrated despite their vacancy. Yet these distant events share a single place, thus highlighting Salama/Kfar Shalem as a site of conjuncture of seemingly unrelated spatial patterns. Thinking spatially enables us to identify what Massey calls the "throwntogetherness of place", and to think of Salama as one of many sites that "implicate us, perforce, in the lives of human others, and in our relations with nonhumans they ask how we shall respond to our temporary meeting-up with these particular rocks and stones and trees".[87] However, the patterns of ruination in Salama/Kfar Shalem are noticeable not only from the safe distance of analytical inspection, but give rise to ground-level confrontations with spatial and historical multiplicities and their political implications.

When the ruin ceases to be the static object that lends itself so well to the melancholic gaze, and when the (almost impulsive) urge to automatically associate it with narratives of victimhood and oppression is suspended, we can begin to unearth the ongoing negotiations that make these sites historically and socially significant. The tensions that surround sites of emptiness and ruination in Salama/Kfar Shalem and their concrete effect on the relations between residents and official bodies of the state and the city will be the focus of Chapter 3.

---

[87] Massey, *For Space*, 141.

3   Fences and Defences: Spaces of Emergency

To the uninformed passer-by, the small, inconspicuous compound on the corner of Moshe Dayan Road and Mahal Street presented no visible feature that would suggest its precarious state. When I visited the compound in October 2007, the dozen or so buildings within its perimeters were barely discernible from the road only a dozen metres away, hidden by makeshift fences and thick vegetation. Indeed, fences are perhaps the most striking feature that sets Salama's Arab houses apart from their more recent urban surroundings. Constructed using numerous materials, from wooden boards and tin slabs to recycled billboards and densely overgrown banana trees, these fences restrict sight and prescribe movement, blocking voyeurs and trespassers from infringing these fenced off enclaves. What is the motivation behind these camouflage tactics? Are these fences merely a mark of the boundary between public and private realms or are they the result of a more complex set of forces? As noted in Chapter 2, the compound was demolished after a long legal battle in which it was concluded that the residents had no legal possession of the houses they occupied, some since 1948. The fate of the Mahal-Moshe Dayan compound suggests that fences surrounding the Arab houses in Kfar Shalem do not merely act to preserve the privacy of those residing behind them, but in fact retain a more urgent function as mechanisms of defence.

Despite being a chronicle of a demolition foretold, this chapter charts the entwined history of space and law, and situates specific spatial phenomena in the interaction between legal, political and cultural forces. The discussion contextualises the struggles over land rights and ownership which have plagued many former Arab neighbourhoods settled by Jews, by examining the formation of "spaces of emergency" – sites in which the clear distinctions between law and action are intentionally blurred, creating a zone of legal and political indeterminacy. The analysis shows how the spatial logic of emergency, which was utilised by the Israeli state in the foundational period of the 1948 War and its aftermath, was later "hijacked" and turned against the state's authority itself. The chapter illustrates the material features that characterise these sites and the profound impact this spatial reality has on relations between citizens and the state.

The demolition of houses in Kfar Shalem is not new. Indeed, as Chapter 2 illustrated, the communal memory of the neighbour-hood's residents is saturated with stories of houses that have been torn down by state authorities since the early 1950s, when official inspectors issued demolition orders on a daily basis. Nonetheless, the Tel Aviv Municipality's eviction operation in Kfar Shalem on 23 December 1982 became a pivotal moment that continues to haunt the neighbourhood to this day. During that day's events, a young man named Shimon Yehoshua stood on the roof of his home in an attempt to delay the demolition of a room he built adjacent to his parents' home – one of Salama's Arab houses. Yehoshua was surrounded by a police force that accompanied the bulldozer sent to carry out the demolition. The standoff lasted only a few minutes. Testimonies from the event are not entirely clear, but suggest that when Yehoshua fired three shots from a pistol in his possession, he was immediately shot by a police officer.[1] Yehoshua died instantly and his body was taken off the roof on the shovel of the bulldozer, which later continued to tear down the house.

An official investigation commission was established to determine the course of events that led to Yehoshua's death, and its report pre-dictably focuses on the legal and criminal aspects of the incident. Nonetheless, in a section dedicated to the phenomenon of illegal sei-zure of houses in the neighbourhood, the report points to the particular use of fences in the struggle over land and property possession. In the case of Yehoshua's family, as in other cases throughout Kfar Shalem where unauthorised construction took place on sites that have previ-ously been subject to evictions, residents erect fences "so that a man from the outside could not see into the grounds".[2] The commission lists 50 such cases in the period that preceded the death of Yehoshua, and notes the determination of the municipal authorities to detect construc-tion in its early stages and execute demolition orders immediately. The commission strongly condemns the attempts to evade the inspecting eye of the law and to conceal evidence of illegal acts. Understandably, the commission's report addresses only the limited legal aspects of the case – and leaves aside other critical aspects, from the precarious status

---

[1] Winograd, Zemach and Mishaeli, "The Committee for the Examination of Events in Kfar Shalem", 13.
[2] Ibid., 17.

of Jewish residents in former Arab property to the history of violence that plagued so many of these urban spaces throughout the country. But the Yehoshua family was not the first to encounter the spite of the authorities. Indeed, we can trace a genealogy of violence and eviction that plagued former Arab spaces, from the shooting of Yaakov Elkarif by police in Haifa's Wadi Salib neighbourhood on 9 July 1959 – which sparked the first major ethnic riots in Israel – to the less known tale of Nahum Khamis, a resident of Malha neighbourhood in Jerusalem, who singlehandedly took control of a bulldozer sent to demolish his house in 1974 and turned it against a police patrol vehicle before he too was shot and jailed. The seemingly mundane object of the fence provides a unique analytical insight into this genealogy of ruination and its intertwined histories of law, territorial sovereignty and social contention.

The case of Mr Shelomo Ram, who immigrated to Israel in 1950 and was given a small lot on which to build a shed for his family, illustrates the legal limbo that haunts hundreds of Jewish families who came to reside on Arab land and in property seized by Israel in 1948. In rather outmoded Hebrew, Ram describes how he was brought to Salama by an employee of the Jewish Agency (JA) – the largest body that dealt with new immigrants in Israel – and was shown "a place that would be mine for generations, ... a plot of land that is my own and I shall work it".[3] While Ram was building a small, temporary home, the JA official, Zechariah Habbani, promised to provide him with a permit that would ensure his legal status over the land. However, "one day Zechariah appears and sabotages the fence around my shack and also destroyed the seeds I have sown". When asked as to the reason for this outburst, Habbani explained that he now held a contract from the Jewish National Fund (JNF), which owned the Arab lands of Salama. Ram reported that he was ordered "to tear down here and tear down there". In his appeal to the JNF, he expressed his confidence that the authorities, "which only want to see the wasteland bloom", would not allow such injustice to take place and would not have agreed to sell off the land while people were still residing on it.

The archive contains no response to Ram's appeal, but this is not necessarily because this case was exceptional. On the contrary, this tale illustrates a pattern of spatial conflict that will emerge around fences, Arab houses, and provisional shacks, in the undetermined interplay between the letter of the law and actions on the grounds.

If fences are at all an indication of Kfar Shalem's spatial conflicts, an interesting typology can be identified in the neighbourhood today.

---

[3] Ram, "Letter to Jewish National Fund".

As in other suburban environments in Israel, many private cottages or semi-detached houses built in the neighbourhood since the 1970s are surrounded by familiar types of hedges and picket fences. These houses were offered by the authorities after other housing solutions, including public tenements built from the late 1950s (see Chapter 5), were rejected by residents of Arab houses in the village. As many as 200 families relocated to these houses under a special governmental redevelopment scheme.[4] In general terms, these houses allowed residents to legitimise and legalise their homes, some for the first time since they immigrated to the country three and four decades earlier. Another type of fence has no pretence to remain innocuous; quite the opposite, these are striking assortments of materials that appear to serve only the most practical and functional of purposes. There is an obvious "anarchic" sense to these constructions, both in terms of their material composition and in their compilation, which at times resembles more a mass of industrial waste than the result of intention and planning. The stark contrast between the two is not merely a result of the owners' taste, nor does it indicate a sharp discrepancy in their financial abilities. Instead, these differences mark the boundary between legitimate and illicit spaces, and attest to a long struggle to rehabilitate the latter, through both law and action.

In his remarkable book on city life in Johannesburg, Ivan Vladislavic records his encounters with the landscapes of the city as an archive of forms and materials through which South Africa's social, political and cultural histories are documented in the most subtle ways.[5] One of the fragments in the book focuses on the emergence of fences and walls following the demise of Apartheid, in a way that enables us to revisit the cultural significance of this spatial phenomenon:

Johannesburg is a frontier city, a place of contested boundaries. Territory must be secured and defended or it will be lost. Today the contest is fierce and so the defences multiply, walls replace fences, high walls replace low ones, even the highest walls acquire electrified wires and spikes. In the wealthier suburbs the pattern is to knock things flat and start all over. Around here people must make the most of what they've already got, and therefore the walls tend to grow by increments. A stone wall is heightened with prefab panels, a prefab wall is heightened with steel palisades, the palisades are topped with razor wire. Wooden pickets on top of brick, ornate wrought-iron panels on top of plaster, blade wire on top of split poles.[6]

[4] Fishbein, "Eviction-Construction".
[5] Vladislavic, *Portrait with Keys*.
[6] Ibid., 173.

These "piggyback walls" suggest a growing desire to isolate the domestic realm from the access of the public in reaction to growing crime rates and a declining sense of personal security in post-Apartheid South Africa. I am, however, interested in Vladislavic's opening statement regarding Johannesburg's characterisation as a frontier city where boundaries are contested. Crime directed at personal property is one form of infringement of boundaries. In these cases the fence is intended to preserve the order that exists within, marking a space of legal possession and ownership, and differentiating what is inside from the lawlessness outside. The fence is therefore a spatial object that distinguishes between social systems and orders. Whether in the scale of a wall surrounding a house, or in a fence that marks the border between states, this object traditionally acts as a marker of landed, territorialised law. It is therefore not surprising that Carl Schmitt refers to the fence as a key feature through which political and social orders become spatially visible: "In the Beginning there was the fence. Fence, enclosure and border are deeply interwoven in the world formed by men, determining its concepts."[7] Schmitt's formulation enables us to think about the function of fences not only as a physical barrier but also as signs of *nomos*, the linkage point of localisation (*Ortung*) and order (*Ordnung*).[8]

The fences built around most of the old Arab houses in Kfar Shalem present, however, a less obvious division between an order within and a looming disorder that reigns outside. As stated above, one of their most distinct functions derives from their ability to conceal the houses they surround, and to keep these houses out of sight. These are not the electrified wires and spikes described by Vladislavic, which could potentially prevent an intruder from entering the premises. Instead, these are methods of camouflage and visual concealment (Figure 3.1). But if we keep in mind the premise that relates fences to order, we are compelled to ask what is the order kept within these fences? How is it different from what is outside, and why does it need to remain hidden? The answer to these questions can be found, to some extent, in the complex spatio-legal reality that has governed many depopulated Arab spaces in Israel for more than half a century.

To this day, more than six decades after the first Jewish inhabitants entered the Arab houses of Salama, the State of Israel, through various governmental and municipal bodies, still retains legal possession of

---

[7] Jost Trier, quoted in Schmitt, *The Nomos of the Earth*, 74.

[8] Diken and Laustsen, *The Culture of Exception*, 40. In his discussion of the term, Schmitt points to its Greek origin, the word *nemein*, meaning both "to divide" and "to pasture". Schmitt, *The Nomos of the Earth*, 70.

Figure 3.1 Makeshift fences surrounding Arab houses in Kfar Shalem. Photo by the author.

this property and supports ambitious construction projects that require the mass demolition of existing houses. To dissuade residents from holding on to their homes, authorities prevent the maintenance of old Arab houses which remain in a precarious state: physically, they are in poor condition and their infrastructure is deteriorating. Residents are prohibited from mending a leaking roof or replacing decaying plumbing due to draconian legal restrictions. Authorities hoped that the dire conditions would hasten the eviction process and make way for new construction. Israel Godovich, who served as Tel Aviv's chief architect in the late 1990s, bluntly outlined the policy carried out against residents of former Arab property: "You don't have to shoot a person. You can kill him from the inside. 'Oh, you don't want to leave? Then you'll die here, rot here, suffocate here'".[9]

For their part, the residents refuse to accept these policies of bureaucratic suffocation and reject the authorities' ongoing attempts to challenge their ownership over their homes. The recurring failure to obtain building permits led to individually driven and unregulated action: from the early 1950s additional rooms were built; lavatories that

[9] Quoted in Rubin and Pinkhasov, *License to Live*.

were situated in the yard were constructed indoors; later on, children built small houses adjacent to their parents'. All these were deemed illegal violations of the residents' tenancy agreements, and could bring about the demolition of the new constructions and even lead to their eviction from the property. In a letter to Mayor Rabinovich, the neighbourhood council points to a family of 14 whose elder sons served on the front during the 1973 War and were obliged to share one room with the rest of the family. According to the appeal, the authorities launched legal action against the family for "adding a wall to a wall next to the house".[10]

It would be a mistake, however, to assume that the controversies over tenancy rights and ownership of land and property are limited to the realm of real-estate and property law, or that it can sufficiently be accounted for as socioeconomic marginalisation and ethnic segregation. There is nothing to suggest, for example, that Shlomo Ram's fence was sabotaged because of his ethnic background, especially when the perpetrator – the JA official – was a Yemenite-Jew himself. Rather, this chapter traces the legal chaos that has plagued the neighbourhood back to the very early days of the State of Israel, the military seizure of Arab lands during the 1948 War, and the attempt to incorporate them into the new national space in the decades that followed. This spatial transformation owes much to the physical actions that took place under the exceptional juridico-political framework of the state of emergency, which was put in place shortly after Israel declared its independence. The fences that still surround the Arab houses of Salama, hiding them from the inspecting eye of municipal or governmental bodies, provide a material illustration of six decades of tensions between state and citizens, law and space, past and present.

Long after the last gun-shots were heard in Salama, regulations drafted during the emergency of war, mass immigration, and their aftermath, determine the material reality of dozens of families in the neighbourhood and throughout Israel. The foundational period of the war and its aftermath stands at the focus of this discussion. The choice of the fence as a juncture between order and space is indicative of the basic contention that cuts through this chapter; namely, that the history of Arab spatial resilience in Salama cannot be fully comprehended without coming to terms with its reliance on the juridical-political foundations that were introduced with the establishment of the State of Israel. This is not an attempt to rewrite the legal history of emergency, but rather foreground the spatiality and materiality that are inherent

---

[10] Kfar Shalem Residents' Council, "Letter to Tel-Aviv Mayor Yehoshua Rabinovich".

in emergency jurisprudence and political philosophy. This grounding of emergency turns critical attention to sites that embody a critical and ironic reversal of emergency land legislation, from a blunt instrument of territorial appropriation to a troubling legacy that incubates disillusion and dissent from those who, like Shlomo Ram, saw themselves as legitimate agents of the state. The following section examines how the proclamation of a state of emergency in the early days of the state derived from specific spatial aspirations, and proved to be one of the most decisive mechanisms through which the Israeli *nomos* – "the constitutive act of spatial ordering"[11] – came to be.

The Space of Emergency

Emergency regulations have a foundational place in Israel's judicial system, and play a pivotal role in the appropriation and management of Arab lands seized in the 1948 War and the decades following it. The Defence (Emergency) Regulations, which grant extensive executive powers over almost every sphere of life, are based on legislation promulgated by the British Mandatory Power in Palestine in September 1945. Ironically, these colonial emergency powers were designed to stave off a Jewish rebellion, and were decried at the time by Jewish jurists in Palestine as reminiscent of a "police state".[12] A notable corpus has dealt with the wide-ranging impact this legal mechanism has had on Israeli governance and social terrain,[13] but relatively little attention has been given to the spatial logic that underlies the state of emergency as a legal-political mechanism. In order to understand the way emergency laws and actions shaped Israel's spatial history and its concrete impact on lived environments like Salama/Kfar Shalem, a brief look at the spatiality of emergency is required.

Legal and political thinkers have long been preoccupied with the intrinsic spatial relations formed by the state of emergency, an extraordinary condition that requires a formal suspension of the existing juridical order, and therefore exists outside the normal legal sphere. But there is a paradox that makes the distinction between "inside"

---

[11] Schmitt, *The Nomos of the Earth*, 71.
[12] Dowty, *The Jewish State*, 95–6.
[13] This process has been broadly discussed and analysed across the disciplines by jurists, legal historians, geographers and sociologists. See, for example: Zamir, "Human Rights and National Security"; Hofnung, "States of Emergency and Ethnic Conflict"; Kedar, "Majority Time, Minority Time"; Forman and Kedar, "From Arab Land to 'Israel Lands'"; Klinghoffer, "On Emergency Regulations in Israel"; Shamir, "Suspended in Space".

and "outside" rather problematic: the suspension of customary law is, after all, permitted by law itself. To account for this tension, Giorgio Agamben suggests that the unique spatiality of emergency be understood as a "no-man's-land between public law and political fact, and between the juridical order and life".[14] Rather than a simple opposition of inside/outside, this condition

> is neither external nor internal to the juridical order, and the problem of defining it concerns precisely a threshold, or a zone of indifference, where inside and outside do not exclude each other but rather blur with each other. The suspension of the norm is not (or at least claims not to be) unrelated to the juridical order. Hence the interest ... [shifts to] a more complex topological relation, in which the very limit of the juridical order is at issue.[15]

This is not an abstract discussion. It illuminates one of the most powerful legal-political mechanisms employed by the modern nation-state. Furthermore, the suspension of law is a tactical one, providing the sovereign power with a space of unrestricted action. What Agamben describes as a "zone of indifference" can be identified in clearly defined spaces where the familiar subordination of political action to legal regulation is challenged and reorganised. This situation does not result in a vacuum of power, but in the rise of a managerial system, what Agamben describes as "the administration of the absence of order".[16] Examining the concrete historical dynamics of this process illustrates that while state apparatuses are often the beneficiaries of the state of emergency, this exceptional legal and political instrument often leaves a highly ambivalent spatial legacy.

An official state of emergency was adopted (rather than declared) as part of the first piece of legislation passed by the Provisional Council of the State of Israel following its declaration of independence on 14 May 1948. Recognising its inability to operate in a legal vacuum, the Council effectively maintained the Mandatory emergency regulations, striking down only those provisions which restricted Jewish immigration and land ownership. According to the *Law and Administration Ordinance* passed five days later,

> the Provisional Government may authorise the Prime Minister or any other Minister to make such emergency regulations as may seem to him expedient in the interests of the defence of the State, public security and the maintenance of supplies and essential services.[17]

---

[14] Agamben, *State of Exception*, 1.
[15] Ibid., 23.
[16] Raulff, "Interview with Giorgio Agamben", 611.
[17] State of Israel Provisional Council, *Law and Administration Ordinance*, section 9(a).

The statute was presented to the Council by Justice Minister Pinchas Rosenblutt (later, Rosen) as "a transitory enactment which really contains only the barest minimum required at this moment so as to establish and provide a legal basis for our whole political system".[18]

One month later, on 24 June, the Provisional Council enacted the first law that was primarily concerned with the status of Arab land that came under Israeli control during the war. The Abandoned Areas Ordinance stated that "The Government may, by order, declare any area or place conquered, surrendered or deserted ... to be an abandoned area", therefore subjecting it "for the purposes of this Ordinance and any regulation made thereunder".[19] This legislation seems to have remained unimplemented because abandoned lands had to be officially designated through a complex bureaucratic procedure.[20] The Ordinance was replaced two years later by the Absentee Property Law, 1950,[21] which substituted "the temporary and vague legal category of 'abandoned' property with the well-defined, soon to be permanent category of 'absentee property' ".[22]

However, the Abandoned Areas Ordinance was more than just an unsuccessful draft for the management of Arab land and property. As a statute borne out of the state of emergency, the decision not to put it into official operation is part of the logic that dominates the founding period of Israel's land legislation. The Ordinance links the emptying of land with the sovereign declaration: to make way for future actions – juristic or physical – that will make use of the new territorial assets, sovereign agencies must first suspend any existing legal system that organises the networks of property, possession and ownership, and the judicial-administrative channels through which protections are granted and redress can be obtained. This primary suspension will consequently be followed by the introduction of new mechanisms that establish the control of the new sovereign regulator. In other words, it will have to incorporate this territory into an existing legal framework. The 1948 Ordinance indeed included the newly conquered land under Israeli regulation and subjected it to further legislation. Moreover, this inclusion was conditioned by an official declaration that would establish the lands' status as *integral and equal* to other lands under Israeli jurisdiction. However, as we have seen, the spatiality of emergency demands

---

[18] Hofnung, *Democracy, Law, and National Security in Israel*, 52, emphasis added.
[19] State of Israel Provisional Council, *Abandoned Areas Ordinance*, section 2(a).
[20] Forman and Kedar, "From Arab Land to 'Israel Lands' ", 814.
[21] State of Israel, *Absentees' Property Law*.
[22] Forman and Kedar, "From Arab Land to 'Israel Lands' ", 814.

the perseverance of indeterminacy – an inclusion that is always subjected to exclusion. Implementing the Abandoned Areas Ordinance would have restricted the relative freedom enjoyed by state actors who operated outside the normative limitations of the law.

The exterritorial status of emergency was fully realised in the Emergency Regulations (Absentee Property) signed by Finance Minister Eliezer Kaplan in December 1948. I refer here specifically to an initial version of the law that underwent substantial revisions culminating in the Absentee Property Law, 1950, because it establishes the juridico-political threshold that epitomises what I describe as the space of emergency. The law stipulated that all property seized by the Israeli authorities is to be defined as "absentee property" and managed by a purposely designed body: the Custodian of Absentees' Property.[23] These regulations prohibited the sale or lease of land for more than five years, which meant that this property retained an abnormal status; namely, neither part of the private real-estate market nor fully declared as an ordinary possession of the state, which would subject it to conventional protections and procedures that govern such assets. By deferring the full inclusion of the Arab spaces into Israeli jurisdiction, a timeframe for unrestricted sovereign action was opened. However, and this is central to the legacy that this emergency deferral left in numerous sites around Israel, "rehabilitating" these spaces and incorporating them back into the normative order of the law proved harder than simply retracting or amending the emergency legislation.

I want to suggest that the time that passed between the physical seizure of Arab lands, and their inclusion as part of the lands administered by the state, maintained their position outside the formal space of law yet still subjected them to actual state power. This ostensibly temporary status, which did not formally expropriate the land, could be overcome by concrete actions of settlement and development. Referring to the various acts legislated during that time with regard to the status of Arab lands, Justice Minister Aharon Tsizling bluntly suggested that "If the law must be a fiction, the development must not be."[24] The provisional legislation that was passed between 1948 and 1950 preserved Arab land and property outside the constraints that limit the state's ability to confiscate, appropriate or reallocate land, and allowed facts

---

[23] Historically, the Absentee Property Regulations were inspired by the British Trading with the Enemy Act (1939), which created an extremely powerful property custodian that was able to officially deny all rights of former owners. See: Domke, *Trading with Enemy in World War II*, 469.

[24] Forman and Kedar, "From Arab Land to 'Israel Lands'", 814.

to be established on the ground. In other words, the vacuum *de jure* allowed for action *de facto*.

The state of emergency declared in Israel on 14 May 1948 was never fully retracted and remains in place to this day, though some restrictions and amendments to its implementation were made during the 1960s and 1990s. A closer examination of spatial history in Salama/Kfar Shalem helps view this maze of legislation through its concrete impacts on people and the environments they inhabit, highlighting the tremors of the emergency years that continue to be felt long after the last gunshots and immigration waves have subsided.

A Genealogy of Emergency

The Jewish resettling of Salama followed its occupation at the end of April 1948, and officially began on 12 May. Comparing the legal timeline of emergency regulation, and that of the settling operation, suggests that the occupation of the Arab houses in fact preceded legislation on the matter: the legislative procedure began only the following week, and decrees regarding the expropriation and handling of Arab land and property were to be finalised and approved toward the end of June. A little under two months passed before Salama's houses could be considered as being under the force of law. However, this legal twilight zone did not prevent the Tel Aviv Municipality from settling the village with Jewish families who were forced to leave their homes during the fighting. To carry this out, the municipal authorities were given 446 rooms in the village by the Department for Arab Property in the Minorities Ministry.[25] Jewish immigrants who began flocking into the country in growing numbers were also settled in Salama's houses by the JA. By January 1949 more than 6,000 Jewish war refugees and immigrants lived in the Arab houses of Salama, but their residence in the village was not legally grounded: the only legal foundation relating to the use of Arab land and property at the time were the Abandoned Areas Ordinance and the Fallow Land Cultivation Regulations, both allowing the "confiscation of property" but falling short of permitting the transfer of control or possession of these properties to new owners.[26]

---

[25] Golan, "From Abandoned Village to Urban Neighbourhood", 74. The department replaced the Committee for Arab Property of the Haganah that dealt with similar issues, and was established at the end of March 1948 by the paramilitary organisation's High Command. See: Golan, "The Transfer to Jewish Control of Abandoned Arabs Lands", 406, 408.

[26] Morris, *Birth of the Palestinian Refugee Problem Revisited*, 364; Forman and Kedar, "From Arab Land to 'Israel Lands'", 817.

Using the Arab houses to settle Jewish refugees and immigrants during the housing shortage of the war and its aftermath proved insufficient less than a year after it began. A report from April 1949 suggests that of the 190,000 Jewish immigrants who arrived in the country after June 1948, 110,000 were settled in Arab houses.[27] For the remainder another solution had to be devised, and, indeed, between September 1948 and March 1949 the Absorption Department of the JA constructed 23 provisional camps that would house immigrants for the immediate stages following their arrival.[28] Between May and July 1949, two camps were built south-west and south of Salama, and by the end of the year these camps housed approximately 1,650 people. The new population in the camps added further pressure to the already strained infrastructure of the village, which was unable to supply running water and electricity to most houses.

The harsh conditions in Salama resembled those found in numerous other immigrant camps around the country. However, Salama's proximity to the country's main urban centre and the consequent prospects of employment for its residents distinguished it from the settlements constructed in the north and south of the country. The village soon began attracting people who were settled by the government in remote peripheral settlements where they were expected to either take up agricultural work or participate in government-initiated projects such as forestation. Disillusioned by harsh conditions and relative isolation, many abandoned these sites and independently relocated closer to the cities. In fact, the authorities' campaign to push immigrants and veterans to voluntarily settle in the remote and isolated strategic frontier failed on many accounts, and turned from a story of hegemonic coercion to one of resistance.[29] In the case of one immigrant camp, for example, the authorities discovered that half of the registered population was no longer resident in the place.[30] Within the government's intention to engineer the settling of immigrants in Arab lands and property, Salama appeared as a microcosm that embodied both the centralised socio-spatial planning, and, at the same time, symbolised the inherent drawbacks and limited success of these policies.

As a space governed by (legal and actual) emergency, Salama quickly demarcated the limits of sovereign action.[31] The suspension of law

---

[27] Morris, *Birth of the Palestinian Refugee Problem Revisited*, 395.
[28] Hacohen, *Immigrants in Turmoil*, 88.
[29] Kemp, "Border Space and National Identity"; Hacohen, *Immigrants in Turmoil*, 225–6.
[30] Felsenstein and Shahar, "The Geography of the Ma'abarot", 94.
[31] I follow here some of the critiques of Agamben's narrow focus on the agency of sovereign power and the passivity of those inhabiting these spaces of emergency exception. See: Papastergiadis, "The Invasion Complex"; Puggioni, "Resisting Sovereign Power".

not only served the official bodies of the state, but invited individual actions by those seeking to make gains from the legal void formed by the governing bodies themselves. In this sense, the independent settlement in Salama was similar to other Arab towns, neighbourhoods and villages around the country, whose empty houses were either illegally occupied or looted.[32] During the late summer and autumn of 1948 the situation in Jaffa, for example, deteriorated to such an extent that army units independently evicted immigrants who invaded Arab property, only to secure those same houses for themselves. The government's attempts to restore control over the city failed time and again, and even Ben-Gurion's personal involvement failed to calm the situation. In a letter to the prime minister, the Custodian for Absentees' Property, Dov Shafrir, reported that "Jaffa was anarchically settled by 'invasions and counter-invasions' by immigrants, soldiers and others".[33] With no other choice, the government was forced to recognise the irreversibility of the mass invasions into Arab property.

The chaos that erupted in Jaffa is indicative of the ambiguity of power that governs spaces of emergency and the delicate balance struck between the licit and the illicit, between the tactical suspension of law and the imposition of a new political order. By designating and shaping whole areas through emergency suspension of normative law, the sovereign power and those acting on its (direct or indirect) behalf can take immediate action without the restraints of standard legal imperatives and procedures. However, it would be naïve to assume that the sovereign suspension of law will not invite clandestine appropriation and popular disregard toward emergency rule itself. Rightly so, Agamben warns that the state of exception opens a "zone of indeterminacy between anomie and law, in which the sphere of creatures and the juridical order are caught up in a single catastrophe".[34]

Is there a single catastrophe that haunts Salama/Kfar Shalem? Aharon Maduel, a resident of the neighbourhood and an active political figure, made a rather daring comparison when he linked the expulsion of the Arab population from Salama with the fate of the Jewish residents who settled the village after 1948:

I feel like we are refugees like them. We left Arab countries; we left property, houses; our parents suffered because of the War of Independence here, [as] they were persecuted in their country because of it ... We are refugees without rights on the land since 1948, because in 1960 my parents and grandparents

[32] Golan, *Wartime Spatial Changes*; Fischbach, *Records of Dispossession*; Segev, *1949*.
[33] Quoted in Morris, *Birth of the Palestinian Refugee Problem Revisited*, 389.
[34] Agamben, *State of Exception*, 57.

were prevented from buying our land … We were left on suitcases for 60 years. At first, they [the authorities] tried to banish us in a brutal way, then things got better and since they've returned to the old ways. The dispossession here is the same as in Jaffa, the same system: leave your home without compensation.[35]

In a later interview, Maduel described the legal disarray that followed the emergency years in Kfar Shalem as "the primal sin" for which the residents of the Arab houses in the neighbourhood continue to pay.[36] However, the agricultural lands in Salama were also used to construct two immigrant camps, known in Hebrew as *Ma'abara* (*Ma'abarot* in plural). Residents of the camps were soon to discover that the suspension and indeterminacy that govern the space of emergency would have a direct and long-lasting impact on them as well.

On the face of it, the hasty construction of immigrant camps was again a consequence of necessity: once other alternatives were exploited or were considered unviable because of a lack of resources,[37] the government was forced to use urgent, albeit temporary, measures. In reality, however, the construction of the first immigrant camps was initiated not by the government but by the Absorption Department of the JA, which decided to independently import some 6,000 cabins and set up temporary encampments on the outskirts of existing towns and villages. The Ministry of Labour planners strongly objected to such initiatives, fearing "that these temporary neighbourhoods would become permanent fixtures and turn into slums".[38] In hindsight, this warning seems prophetic: the immigrant camps, either in their initial form in Salama or as they later developed to house one sixth of the country's population by 1952, were not as easily abolished as the government hoped and "remained as scars on the map".[39]

The spatial logic that guided the location and dispersion of immigrant camps provides the initial explanation to the "scarring" effect they had on the Israeli landscape and on the collective memory of the Israeli society. In addition to the work conducted by the Absorption Department of the JA, Prime Minister Ben-Gurion appointed architect Arieh Sharon[40] to form the Governmental Planning Department.

---

[35] Baruch, "Operation Bi'ur Hametz", 86.

[36] Maduel, Interview with the author.

[37] According to calculations made by governmental bodies in autumn 1948, 55 million Israel Liras were required to house 250,000 immigrants in the period of 1940–1950. The entire state budget for that fiscal year reached a mere 7.8 million Liras, not including defence expenditure. Efrat, *The Israeli Project*, 516.

[38] Hacohen, *Immigrants in Turmoil*, 131.

[39] Efrat, *The Israeli Project*, 521.

[40] Not to be confused with Ariel Sharon, an Israeli general who became one of the country's most revered yet controversial political figures, and who was elected as prime minister in 2001.

Sharon, who faced the urgent task of supplying immediate housing solutions to the new immigrants, devised a network of camps, villages, work bases and outposts that provided ad hoc housing and employment, while at the same time securing Jewish presence along the country's borders. Sharon's concepts culminated in the first National Planning Scheme, which was presented in 1950 and emphasised dispersal of population in the country's northern and southern peripheries, along the borders and in strategically designated areas (Jerusalem's western foothills, for example). However, during the first years of the Planning Department's work, most immigrant camps were in fact situated adjacent to existing villages, towns or cities, mostly due to lack of time and scarcity of financial resources.[41]

From the moment of their inception, camps like the ones in Salama – which were named Salama A and Salama B – became visible symbols of social exclusion and economic deprivation. People lodged in rough fabric or tin cabins often managed to build improvised structures and slightly improve their extremely basic living conditions. The governmental survey of Kfar Shalem carried out in 1969 recorded this process:

The houses of the village, which were never known for their excellence, began crumbling in time. In addition, the increase of population – caused by the large proportions of natural growth and the flow of deprived population to the village – encouraged extensive illegal construction, of extremely low quality. This construction enhanced the poor impression of the village's dilapidated houses and the sight of a "slum".[42]

Reading the spatiality of the camps through its relation to a regulating legal framework (or lack thereof), underscores the constitution of a *threshold condition*, from which socioeconomic, cultural and political identities are forged. At the outset, the camps' proximity to existing settlement was supposed to allow the residents access to local services and provide the grounds for integration between the new residents and the veteran communities. But the legal aspects of jurisdiction and the subsequent responsibilities placed on local councils were only officially defined in a 1951 statutory order which was only partially implemented and did not bridge the social, economic and cultural gaps that divided the camps from their surroundings. In effect, many of the councils rejected the order, claiming that it was beyond their financial and administrative means to take responsibility for the new encampments and their residents. The head of the camps subdivision

---

[41] Hacohen, *Immigrants in Turmoil*, 165.
[42] Halamish, Municipal-Governmental Company for Housing in Gush Dan, "Kfar Shalem Survey. The Construction and Eviction of Development Areas", 1.

in the JA admitted that "for the sake of historical truth, we did not ask local councils. The pressure was so great, the waves of immigration so immense, that if we could only find an empty space – we went up and constructed a camp."[43] These conflicting priorities – the government's need to house immigrants and the councils' inability to cater to their socioeconomic requirements – took place to a large extent in a legal limbo in which authorities and semi-official bodies acted with little or no coordination, abiding solely by the law of immediate necessity.

The Hebrew name assigned to the immigrant camp – *Maabara* – literally meaning "a place of passage", reiterates its position in between – not fully integrated into the unambiguous "Israeli Space" or simply marked as its antithesis. Hannan Hever identifies the *Maabara* as a heterotopia in Foucault's terms,[44] a real place that retains an ambivalent relation to the space of Zionist hegemony:

> On the one hand, the *Maabara* is the destination-of-Zionist-space to which immigrants arrive, and on the other, it is a place left outside the camp, it is not a place – it is a place that exists in the world, but at the same time it is a non-place to the Zionist collective … This contrast between place and non-place penetrates the innermost structure of the *Maabara*: The *Maabara* is a non-place because of its dilapidated and neglected state; yet it is still a place because people build a shack for themselves in it.[45]

Hever points to the fact that the socio-cultural exception constituted in the *Maabara* should not be understood as a simple state of exclusion. Instead, it is designated as a liminal position between those spaces identified with the Zionist centre and its other; namely, Arab space. Embodying the various forms of an in-between existence – the physical, socio-cultural and legal divides that separate the transient immigrant from the permanent resident – the *Maabara* marked a space of passage where the dichotomy between the space of the self and that of the other can be renegotiated.

Hever, for example, identifies the ways Shimon Ballas, a Jewish-Arab writer, forms the transit camp in his novella *Ma'abara*[46] as a space in which Arab-Jewish identity makes its marks on the landscape. One example Hever discusses is the tale of a café opened by one of the camp's residents in his tent. The name chosen for this establishment is an Arabic one, "*al-Nasser*", meaning "the victory". The victory suggested in the name chosen for the tent-café derives from the

---

[43] Quoted in Felsenstein and Shahar, "The Geography of the Ma'abarot", 96.
[44] Foucault, "Of Other Spaces".
[45] Hever, *Producing the Modern Hebrew Canon*, 207.
[46] Ballas, *Outcast*.

territorialisation of an identity that was denied a place. The Eurocentric cultural uniformity of hegemonic Israeli culture in the first decades of the state provided no room for the Arab-Jewish identity to make its mark on the production of the Israeli space. Despite this institutional deterritorialisation of the Arab-Jews, individuals and communities found ways to claim small, ephemeral stakes in the land, making use of spaces that were already "flawed" – like the immigrant camp in the 1950s, the development towns, or the public tenement projects built in the 1950s and 1960s (see Chapter 5).

And yet this victory of an Arab-Jew that succeeds in forming an enclave of hybrid identities in the Israeli space appears, perhaps, as a pyrrhic victory. The alien materiality of the Arab village and the immigrant camp marked a sign of foreign existence, an anachronism that did not abide by the demand for the new order of space. Within the space of emergency, forged as a site in which state power can be put into operation in relative freedom, Salama – the village and the immigrant camps adjacent to it – became a marker of resistance to spatial and socio-ethnic regularisation. The ambivalence toward dominant political and cultural dichotomies brought some critics to celebrate the subversive politics harboured by these liminal spaces.[47] There is indeed strong evidence to suggest that residents in these "third-spaces" challenged the Zionist ethno-national logic that stipulated Jew and Arab as two mutually exclusive categories. But this liminality came at a heavy price: it meant that those inhabiting this in-between space were criminalised and forced to hide behind elaborate makeshift fences, their houses under constant threat of demolition.

Shortly after *Ma'abara* was published, Shimon Ballas wrote *Beyond the Wadi*, a novella that follows the protagonists of the immigrant camp as they relocate to a neighbourhood in the eastern suburbs of Tel Aviv. The work was completed in 1966, but was rejected by the author's publisher and only published in 1998 under a new title, *Tel-Aviv East*.[48] In one of the opening scenes, as the mailman stops in front of "a pile of shattered bricks", Ballas already hints that the relocation to the new neighbourhood does not overcome the precarious spatial legacy of the camp. When one of the neighbours tells him that the residents tore down the house after they were promised a construction permit from the council, the mailman remains sceptical: " 'Now the council will start harassing

---

[47] See for example: Nuriely, "Strangers in a National Space"; Benjamin, " 'Present-Absent' ". I have discussed this approach at some length in Chapter 1.
[48] Shimony, *On the Threshold of Redemption*, 72–3.

everybody', he said. Where will they go? All the houses are without a permit. Is there a house here with a permit?"[49]

The permits noted here exceed the legal status of houses and allude to the actual ability to overcome the disturbing sense of foreignness carried by Mizrahi immigrants. As Batya Shiloni suggests, the inner-city neighbourhood (*Shekhuna*) carries with it the legacy of the *Maabara*, yet asserts that the liminal condition of the former is determined by social reality and not by geographical peripherality.[50] This assertion locates the lines of conflict along socio-ethnic divides, which explains how liminality "migrates" from the *Maabara* to the neighbourhoods, since it is imprinted in peoples' social and cultural identities. While this may be true to a degree, it often overlooks the inherently spatial aspects of being "neither here nor there", as one of protagonists in *Beyond the Wadi* describes it. The following section returns to Salama/Kfar Shalem and illustrates how social stigmatisation and marginalisation result from concrete spatial conditions that echo the persistent legacy of emergency.

Illicit Pioneers: The Legacy of Emergency

In the immediate period following the proclamation of the State of Israel, it is possible to chart a "geography of defiance" that would be congruent to the Arab areas seized during the 1948 War. The mixed cities of Jerusalem, Haifa, Jaffa, Lod, and Arab settlements in their vicinity, experienced similar phenomena to those seen in Salama – from vandalism and looting, to seizure of property for the housing of Jews. In more remote regions of the country, where Arab land was used to house new immigrants in provisional labour encampments or in frontier settlements, this defiance was expressed in the steady stream of people who "deserted" the settling mission imposed on them, and returned to the urban centres in search of improved living conditions.

Was this defiance solely the result of the unique legal status of emergency imposed in all these regions? Perhaps not. The plight of tens of thousands of people was not exclusively dictated by specific legal stipulations. Nonetheless, the declaration of a state of emergency and the employment of emergency powers were made with the intention to construct, organise and legitimise a given social and spatial order. In effect, the means employed to exert national sovereignty designated these spaces as a no-man's land, vacated from rightful owners or a regulating

---

[49] Ballas, "Tel-Aviv East", 9.
[50] Shimony, *On the Threshold of Redemption*, 160.

system of law. These new conditions resulted in a normative vacuum that appealed not only to official bodies working to realise the government's territorial policies.

As indicated above, the initial resettling of Jews in former Arab towns and neighbourhoods was devised as a solution to the housing shortage of the time and as a way of blocking the return of Palestinian refugees. For this purpose, emergency measures provided the perfect tool in the hand of the sovereign power. However, it was not long before these areas begin to be characterised as "troublesome" and "unruly".[51] What was initially a mission on behalf of the state and in accordance with a long-time Zionist ethos of settling the land, turned in a rather short period into clearly defined sites that challenged prevailing social and spatial orders. The effect of this transformation was felt decades after the "primal sin" of the emergency period.

Throughout this book, I cite numerous examples of the conflicts that emerge in Salama/Kfar Shalem around specific spatial phenomena, from roads to ruins, sacred sites and public tenements. However, the Tel Aviv Council meeting that followed the death of Shimon Yehoshua during the demolition of his house in December 1982 provides perhaps the most vivid illustration of the threat associated with the neighbourhood by members of the council. The meeting began with a statement by Mayor Shlomo Lahat, who expressed his "deep sorrow" following the incident, but also noted that acts of vandalism were carried out in northern neighbourhoods of the city,[52] swastikas were painted on walls, and threats were made against the mayor and his family.[53] Several comments by council members were made following the mayor's statement, which are surprising in their severity: Council Member Basouk opened by saying that "the struggle over [the execution of] demolition orders is a struggle for our lives and for a true democracy"; Mr Onikowsky stated that "what happened in Kfar Shalem was a transgression of extreme social norms, that provides reasons to fear for the

---

[51] To give a few examples, Haim Yacobi ("The Daily Life in Lod") and Benny Nuriely ("Strangers in a National Space") describe this process in the "ghetto" of downtown Lod in the 1950s; Shlomit Binyamin ("'Present-Absent'") illustrates this process in Qubeiba/Kfar Gvirol, now a suburb of Rehovot; Weiss, *A Confiscated Memory*, explores similar tensions in Wadi Salib, one of Haifa's downtown neighbourhoods.

[52] Tel Aviv is traditionally divided into the well-off northern neighbourhoods and the poorer neighbourhoods of the south, which range from Jaffa in the south-west, to Kfar Shalem in the south-east. It is important to note that gentrification processes, which have accelerated in the past two decades, have changed the demographic composition of certain areas, but have at the same time increased the sense of marginalisation among local communities, including Arab, Mizrahi-Jews and migrant workers in the southern and south-eastern suburbs. See: LeVine, *Overthrowing Geography*.

[53] Tel Aviv Municipal Council, "Meeting Protocol", 2.

fate of the state"; Council Member Youtan refuted the criticism against the mayor by determining that "the war is not about the mayor's prestige, but about the existence of the Israeli society".[54]

It is rather surprising that the case of Shimon Yehoshua instigated such blunt responses which portray a local incident – tragic as it may be – as a matter of national calamity and a social peril of enormous magnitude. What is at stake here, it seems, goes beyond the threat posed by the misuse of firearms: the speakers repeat time and again the need to carry on with the implementation of demolition orders as the prime means to prevent "illegal invasions". "Our policy", suggested Council Member Fishler, "must be decisive, not to agree to the robbery of lands or to *construction that constitutes facts*".[55] The law, he suggests, cannot succumb to actions on the ground. Yet it was exactly this formulation that was expressed by the first justice minister of Israel during a meeting of the Ministerial Abandoned Property Committee in August 1948, as the settling of Jews in Salama was gaining pace. I have already noted this above, but it is worth recalling: reassuring ministers that the temporary nature of land expropriation laws would not jeopardise the seizure of Arab property, Aharon Tsizling stressed, "If the law must be a fiction, the development must not be".[56] The prevalent logic of emergency, which prioritised action over procedure, was initially intended to deal with the conditions of war and mass immigration, but the patterns of spatial practice established during that period were hard to override, even when the initial grounds for their inception were no longer present.

The tension between law and practice was also considered by the investigation commission that looked into Yehoshua's death. In its closing remarks, after strongly reprimanding the attempt to harm the evicting force, the commission stressed the danger posed to the existence of a democratic society by the use of violence in general and against civil servants in particular:

Conceding to illegal pressures and to violence paves the way for more violence. An uncompromising war on violence can contribute toward its eradication or significant reduction. This is a fundamental lesson of civil discipline. This is the actualisation of the principle of the "rule of law" *de jure* and *de facto*. *And practice matters here no less, perhaps even more than principle.*[57]

---

[54] Ibid., 3–4.
[55] Ibid., 3, emphasis added.
[56] Quoted in Forman and Kedar, "From Arab Land to 'Israel Lands'", 814.
[57] Winograd, Zemach, and Mishaeli, "The Committee for the Examination of Events in Kfar Shalem", 24–5, emphasis added.

The commission is guided by a Weberian logic that sanctifies the state's monopoly on the legitimate use of violence. This applies equally to the use of firearms as it does to the appropriation of land and the demolition of houses: only those sanctioned by the state may claim their acts to be within the normative realm or "the rule of law". However, while uniforms and badges make the identification of those sanctioned to bear arms presumably simple, the identification of state agents is rather more difficult when territorial and spatial violence is concerned. Who is sanctioned, for example, to carry out settling missions that result in the seizure of land and property? According to one stance the division seems to adhere to simple Manichean logic:

On one hand, state authorities move agents, that is, groups which are intended to perform a function on behalf of the state. State agents are normally settled, that is made provision for, and they are normally moved to peripheral parts of the state occupied by minorities. On the other hand, the authorities move enemies, that is, groups, which in their present location pose a problem for the authorities and an obstacle to their goals. 'Enemy' status is subjectively assigned by the authorities, and need not correspond with anti-state activity on the part of targeted groups.[58]

But who assumes the role of "the enemy" in the case of Salama, and who functions as a legitimate "agent"? Can the former be applied only to the Arab population that was forced to flee their homes during the war? Similarly, is "agency" assumed by the immigrants who came to inhabit the confiscated lands, or is it held by municipal officials, state custodians and inspectors who retain bureaucratic powers over the utility of this property? A schematic illustration of relations that fails to account for the liquidity of these categories and the terms according to which one's position is determined and redefined over time and space, is insufficient when we look to untangle the spatial and legal conundrum of repopulated Arab lands in Israel. Indeed, this exact confusion appears several times in correspondence between residents in Kfar Shalem and the authorities, always at a critical moment of realisation that they are no longer considered to be legitimate agents. When, for example, Shlomo Ram wrote to the JNF in 1956, he assumed that his personal act of settlement in a former Arab village necessarily corresponded with the larger Zionist ethos that guided the operation of the settling authorities. While that may have been the case, Ram also presumed that this identity of interests would continue once slogans were made into concrete policy: surely, he asserted, referring to the

---

[58] McGarry, "'Demographic Engineering'", 614–15.

suggestion that his property had been given to others, "you [the JNF] would not have sold on a place in which people live".[59] Evidence suggests this was exactly the case.

This is not just a case of one man's naïvety regarding the operation of state bureaucracy. The blurring of the distinction between "ordinary" citizens and state officials was one of the trademarks of the Zionist settling operations, which highlighted the role of the "pioneers" (*halutzim*) in realising the movements' territorial aspirations. The emergence of the Stockade and Tower (*Homa u-Migdal*) settlements in the latter half of the 1930s provides a clear illustration of the bottom-up settlement model that continues to resonate in the Israeli cultural memory and spatial practices decades later. This was an effort to erect "instant" settlements that could be constructed in a matter of hours and create, in a rather short period of time, a new territorial reality. This was more than architectural ingenuity responding to local practical needs, but rather an idea that was borne out of an attempt to influence legal and political decisions. Once again, the understanding that law can be subordinated to spatial practice was a motif that guided the initiators of the project.

Following the eruption of violence throughout Mandatory Palestine in April 1936, the British government appointed an investigation commission headed by Lord Peel, which was charged with determining the cause of the riots and judging the merit of grievances on both sides.[60] The Commission's recommendation for a partition of Palestine was deemed unattainable by the Woodhead Commission and in November 1938 the British government announced the complete abandonment of partition.[61] Instead, a White Paper published on 17 May 1939 outlined the British intention to preserve the status quo between Jews and Arabs by limiting Jewish immigration and restricting Jewish land purchases. These political developments led to a realisation among the Jewish leadership that settlement and land acquisition must be directed and coordinated by a broader geopolitical strategy. Two years earlier, in 1937, Haganah leaders reached the conclusion that settlements were to become an instrument to "defend the boundaries of the state, to strengthen areas which were 'weak links' in the Jewish territorial continuum and to establish new territorial 'facts' – all on the basis of an integrative *territorial conception*".[62]

A method for realising this policy had already been implemented in the north of Israel since the winter of 1936. Kibbutz Tel Amal (later, Nir

---

[59] Ram, "Letter to Jewish National Fund".
[60] Palestine Royal Commission, "The Peel Commission".
[61] Kimmerling, *Zionism and Territory*, 55.
[62] Ibid., 56, emphasis in the original.

David) in the Lower Galilee region was the first to be constructed in the form of four barracks surrounded by a defensive wall and a watch-tower that overlooked the surroundings. The idea was the brainchild of Shelomo Grazovski (Gur), one of Tel Amal's founders, and architect Yochanan Ratner. Initially, the kibbutz was to be established on lands purchased from its Beirut owners by the JNF, but the founding group could not claim possession of the land due to a large Bedouin camp that used it for seasonal grazing, and therefore enjoyed the protection of Ottoman land laws.[63] Determined to establish the new kibbutz, but fearing violent retaliation by the Bedouins, Grazovski and Ratner devised a construction method that would erect the gated farm using prefabricated parts, shipped to the site with lorries and assembled in a short period by the settling group and members of surrounding communities. Although – as the Haganah policy document suggests – these "settlement attacks" were consistent with broader policies of the Zionist leadership, the driving force behind them came from the grass-roots level. Nonetheless, these groups enjoyed institutional support: when the settling group lacked sufficient funds to carry out the plan, it was able to use its connections with the JNF and the JA to put together the needed sum. Once established, Tel Amal provided the precedent for 56 other Stockade and Tower "points".[64]

The impact of this endeavour went beyond the geopolitical aspects of Jewish settlement in Palestine and obscured (though did not completely erase) the boundaries between settler and soldier in the pre-state period.[65] The category of the *halutz* (pioneer) merged previously conflicted identities[66] and solidified the ethos of an entire community that collectively bears the burden of national realisation. More than 20 years after Jewish settlers foiled an attack on Hanita – a Stockade

---

[63] Rotbard, "Stockade and Tower", 39. On Ottoman land legislation, which prevailed during the British Mandate and, indeed, provided the basis for Israeli legislation as well, see Kimmerling, *Zionism and Territory*, 31–8.

[64] Rotbard notes 57 such settlements, while Gvati lists 53. Compare: Rotbard, "Stockade and Tower", 38; and Gvati, *A Hundred Years of Settlement*, 102.

[65] Shapira, *Land and Power*, 252–4.

[66] Jewish society in Palestine during the early twentieth century was ravaged with ideological and social conflicts. One famous example which was documented in the literature of the time was the tension between Jewish farm owners and young Jewish labourers during the second and third *Aliyah*. This period saw growing tensions between groups of young Jewish immigrants who hoped to fulfill the dream of becoming agricultural workers, and farm owners who refused to replace their skilled Arab workforce. See, for example, Kimmerling, *Zionism and Territory*, 99–103. The general category of the *Halutz* also merged more symbolic and spiritual aspects. A genre of pioneer plays in the 1930s and 1940s depicted the *Halutz* as the figure who brings together the earth and the heavens, thus overcoming the strong division between the

and Tower settlement built overnight in May 1938 in western Galilee – a Haganah chronicler wrote that "the Arabs learned once again ... that a place where the foot of a *Jewish settler* has tread, where the blood of a *Hebrew defender* has been spilled, will not be abandoned by its builders and defenders".[67] The mythic status of the Stockade and Tower era extracted it from the specific historical and political context in which it first appeared, allowing it to form one of the foundational relationships in the act of settlement and the conquest of land. According to one leading geographer, writing in 1981:

> The settlement of new areas ... if you will, frontier areas, [always required] the securing of ownership over land, territorial continuity, securing the borders [and] the establishment of settlements clusters. The conclusion is clear – since 1936 and till 1980s, the Tower and Stockade era has been continuing, and only the ways of implementing that strategy have changed.[68]

If it was still legitimate to identify the traces of Tower and Stockade in 1970s settlements, it is no wonder that Shelomo Ram saw his small shack in Salama as yet another manifestation of the pioneering mission, and himself as a legitimate *halutz*. The moment in which Ram is confronted with an official denial of his status as a rightful member of an imagined community of pioneers, is a moment of crisis that conveys a sense of deep disillusion:

> Can such a thing be done, to sell to that Jew [Habbani] this place on which I live since 1950 all the time, and I have a right [sic]. Will this thing not bring about grave consequences, and who will be responsible if not the authorities entrusted with this matter?[69]

Ram's unanswered question was repeated time and again in the following years as more residents in Salama/Kfar Shalem discovered that actions, which were encouraged in the first years of war and mass immigration, became illegitimate once the emergency period was over. In

---

sky – the spiritual domain of the religious, diasporic and intellectual Jew – and the earth, the object of desire for the young workers of the second and third *Aliyah*. Ofrat, *Earth, Man, Blood*, 79–83.

[67] Dinur, Slutsky, and Avigur, *History of the Haganah*, vol. 3: 877. The origins of the farmer-fighter image can be traced to the events that surrounded the fall of Tel Hai, a remote Jewish settlement in Upper Galilee, and to Joseph Trumpeldor who headed the defending group and was killed during the fighting. See Shapira, *Land and Power*, 98–109; Zerubavel, *Recovered Roots*. Indeed, Tel Hai became a mythic precursor to the Stockade and Tower settlements, but it was only with the emergence of the latter that the pioneering settlement gains a dominant status and provides the arch-pattern of Israeli architecture, as Sharon Rotbard indeed argues. Rotbard, "Stockade and Tower". Quoted in Katriel and Shenhar, "Tower and Stockade", 360, emphasis added.

[68] Katriel and Shenhar, "Tower and Stockade", 360.

[69] Ram, "Letter to Jewish National Fund".

their correspondences with the authorities, residents repeatedly high-lighted their participation in what they saw as (or were led to believe to be) a pioneering settling mission on behalf of the state. The realisation that the same authorities now saw them as transgressors inevitably gave rise to a sense of betrayal. When residents were prosecuted and ordered to leave their homes in the 1970s, a group from Kfar Shalem wrote a petition to the Tel Aviv mayor, noting the dire conditions they endured during the first years in the village and conveying the deep disillusion from the myth of a collective settling mission:

We knew what suffering was, we did not set out demands or demonstrations to improve our lives, [and] we were satisfied with the little we had. We *sanctified the imperative of settling the land*, and in those days we were very good! We were not considered intruders or invaders.[70]

The Law of the Land: Reflections on the Spatial Afterlife of Emergency

The literature on the intersection of space and law in Israel's emergency period focuses primarily on the objectives of official bodies toward the Arab lands seized during the 1948 War, and the prevention of the return of Palestinian refugees. According to this strand of Israeli legal geography,[71] the Jewish population settled on Arab land and in Arab property is given little attention. Without thorough examination, these communities are identified as simply the agents of the state or as its beneficiaries. As such, one may assume that a complete identity of interests existed between the new residents and the state, the former reaping the (property) fruits that were militarily seized and legally expropriated by the latter. Nonetheless, a small number of scholarly accounts have sought to unpack the all-inclusive category of "the state" and point to the intense internal competition and conflicts between various government branches, building societies and interest groups.[72] The individuals and communities who settled on Arab land and property were mostly

---

[70] Zerubavel, *Recovered Roots*, emphasis added.
[71] Issachar Rosen-Zvi's book is perhaps the most comprehensive example of this analytical trend, examining the legal forces that take part in shaping the social map of Israeli society. Rosen-Zvi, *Taking Space Seriously*; see also Blank, "Space, Community, Subject". Others have focused on the specific operation of legal mechanisms in the appropriation of Arab lands following the 1948 War: Kedar, "The Legal Transformation of Ethnic Geography"; Forman and Kedar, "From Arab Land to 'Israel Lands'". For similar patterns in the attitude of the State of Israel to the Bedouin minority, see Shamir, "Suspended in Space".
[72] For instance, Golan, *Wartime Spatial Changes*; Golan, "Jewish Settlement of Former Arab Towns and Their Incorporation into the Israeli Urban System (1948–50)".

featured in analyses conducted by Israeli social and cultural historians, who illustrated the ambiguities and tensions that characterised these places: the ethnic composition of these communities, their socioeconomic and cultural marginalisation, and the attitudes of local and state institutions which ranged from indifference to outright confrontation.[73]

In these accounts, however, categories of criminality are analysed through their relation to the socio-ethnic discourse that dominated Israeli society in the first decades. Beyond the social and economic aspects that breed criminal activity, the origins and history of "spatial criminality" of the sort found in former Arab areas seem to have been largely overlooked.

The need for a synthesis of historical legal and social analysis is not just an academic exercise, but a reflection of a pressing reality in which "building violations", "invasions" and "illegal occupancy" become dominant tropes for the classification of entire communities, and in turn determines the operation of official bodies.[74] My argument here, which draws on both the corpus of legal geography and historical socio-cultural analysis, seeks to overcome some of the disciplinary boundaries that still divide these spheres. First, it looks to bypass the tendency of legal-geographical analysis to operate within a rigid socio-ethnic grid that compartmentalises religious and socio-ethnic identities. The spatial history of Salama/Kfar Shalem illustrates how legal mechanisms devised under specific historical conditions ossify and shape spatial reality long after their original trigger was no longer relevant. The emergency laws and regulations instated in the aftermath of the 1948 War had a direct impact on the Arab residents who were forced to flee and cede their ownership over land and property. However, the Jewish population that was settled in the village in the decades that followed was also bound by strict legal constraints that emanated from the same body of legislation and was imposed by an administrative mechanism formed specifically to deal with these exceptional spaces. The endemic phenomena of illicit construction, invasions and disputes over ownership and compensation are all symptoms of space haunted by a 60-year-old emergency, which still struggles to distinguish between friends and foes.

---

[73] Weiss, *A Confiscated Memory*; Benjamin, " 'Present-Absent' "; Nuriely, "Strangers in a National Space", to give some examples.

[74] These are tropes that can be found in debates regarding illegal construction in Kfar Shalem as well as in relation to the Bedouin communities in the Negev and Palestinians in East Jerusalem. While each case retains unique characteristics, all are manifestations of the space of emergency. See Note 67, above.

This was not, however, a one-sided process. The legal production of space had a direct effect on the residents' relation to the state and its representative branches. Despite the conviction that the hardships endured in the "settling mission" of the Arab territory validated them as equal members of the national community, if not actual pioneers, many residents of Kfar Shalem were sooner or later to discover that it was the law, not the land, that provided the right of passage into the realm of national legitimisation and recognition. While the emergency period focused its efforts on the integration of Arab lands into the space of the new state and understood settlement as an instrument to assert one's territorial possession, the years that followed saw a gradual change in this policy. The introduction of centralised planning mechanisms and an extensive system of legislation to support it also changed the status of those who were sent to inhabit these lands during the years of emergency. Once comprehensive plans were made in the early 1960s for the abolition of the Arab built environment in favour of government housing projects, the residents of Salama's Arab houses were seen as "invaders" who stood in the way of "modernising progress". The effects official planning had on Salama are discussed at length in Chapter 5, but it is worth noting that in this transition, the residents of Salama were transformed from agents of the state to representatives of a foreign spatial order. By virtue of inhabiting an "Arab space", the Jewish inhabitants of Salama found themselves, as it were, on the wrong side of the fence. This was not merely the result of official aesthetic, cultural or moral predispositions, but emanated from a legal framework that reflected a new desired spatial order.

Unlike other Arab towns or villages, the modest appearance of Salama meant that it did not qualify to be "rehabilitated" and preserved as a tourist destination (like Jaffa or Safed) or an artist colony (Ein Hod). Salama was seen as a chaotic compilation that did not include any remarkable buildings "worthy of restoration and protection", except the structure of the village mosque and shrine.[75] Without the virtues that would legitimate it under the new legal, social and spatial order that gained pace in the early 1960s, Salama and its Jewish residents were required to make way for Kfar Shalem, a neighbourhood designed according to the era's prevailing conceptions of spatial order: a planned, regulated, and fully "modern" neighbourhood.

---

[75] Halamish, Municipal-Governmental Company for Housing in Gush Dan, "Kfar Shalem Survey. The Construction and Eviction of Development Areas", 30.

This goal, however, was only partly and very gradually fulfilled. The spatial patterns that dominated the emergency era, which resembled, to some extent, pre-state settlement practices, were not easily replaced by centralised procedures of planning, regulation and standardisation. The penetrability of the Arab space and the Arab house in particular,[76] an intrinsic result of the emergency legislation that enabled its expropriation and reallocation, became a defining characteristic of Salama as a whole, allowing for houses vacated by their residents to be reoccupied by others seeking affordable accommodation in proximity to the urban centre of Tel Aviv. As such, the neighbourhood attracted other communities that were marginalised from the mainstream of Israeli society – from Palestinian construction workers from Gaza who lived in the neighbourhood during the 1980s, to migrant workers from the Philippines in the present.

It is important to note that Kfar Shalem also attracted people who sought to take advantage of the compensation payments given to residents who agreed to relocate from their homes. One report suggests that the southern areas of Salama, now identified as Shekhunat Ha'argazim, attracted a small community of ex-convicts, which to this day demands to be included in an eviction-construction scheme devised to allow a large development on the site.[77]

Spaces of emergency, defined here as sites subjected to legal and physical activity under an emergency framework, provide rich historical grounds for the analysis of the relations between the social, spatial and legal spheres. In the specific case of Salama/Kfar Shalem, the 1948 War and its aftermath were a defining period during which the legal and physical foundations for the neighbourhood's evolution were laid. Without comprehending the emergency *modus operandi*, its inherent tension between exclusion and inclusion, and the purposely indefinite status of the regulations and decrees it produces, spaces like Salama are viewed only through the important, yet incomplete, prism of ethnic and cultural identity politics. As the evidence provided in this chapter indicates, the unique spatial and legal status of Salama was a determining factor in the stigmatisation and social marginalisation of its residents. This analysis of Salama's spatial and legal history illustrates how spaces of emergency provide a rich, yet still under-theorised, environment in which the dynamic interplay between spatiality, law and identity can be revisited and re-evaluated.

---

[76] Ariella Azoulay illustrates this aspect with relation to the use Israeli military forces make of Palestinian homes to this day. Azoulay, "Sleeping in a Sterile Zone"; Azoulay, "Who Needs the Truth (in Photography)?"

[77] Fishbein, "Eviction-Construction", 11.

This discussion touches on the intimate, though ambiguous, relation between the nation-state and the sanctioned use of violence. At first sight, the period that surrounded the constitution of the Jewish nation-state captures the appearance of what Walter Benjamin describes as law-making violence, the emergence *ex nihilo* of a new legal-political order; from this constitutive point, a system of law-preserving violence is developed, designed to maintain and fortify the existing order.[78] But as Jacques Derrida noted in his discussion of Benjamin's "Critique of Violence", the two forms are not distinct: law never quite rids itself of the original founding violence and continues to engage in a kind of secret relegitimation of the original moment of its own inception.[79] Exceeding the philosophical discussion of law and violence, the analysis here shows how the foundational violence of 1948 continues to haunt and disrupt law-preserving efforts to regulate, reorganise and ensure the formation of a normative space in accordance with national and modern ideals. Salama/Kfar Shalem illustrates how law is never fully constituted, continuously requiring validation and maintenance and therefore constantly bound to repetition in letter and action.

By broadening the historical scope to include events spanning almost eight decades, we find the fictional nature of any singular "zero point": there is always a prehistory of violence and a prehistory of law on which inception moments of social, political and legal orders rely.[80] In turn, the analysis shows how more or less violent practices of spatial seizure, appropriation and control are repeatedly enacted, signalling the ever-open negotiation of power and the ongoing labour of fusing people and land.

The lingering effects of emergency, from the pre-state years under Mandatory rule through the establishment of sovereignty in and following the 1948 War, and their recurring appearance in the ongoing struggles in Salama/Kfar Shalem, clearly illustrate the scope and concerns of spatial history. They turn our attention "to what remains, to the aftershock of empire, to the material and social afterlife of structures, sensibilities and things".[81] It is a non-linear endeavour that spirals from the site- and time-specific event to trace its prehistory and reverberations, in spatio-physical forms and in legal-political norms: in fences and defences. In an analysis of this sort, state mechanisms reappear as unstable and dynamic, and their operations often indecisive and

---

[78] Benjamin, "Critique of Violence".
[79] Derrida, "Force of Law", 269.
[80] Benjamin, "Critique of Violence", 244.
[81] Stoler, "Imperial Debris", 194.

contradictory. As such, spatial history is able to remain attentive to the ironies and slippages of power: to illustrate how the legal tools directed at the Arabs of Salama spill beyond the confines of national conflict to affect the Jews who settled in the village. Similarly, this analysis shows the mocking reversal of power, how the logic of invasion and appropriation that guided state activities in the formative period are directed against it by individuals and communities who demand to be recognised as legitimate and rightful actors, even when they, or the space they inhabit, do not conform to the normative law of the land.

4   On the Road: From Salama to Kfar Shalem and Back

According to the records of the Israeli Government Names Committee, the name "Salama" officially ceased to exist on 28 October 1952.[1] In a routine meeting, members of the committee came up with several dozen new names for new or existing settlements. Salama, by then an urban settlement[2] with a population of more than 10,000 people,[3] was from that moment to be known as Kfar Shalem.

Although the committee's decisions are made public and oblige all the official bodies of the Israeli government to make use of the new names,[4] it seems that the news failed to reach the clerks of the Tel Aviv Municipal Council, who in August 1953 published a document listing the neighbourhoods within the city's municipal boundaries that were in need of renovation, or, alternatively, were to be demolished for the construction of new housing projects. What is noteworthy in this document – which contains a map, a list of neighbourhoods and data regarding the population and the possible gain of land from the eviction – is that it cites the name Salama not once but three times: once as the "Village of Salama" (כפר סלמה), and twice more as "Salama A" (סלמה א') and "Salama B" (סלמה ב'). Was this an honest mistake on behalf of the Engineering and Planning Department at the Tel Aviv-Jaffa municipality? Perhaps the news regarding the changing of the name travelled slowly over the 60-odd kilometres separating the governmental offices in Jerusalem and Tel Aviv's town hall?

A quick review of sources indicates that this ambiguity does not simply fade away in the following years: Kfar Shalem, Salama, "the village" all appear interchangeably. The name is also subject to various,

---

[1] Kadmon, *Toponomasticon*, 58.
[2] According to Israeli legal definitions, an "urban settlement" would apply to any settlement with 2,000 residents or more.
[3] Golan, "From Abandoned Village to Urban Neighbourhood", 79.
[4] All of the committee's decisions are forwarded to the governmental executive branches including the Ministry of Interior, the national Public Work Department that places road signs throughout the country, the National Mapping Authority, and so on.

somewhat baffling, misspellings: on a road sign designating "Derekh Salama" (Salama Road) – the historic route leading from Jaffa eastward, toward Salama and onwards to the towns of Lydda, Ramla and the city of Jerusalem – the name appears at first to have been changed to "Derekh Shlomo" (Solomon Way).[5] A closer look clarifies that it in fact reads "Shalma" (שְׁלְמַה).[6] The small print that was added to clarify the historical background of the name on the sign does little to resolve the problem of multiplicity when it reads: "The road leading from Jaffa to Kfar Shalem (Seleme) [sic] where Judah the Maccabee defeated Nicanor (Maccabee 1:11)". Shlomo, Shalma, Kfar Shalem, or the oddly-punctuated Seleme – all crammed into the small rectangular space of a street sign.

Salama is not the only place bearing multiple names – old, new, abbreviated or mispronounced. Yet two issues suggest that this multiplicity is an anomaly that deserves closer critical consideration. The first relates to the way toponyms convey spatial and cultural histories. As I show, whereas names are justly understood as historical landmarks signifying events or people that are deemed worthy of public commemoration, the reception of these histories is often a protracted process of negotiation between various forces and actors. In the case of Salama, the multiplicity of names encourages us to re-evaluate the triangulation of name, place and history as it orients us in time and space; or, perhaps, how it fails to do so. The second issue regards the specific ideological and political contestation that lies at the heart of the mass alteration of names in Palestine since the end of the nineteenth century. My aim in this regard will be to question the direct correlation between ideological agendas and their actual manifestation. I posit that in order to account for the complexities and ambiguities of the spatial reality in present-day Israel, one has to interrogate the official apparatuses that are assigned with the authority to designate place-names and symbolic meaning. In parallel, the analysis must follow the actual forms official resolutions take, their paper trails and bureaucratic mishaps. And, in turn, we must explore how these decisions transform and mutate as they are practised in the lived space of the city.

[5] Some English maps do refer to the street as such. See for example: www.mapquest.com/maps/map.adp?formtype=address&country=IL&addtohistory=&city=Tel+Aviv

[6] The only distinction between the two forms lies in the Hebrew punctuation marks; without these, there is no difference in spelling.

Roadside Assistance: Space-Time Narratives

To further interrogate these questions, it is perhaps worth returning to the innocuous road sign on Derekh Salama. Taking the time in front of this mundane urban feature, with less than two-dozen words on its face, may hardly count as a worthwhile critical exercise. Yet in its unassuming way, through intricate temporalities and spatialities, this road sign distils a rich political history and exposes the unfinished effort to remake the spatial history of Israel-Palestine.

The information contained in this sign not only provides a designation of location, but signifies a direction, as it reads: "The road leading from Jaffa to Kfar Shalem (Seleme)." Setting aside what might well be a mispunctuation of the Arabic name *Salama*, one has to wonder what was the guiding logic that led the municipal authorities' decision to include the Arab name in this short narrative on a street sign? The parenthesis into which the Arab name is inserted provides a useful clue that ties this sign to a wider practice. A photograph in the Israeli National Photo Collection documents the erection of a sign bearing the name of the village of Elyakim, which was founded on the ruins of the former Arab village of Um al-Zinat (Figure 4.1). The photo captures a moment of birth; the marking of a new settlement. Yet the sign put up by the two young men in the image includes not only the Hebrew name of the new village but also the Arab name – underneath it, in parentheses. Reading this photo, Ariella Azoulay suggests that until the introduction of a forceful governmental name alteration policy in 1952, the presence of both Hebrew and Arab names was possible, if only for pragmatic reasons: "How will new immigrants find their way ... when old-timers still referred to the villages by their original Arab names?"[7]

Over half a century later, in mid-2008, the Jerusalem municipality erected new signs bearing neighbourhood names. In the city's former Arab neighbourhoods like Musrara, Talbiyeh and Malha, the council highlighted the Hebrew names assigned to them in the early 1950s – perhaps to compensate for the complete ignorance of residents to these names. The Arab names, widely used by all the residents of the city to this very day, are not erased from the new signs; rather, repeating the familiar form, they are there, only in parentheses.

The parenthetical enclosure of the Arab name points to two important issues: first, it attests to the resilience of the Arabic names as part of the spatial knowledge of the people who encounter these signs, a knowledge that cannot simply be ignored or erased; at best, it can be

---

[7] Azoulay, *From Palestine to Israel*, 116.

Figure 4.1 Putting up a sign for the Israeli village "Elyakim" on the site of former Arab village "Umm Al-Zinat", 1950.
Photographer: Teddy Brauner, Government Press Office Collection.

contained by a written gesture, to be put in parentheses. By the time the Arab toponym "Salama" was renamed as Kfar Shalem, "Derekh Salama" was already part of the spatial vocabulary of the residents of Jaffa and Tel Aviv, Jews and Arab alike – part of the spatial knowledge through which they comprehend and practise their city. Although the act of renaming is an age-old attempt to claim unlimited control over the signified space,[8] leaving the previous name in parentheses points, perhaps, to the limits of this signifying power.

The street sign in Derekh Salama also seeks to establish, or more precisely to duplicate, a specific temporal sequence. The short narrative that the sign conveys is an ungainly attempt to replay what Yael Zerubavel describes as the intentional anachronism that rests at the foundation of Zionism's temporal imagination: present-day Jewish sovereignty reinstates the heroic past of the ancient Israelite kingdoms, thus assigning historical significance only to the teleological ascension from exile to sovereignty. Any period that does not fit the "sovereign

---

[8] Benvenisti, *Sacred Landscape*, chapter 1; Azaryahu and Golan, "(Re)naming the Landscape".

threshold" of Jewish history is bound to remain outside official national commemoration:

> The alignment of the national periods on the one hand and Exile on the other plays up the positive images of the first and third periods [the ancient Israelite kingdom and the sovereign nation-state] against the highly negative image of the middle period. Even though Zionist memory acknowledges Exile as a very long period (often marked by the formulaic reference to "two thousand years") it defines it by its lack as if it were "empty" in substance.[9]

Zerubavel points to the "emptying" mechanisms that aspired to reconstruct the image of the past as an uninterrupted, teleological historical advancement that reaches its realisation with the establishment of the State of Israel. To compensate for the disruption of historical continuity, "the Zionist commemorative narrative constructs a *symbolic bridge* between Antiquity and the modern period"[10] that emphasises the affinity between the two. Furthermore, the State of Israel was perceived as the realisation of the aspiration of those who revolted, yet failed to fulfill their hopes for independent sovereignty: state symbols are therefore assumed to act as symbolic bridges that would bring together heroic past and present into a single, uninterrupted commemorative narrative, "a story about a particular past that … provides a moral message for the group members".[11]

At first, the street sign on Derekh Salama is a striking example of the intentional displacement of space and time: on the one hand, Kfar Shalem as part of present-day Israel; and on the other, Kfar Shalma, a symbol of the Maccabean rebellion against Antiochus IV Epiphanes (215–164 BCE), the former simply providing a contemporary alliteration of the latter. As Azaryahu and Kellerman note, the concentration on the specific historical period of the Second Temple, which also appears in the street sign on Derekh Salama, is "an attempt to reject the history of 'exile' through the recovery of a pre-exilic Jewish history, a history directly linked to the territory of the newly arising homeland".[12] The sign's narrative of national revival echoes Theodore Herzl's words in the conclusion to his 1896 pamphlet, "The Jews' State" (*Der Judenstaat*), in which he imagined "that a generation of wonderful Jews will grow out of the earth. The Maccabees shall rise again".[13] The street sign functions here as a commemorative designation that assigns historic and mythic

---

[9] Zerubavel, *Recovered Roots*, 33.
[10] Ibid., 32.
[11] Ibid., 6.
[12] Azaryahu and Kellerman, "Symbolic Places of National History and Revival", 112–13.
[13] Herzl, *The Jews' State*, 212.

significance through a semantic displacement: the historical location is dissociated from its commemorative site. While this displacement is not in itself a unique phenomenon,[14] the significance of this street sign lies in the way it uses the semantic displacement to overcome the *presence* of a contesting spatial and temporal order. Moreover, it does so not by a simple erasure of the Arab text, but by gestures of imitation (by means of alliteration) and inclusion (in the text of the street sign). The street sign does not simply direct us from one historical period to another, nor does it pretend to obliviously bridge between two historical eras on its far-from-pristine surface. To follow Zerubavel's metaphor, the road as a symbolic bridge cannot reach its destination without encountering the obstacle of Arab history, which creates a caesura in the narrative of the redeemed, national Hebrew Space.

The syntactic form of the sign's narrative presents the ambiguous way Salama – and the Arab space more broadly – is *contained* in and by its Jewish-Israeli environment: on the one hand, it is maintained in and as part of what would seem as the hegemonic Zionist narrative. However, Salama is also confined or restrained by this same structure that keeps it publicly visible, enclosed within the confinements of a Zionist historical leap from antiquity to national revival. Contrary to the claim that Zionist history treated the historical period in-between the two sovereignties "as if it were empty' in substance",[15] what we see here is the intricate persistence of substance (matter and meaning) and the consequent implications it has on the shaping of historical time-space.

The ploysemic nature of Salama's appearances – at one and the same time maintained and restrained by the Jewish-Israeli, Hebrew sign – operates mostly at the symbolic level of place-naming, but its potential should not be restricted to these manifestations only. In what follows, the duality of containment will return to surface in concrete and material expressions, undermining the seemingly stable power matrix of ethno-national space.

In the Name of Power: Historical and Comparative Framework

The identification of an Arab trace within the Hebrew-Israeli text of the street sign may seem to abide by the geological Principle of

---

[14] Monuments and memorial sites often serve to commemorate people or events that have no direct relation to the specific sites in which they are located. Thus, cities can memorialise national heroes or events that occurred in other historical contexts and other geographical settings.

[15] Zerubavel, *Recovered Roots*, 33.

Superposition, where each spatial layer is deposited on the foundations of the layer that preceded it.[16] But the historical context in which this sign exists and to which it relates, suggests that the persistence of an Arab name is an exception, rather than the rule. Numerous examples from other geographical locations and historical periods have shown that major political transformations are often accompanied or followed by transformations of symbolic representations through which a community imagines itself. This is often woven into a collective narrative that conveys the group's history, and is disseminated through various cultural forms and practices. In this respect, place-naming is one of many methods used by the sovereign power to transmit this narrative and embed it in the collective cultural fabric. The correlation between military conquest and symbolic renaming is a common phenomenon in human history, dating back to biblical times, as illustrated in the following verse: "And Judah went with Simeon his brother, and they slew the Canaanites that inhabited Zephath, and utterly destroyed it. And the name of the city was called Hormah" (Judges 1:17).[17]

Changes to the collective symbolic order can occur not only in cases of external conquest but also as a result of internal changes in political order or cultural values. Two examples come to mind in this sense, the first being the renaming in 1793 of "Place Louis XV" in Paris to "Place de la Revolution". Maoz Azaryahu notes that this act targeted the symbolic presence of the monarchist past and aspired to replace it with the new symbols of the revolutionary order.[18] This, however, lasted only two years and in 1795 the government decided to rename it once more, this time as "Place de la Concorde", hoping to somewhat obscure its bloody years of hosting public executions. It is perhaps the first example in which the process of renaming occurs within the context of the nation-state and as part of the internal tensions that accompany the development of its symbolic identity.

Another, later example, which highlights the changes in symbolic naming as a result of internal normative shifts within the national collective, is a 1962 decision of the United States Board on Geographic

---

[16] Hamblin, *The Earth's Dynamic Systems*, 116.

[17] This example is cited in Azaryahu, "The Purge of Bismarck and Saladin". The Bible notes several other incidents in which renaming was conducted as a symbolic act through which sovereignty was assigned, with the renaming of Jerusalem as the "City of David" following its conquest (II Samuel 5:9) as a prime example. Isaac Leo Zeeligman suggests that the origin of this transformation lies in the biblical legal tradition of declaring the owners of a newly acquired property. Zeeligman, "Signs of Changes and Editorial Alterations", 223–4. For further discussion of biblical naming traditions, see Mazor, "Between Bible and Zionism".

[18] Azaryahu, "The Purge of Bismarck and Saladin", 352.

Names – the federal agency authorised to establish and maintain uni-
form geographic name usage throughout the American federal government – to abolish the use of the words "Nigger" and "Nip" (a derogatory
term for Japanese) for official place-names in the United States.[19] These
were the only racially insulting words banned from use as toponyms.
On the face of it, the USBGN's decision reflects the growing sensitivity
of American society to racially offensive language and its dissemination through cultural practices such as place-names. The shifts in the
American normative climate regarding minority rights made their
mark on various aspects of American culture; place-names were but
one reflection of these changes. But the actual practice of change is
worth noting: most of the toponyms that previously contained the word
"Nigger" were changed to "Negro"[20] and were accordingly changed
in official documentation. This was, as one American columnist put it,
an attempt at "taking the sting out of place names".[21] Considering the
French and the American examples cited here, the process of renaming
cannot be understood separately from the socio-political climate within
which it occurs. Moreover, place-names reflect the decisive role played
by authoritative apparatuses and their ideological agendas.

The focus on the symbolic force of place-names and street names in
particular is not detached from other physical manifestations of power.
In the context of historical Palestine, roads were officially considered
as territory owned by the state and therefore as places of sovereign
presence. Initial classification of land ownership was presented in the
Ottoman Land Code of 1858. This legislation distinguished between
five classes of ownership, which differentiated between public and private ownerships and additionally classified the various sub-categories
within each.[22] According to this legal taxonomy, roads were classified as
matrūk maḥmiyya, or property for general public use. Granovsky notes
that "The object of the law of 1858, which dealt primarily with these
three classes of [public] property, was to maintain the rights of the State
over them."[23] Similarly, Eisenman concludes that the principle aim of
the Land Code of 1858 "was the reassertion of Government control over

---

[19] "News and Views: 'Nigger Creeks' Are Gone".
[20] The Geographic Names Information System (GNIS) lists 754 geographical features
containing the term "Negro". Some of these, mostly in the south-west, arise from the
Spanish word used to describe geographical features, not skin colour. Many other
features, however, are related to a specific historical context in which the derogative
term was used. "US Board on Geographic Names (BGN)".
[21] Jamieson, "Taking the Sting Out of Place Names".
[22] Granovsky, *The Land System in Palestine*, 88–90.
[23] Ibid., 87.

State Domain".[24] Roads were therefore not merely physical, utilitarian spaces, but manifestations of a legal administration and an arena in which sovereign power is played out. Controlling the procedures of ownership is but one expression of the state's claim over its territory, enacted mostly in the limited discursive realms of law and planning regulations. To gain recognition of roads as part of the sovereign power's territory, additional interventions that emphasise its public nature are called for: architectural forms or street names function as part of the symbolic system through which the sovereign asserts its power over territory. Roads are thus manifestations of power *de jure*, as they are claimed by the state or the city authorities in the text of law, but also function as *de facto* signs of power by bearing the visible marks and scripts of their administrators.

If roads are a socio-political arena, and if street names are "instrumental in substantiating the socio-political order and its particular 'theory of the world' in the cityscape",[25] then the street sign in Derekh Salama is far from a banal remnant of Jaffa's history, or an incidental "cultural leftover". Several questions come into mind in this regard: what impact does the resilience of the Arab name have on the Israeli cultural setting? How does it constitute a "spatial disturbance" that disrupts the conventional flows of power and knowledge? What are the mechanisms that enable the appearance of such disruptions, and what are the dynamics that enable their persistence? Paul Carter's poetic definition of spatial history – "a history of roads, footprints, trails of dust"[26] – is an important starting point of this interrogation, enabling us to consider the very literal and concrete forces that shape these spaces.

The historical link between sovereign power and spatial phenomena like roads and streets interestingly reappears in the debate that followed the annexation of Jaffa to Tel Aviv in October 1949. Not merely a legalistic, formal discussion between administrative levels, the debate presented key figures with the opportunity to publicly articulate the historical imperative of street naming in Tel Aviv. The Municipal Names Committee was established in 1934 and received its guiding principles from the Tel Aviv Municipal Council in 1942. According to these guidelines, the committee should prioritise "symbolic names related to the chronicles of Israel and its land".[27] However, following the annexation,

---

[24] Eisenman, *Islamic Law in Palestine and Israel*, 56.
[25] Azaryahu, "The Power of Commemorative Street Names", 312.
[26] Carter, *The Road to Botany Bay*, xxi–xxii.
[27] Tel Aviv Municipal Names Committee, "For the assignment of names to Tel Aviv's streets".

a whole new space was opened for the inscription of the "appropriate" narratives of Jewish and Zionist history. In an essay published in
the municipality's official gazette, the committee's secretary, A.Z. Ben-
Yishai, states that the newly named streets form a "key to the history of
Israel throughout the generations".[28] Ben-Yishai clearly sees the renaming of streets in Jaffa as a symbolic action that completes the military
occupation of the city by the Israeli forces, "retrieving to Jaffa, through
its street names, its Jewish and Hebrew-historical character".[29]

But the assumption that historical knowledge can and should be con-
veyed through spatial signs and names seems to be part of a broader
discourse in the first years following the encounter between Jaffa and
Tel Aviv. The hyphen that tied the names of the two cities – a matter that
required no less than a government debate on 4 October 1949 – did not
suffice. In a special municipal council meeting two days later, Council
Member Sa'adia Shoshani rejected the government's decision to name
the new unified city "Jaffa-Tel Aviv", stating that "Tel Aviv conquered
Jaffa, and one must not agree that Jaffa would 'conquer' Tel Aviv."[30] For
Shoshani, as for many others at the time,[31] the symbolic gesture that
allows Jaffa to appear ahead of Tel Aviv in the official name was enough
to jeopardise the significance of the military achievements gained by the
occupation of the largest Arab urban centre in Palestine. In the following sections, a more focused analysis will follow the way Tel Aviv dealt
with the expansion of its borders, with the inclusion of Jaffa and the
Arab villages in its periphery into the new municipal boundaries, and
the specific issue of street names in the negotiation of power and place.

"Old Habits Die Hard": Ambiguity, Fear and the Impediments of Spatial Control

The interrogation of street naming politics often focuses on the political
and ideological forces that take part in the production of such "city-
texts". But the ambiguities that appear in the process of scripting space
are often left unaccounted for. In this sense, the centrality of names
in the early debates regarding the annexation of Jaffa to Tel Aviv presents, perhaps, the ambivalence and uncertainties of the cities' new

---

[28] Ben-Yishai, "The Street Names of Tel Aviv", 39.
[29] Ibid., 40.
[30] Quoted in: Ben-Yishai, "The City Council on the Question of Annexation and the
Name", 74.
[31] Israeli daily newspapers of the day strongly rejected the prevalence given to Jaffa
in the government's decision, including the official publication of the ruling Mapai
party, *ha-Dor*, and in the left-wing *Al-Hamishmar*.

administrators and not simply the voice of self-assured, authoritative control per se. It is important to note once again that these ambiguities are not external to official centres of power, and must not be sought solely in the subversive spatial tactics of subaltern groups. This critical reconsideration of colonial authority has been a hallmark of postcolonial theorists who challenged simplistic portrayals of an omnipotent coloniser.[32] This was not only an effort to draw attention to multiple forms of resistance to colonial hierarchies, but a refined understanding of the ambiguities and contradictions that were inherent to the colonising power itself. Through this particular critical prism, the following analysis closely reads the way key Zionist political figures narrate the symbolic appropriation of the Arab space, and illuminates the slippages and incongruities that plague the attempt to stabilise a settler-colonial master narrative.

In a short article published in the *Tel Aviv Gazette* in 1954,[33] the author notes that "With the occupation of Jaffa by Israel's Defence Forces, the few street names in the city were changed to numbers by a temporary order, in the fashion of the big American cities (New York in particular)".[34] However, the endeavour to duplicate the American method was soon to encounter an unexpected difficulty:

The winding and unplanned shape of the roads and alleyways of Jaffa – most of which are unpaved and some [resembling] actual demolition sites that are expected to be planned and rebuilt – prevented the establishment of a convenient numerical order in the streets, which is why numbers were assigned with no method or order, high [numbers] next to low, which resulted in confusion and chaos in the city. Out of habit and for convenience sake, the old-time residents – and under their influence, the new immigrants who comprise the majority of Jaffa's residents – *continued to use some of the Arab names for the main arteries, which we intended to obscure from memory.* Governmental and military offices also continued to use these names in order to avoid inaccuracies.[35]

Instead of projecting a desired narrative on space, the process of naming appears here as a negotiation between the linguistic practices of space and its physicality – an unresolved tension between a supposedly passive and obedient realm of names and the "unplanned" physical

---

[32] The work of Ann Laura Stoler stands out in this effort, but joins others who explored the inherent anxieties that make up settler colonial rule, from German South West Africa to Australia and Canada. See Stoler, *Along the Archival Grain*; Noyes, *Colonial Space*; Jacobs, *Edge of Empire*; Mawani, *Colonial Proximities*.

[33] Although anonymously published, there is reason to assume that it was written by A. Z. Ben-Yishai, chair of the Municipal Names Committee and editor of the journal.

[34] "The Street Names of Israeli Jaffa".

[35] Ibid.

inheritance of a "disorderly order" that dominated the Arab space of Jaffa. This obstructive legacy was not confined to the physical aspects of Jaffa's streets. Another system that remained present in the local cultural memory was a method of linguistic orientation through which the Arab areas annexed to Tel Aviv were experienced by their "old time" inhabitants.[36] Moreover, the symbolic system of Arab street names was not confined to the minority of the older residents of Jaffa, but was disseminated and circulated among the masses of new immigrants who populated the city after its conquest in the 1948 War. The attempt to superimpose a new, external system of spatial ordering encountered both physical and cultural resistance that disrupted its absorption.

The intricacies of this case challenge, without completely refuting, the customary association between political interventions in street naming, and questions of memory and forgetfulness. In his influential work "The Power of Commemorative Street Names", Maoz Azaryahu asserts that, "A politically motivated renaming involves a twofold procedure: decommemoration and commemoration."[37] Undeniably, both processes can be identified in the actions of the Israeli authorities during the renaming of Jaffa's streets, but it is unclear whether one system of commemoration simply *replaces* the previous one, and to what degree this process of resignification is compelled to *negotiate* its presence in space for an extended period of time. In order to advance the analysis beyond binary divisions and closer to the subtleties that constitute spatial history, I would like to show how this official record of the street naming of Jaffa can be understood as evidence of the limitations of political power; or, more precisely, of the effort invested in resolving the tension between the way space is imagined and the way it is practised. For example, once mentioning the failure to number the streets of Jaffa, the writer in the municipal gazette moves swiftly to remind us that

After the unification of Tel Aviv and Jaffa to a single city, under one municipal governance, the Tel Aviv municipality immediately changed some of the names of the main streets that connect Jaffa with Tel Aviv and with other state roads … That is how the arteries of Jaffa were given pure Hebrew names, some which recall Jaffa in biblical days, Israel's Jaffa.[38]

The author also reminds his readers that despite these initial efforts, "the Israeli Jaffa, which became an almost purely Jewish city in the seven

---

[36] This likely refers to the Arab residents of the city, though there is no reason to dismiss the possibility that this definition would include the Jews who resided in the city and equally absorbed it into their vocabulary.

[37] Azaryahu, "The Power of Commemorative Street Names", 317.

[38] "The Street Names of Israeli Jaffa".

years of the existence of the State of Israel, also awaits the redemption of its street names to restore its Hebrew character of old". The realisation of Jaffa's historical redemption began, therefore, in August 1954 with the naming of 100 streets throughout the city:

In determining the first 100 names – which will be followed, in due course, by other names – all of Israeli Jaffa's virtues and desires were taken into account: ancient history, legend and myth, new Hebrew history, landscape and seaside and the "internationalism" of its minorities. These names came to mark Jaffa with a Hebrew-Jewish-Israeli seal, to place clear names instead of obscure numbers in the mouths of its diverse population, Hebrew names instead of foreign ones ... Naming streets is undoubtedly one of the most important instruments to redeem Jaffa from *the burden of its foreign past* and its transformation to a fully Jewish city, an inseparable part of the great city of "Tel Aviv – Jaffa".

Despite the celebratory tone of this account, the "burden" of Jaffa's past was not easily lifted and the text illustrates just how unsettling spatial multiplicity actually is. On the one hand, it reiterates the narrative through which the Zionist vision portrayed the continuum of Jewish presence in the land – "biblical days, Israel's kingdoms, the days of the Talmud, the immigrations in various times, the attempts to seize and settle, the new return to Zion, the War of Independence and the latest occupation". Much like certain colonial maps, this text "presupposes a conception of the world as semiotic invention rather than a representation of reality that would purportedly reflect natural spatial relations".[39] At the same time, this new spatial imagination encounters components that already make up spatial reality – both physical and linguistic-cultural – of the people who lived in Jaffa and its Arab environs. To resolve this impasse, the text resorts to the power of names, hoping that what failed with numbers will succeed with words. It assumes that the Arab spatial history practised by both Arabs and Jews, with its history and cultural significance, will be eroded only by providing an alternative narrative of history and space. As illustrated in the case of Derekh Salama, this was never fully accomplished.

It is hard to overstate the emphasis placed on historical meaning in the debates that surrounded the unification of Jaffa and Tel Aviv. While the process that led to the creation of a single municipal entity clearly involved practical issues such as municipal borders, taxation, welfare services and rubbish disposal, the most heated debates regarding this process often revolved around the organising narratives of each city's history. Arguments in this debate expressed two related anxieties, while sharing the underlying fear that the central, authoritative

---

[39] Rabasa, *Inventing America*, 185.

control over space would be lost. In the first instance, it was feared that the cohesive urban mythography that surrounded Tel Aviv in the first decades of its establishment would dissolve into a multicultural muddle. Integrating the Arab history of Jaffa, a history that was written into its streets and architecture and embedded into the vocabulary of its residents, could potentially fracture the self-assuring homogeneity of Tel Aviv's historical narrative. Others used the opposite argument, without deviating from the same logic: fear this time was directed not at the possible loss of control in case of unification, but at the possible threat of isolating Jaffa, maintaining its separate status and the possible inability to ensure control and governance over it. These parallel anxieties were each expressed in December 1949 by two of the key figures involved in the process – Interior Minister Moshe Shapira and Tel Aviv Mayor Israel Rokach – in two short articles printed side by side in the municipality's official publication.

Rokach begins his column with a biographical note entitled "Bleak memories of Jaffa",[40] in which he reminisces on "grim childhood memories that have not been forgotten from my heart to this day: The rocks, which the Arabs used to throw in the narrow and filthy alleyways of Jaffa, the victims of the wild assault of 1921, where some of my friends … were martyred".[41] The mayor continues to describe the persecution of Jews during the 1929 riots, commonly remembered for the massacre of the Jewish community of Hebron, and those of 1936. Rokach's choice of opening with his own hardships and sufferings is not incidental, as he proceeds to remind his readers of the "war I fought for the separation from Arab Jaffa and for the independence of Tel Aviv".[42] From this point, Tel Aviv's mythography begins to appear: the departure from the Arab city to establish a separate, Jewish, town; the emergence of self-reliant defence activity; the solidarity that existed between the members of the new community; and Tel Aviv's role in the national mission of immigrant absorption. Concluding the first part of his article, Rokach chooses to juxtapose the role of each city in history:

Jaffa has not played any role in the world's history, or in the history of Israel. One cannot find any relic of ancient periods aside from a short period during the Hashmonaim time[43] … Tel Aviv itself lies mostly in the region of the [biblical tribe of] Dan, and in part in that of Ephraim. A whole generation strived and laboured to build the first Hebrew city and make it a fortress in the service

---

[40] Rokach, "On Greater Tel Aviv".
[41] Ibid., 73.
[42] Ibid.
[43] Reference to the ruling dynasty of the Hasmonean Kingdom of Israel (140–37 BCE).

the young Hebrew state in terms of economy, policy, society and culture, and a symbol of the remarkable struggle for creative work and construction.

The historical opposition between the two cities preludes the civilising mission "imposed" on Tel Aviv, which needs to make sense of a place "without any sanitary or engineering order":

The Tel Aviv municipality now faces tremendous work to change Jaffa's plan from the foundation ... A heavy burden has been placed on the citizens of broader Tel Aviv in fulfilling a financial and cultural mission involved in the cohesion of the masses of immigrants into our society, despite the mishmash of languages, customs, and cultures still practiced by them. We will be required to organise these spaces with a unified system of construction, to establish cultural institutions, schools and kindergartens, to plant gardens and also educate the population to help and carry the joint burden.[44]

For Rokach, the historical difference between the two cities is manifested in spatial terms – from filthy streets to planning disorder – and this difference must be overcome by a civilising endeavour "that will prove the justification for our destiny, that fate imposed upon us".[45] This gesture of "benevolent assimilation"[46] does little to conceal the threat Rokach identifies in the incorporation of Jaffa into the imagined narrative Tel Aviv has plotted: Jaffa "contaminates" the imagined birth of Tel Aviv with an "impure" ancestry, confronting the Hebrew city with the urban image from which it sought to distance itself. This was a substantial challenge to the city that hoped to invent itself as the diametrical opposition to Jaffa and all it was understood to represent in the eyes of Tel Aviv's forefathers.[47] To defuse this threat, the spatial changes of 1949 (the redrawing of the municipal boundaries) must be reframed and rephrased in a way that will reinstate a hierarchy of difference; or in Rokach's words, "not unification, but annexation". Rokach saw how the seemingly technical changes to the city's borders challenge Tel Aviv's self-image as "the city born out of the sands",[48]

---

[44] Rokach, "On Greater Tel Aviv", 73–4.
[45] Ibid., 74.
[46] Miller, *Benevolent Assimilation*.
[47] The various components of Tel Aviv's mythography and its historical evolution have been noted in several recent accounts; for example, Azaryahu, *Tel Aviv*; Rotbard, *White City, Black City*; Mann, *A Place in History*; LeVine, *Overthrowing Geography*. My focus here is placed on the unavoidable ambivalence of these founding narratives toward the Arab space it encounters.
[48] Sharon Rotbard dedicates an illuminating chapter in his book *White City, Black City* to the motif of "the sands" in the Zionist narration of Tel Aviv's history – and to the "professionalisation" of this motif from the mid-1990s – as it penetrates contemporary architectural discourse in Israel. Another aspect of the sands and their nostalgic role in Tel Aviv's founding narrative appears in Azaryahu, *Tel Aviv*, 54–8, 102.

and requires its narrators to shift from the "glorious seclusion" of the past to the "redeeming civilising mission" it is about to embark on.

There was, however, another narrative regarding the unification of Jaffa and Tel Aviv, and although it runs along similar veins that emphasise the mission Tel Aviv faces in absorbing Jaffa and bestowing it with its cultural, social and economic wealth, it nonetheless emerges out of a distinct concern. In a column published alongside the one written by Rokach, Moshe Haim Shapira, the then interior minister and one of the notable leaders of the religious-Zionist movement, suggested that the threat lay not in the inclusion of Jaffa, but with its exclusion and isolation. If Rokach feared that Jaffa's insertion into the borders (both concrete and imagined) of Tel Aviv would undermine the narrative upon which the city was founded, Shapira pointed out the dangers of seclusion:

> As I tour the new towns and the abandoned villages where only new immigrants were settled my heart fills with anxiety and fear. One gets the impression that diasporic towns were uprooted from their place and planted in our country with all their side effects. Therefore, the Ministry of Interior is doing all it can to adjoin the new settlements inhabited by new immigrants to veteran towns and cities in order to accelerate the process of assimilation and incorporation … and from this point of view we must not establish a backward immigrant city, to leave its inhabitants deserted to their own fate and isolated from the springs of spirit and wealth of the Land of Israel.[49]

Shapira's concerns emerge from the harsh conditions that existed in many of the immigrant towns and settlements, and their ambivalent place in Israel's historiography and cultural memory (as discussed in Chapter 3). The "anxiety and fear" Shapira expresses are directed at the recurring phenomenon of cultural enclaves of secluded immigrant communities that were yet to become an integral part of the Israeli social and cultural space, and maintained – partly by choice, and more often by the lack thereof – a degree of foreignness. Confined to the hinterland of the Galilee or the Negev desert, these marginalised enclaves had little effect on the cultural and social centres; however, similar enclaves in Jaffa or in the Arab villages adjacent to Tel Aviv would have a destabilising impact on the commonly used notion of the "melting pot" adopted by Tel Aviv and used to symbolise the forging of a new society for the new nation.[50] The anxiety here emerges out of the potential autonomy that these spaces may claim, thus transplanting the space of the diaspora into the heart of the national territory. Much like Rokach's

---

[49] Shapira, "On the Annexation and it Causes", 74.
[50] Azaryahu, *Tel Aviv*, 76.

conclusion regarding Tel Aviv's civilising mission, Shapira states that despite the differences between the two cities, he hopes "Tel Aviv will bestow some of its gleam and glitter upon the residents of Jaffa".[51]

The two trajectories I have thus far described are not mutually exclusive. They illustrate the familiar dynamic of ambivalence that moves restlessly between the desire for conquest and the fear of the corruption of a (mostly imagined) cultural and spatial cohesion. The uneasy fluctuation between these two poles, which I have already indicated in Chapter 2, resulted in the recruitment of a wide variety of resources through which, it was hoped, this ambivalence could be resolved and "order" restored. As Minister Shapira elsewhere noted, in addition to being a legal act with economic, political and administrative consequences, the annexation is also "an historical-symbolic act, with great value to our generation and those to follow".[52] Yet six decades after Jaffa and Tel Aviv were officially united, the two cities remain physically and symbolically distinct. Furthermore, Tel Aviv continues to grapple with the dissonant conjuncture between its own mythography and the histories it encountered once it was – administratively at least – required to contain a heterogeneous collection of spaces and histories.[53] The unfinished task of absorption and the ongoing effort invested in eliminating Jaffa's "disturbing" features raises the question of whether this ambivalence was meant to be resolved at all, or whether it was intended to allow Tel Aviv to cling on to its cohesive foundation narrative even after unification. In any case, street-level practices continued to present authorities with concrete challenges.

As noted above, the physical shape of the streets in Jaffa and the Arab periphery of Tel Aviv defied the numerical street system introduced after the war. This phenomenon was not marginal and its effects were not restricted to some "clandestine" locals in Jaffa. A letter sent in 1953 by Tel Aviv's vice-mayor, Haim Levanon, to the Government Names Committee regarding the names of neighbourhoods and streets in Jaffa clarifies the gravity of this issue. Levanon begins his letter with a general remark: "It is difficult to instantaneously uproot the names of the neighbourhoods in Jaffa and in the abandoned villages annexed to the municipal jurisdiction of Tel Aviv – names which were absorbed during

---

[51] Shapira, "On the Annexation and it Causes", 74.
[52] Shapira, "The Annexation of Jaffa".
[53] This included not only Arab areas but also Jewish neighbourhoods that were not included in the city's original municipal borders like Shapira and Hatikva neighbourhoods, each with its own history that was, as one book title suggests, neither that of Jaffa nor that of Tel Aviv. See, for example, the collection of local history in the Shapira neighbourhood compiled in Tzur and Rotbard, *Neither in Jaffa Nor in Tel Aviv*.

many years."[54] However, Levanon goes on to suggest that the perseverance of Arab names was not just the consequence of their use by Jaffa's
residents; in fact, it was the negligence of none other than the governmental authorities that was to blame for upholding the Arab spatial history: "the [military] recruitment offices, tax departments etc. – continue
to this day to use in their publications Arab names of the streets of Jaffa,
even those who have already been assigned with Hebrew names".[55]

Ironically, less than a year later, the Tel Aviv Municipality was itself
accused of similar negligence in a memo sent by the Tel Aviv Regional
Governance office. What thus far appeared as either a technical problem
or an issue of symbolic importance, now became a matter of national
security:

> Recently, government authorities have become aware of difficulties in finding
> addresses in many urban settlements in the country, in which the indication of
> streets and house numbers is extremely inadequate. This has been especially
> pointed out by the Chief of Staff, as unmarking streets and houses complicate
> personal summoning to reserve service by the military ... It is advised therefore
> to include the local Civil Defence Command in the municipal committees to
> determine names and regulate the demarcation of streets and houses.[56]

If indeed, as this memo concludes, street naming and demarcation are
a "problem that requires military handling", then streets are rather
more than a symbolic conflation of histories, "traces and ruins of their
former selves", or "tokens and hieroglyphs from the past" – as Boyer
suggests.[57] Rather, they are arenas of conflict where authorities, communities and cultural histories present and negotiate their rights and
powers.

The Other Side of Town: A Spatial History of City Borders

In 1950, Derekh Salama not only marked the way to Salama but
charted the movement from the recognised boundaries of the city to
the unmarked urban peripheries. Already a densely populated area
housing more than 14,000 people, Salama was the largest concentration of immigrants and Jewish war refugees in the entire region of Tel
Aviv, surpassed only by the city of Jaffa itself. However, despite its size

---

[54] Levanon, Memo to the Government Names Committee, "Names of neighbourhoods
in Jaffa".
[55] Ibid.
[56] Tel Aviv Regional Governance. "Demarcation of Streets and Houses". Letter to Tel
Aviv Mayor, February 1954. TAMHA 4/2212.
[57] Boyer, *The City of Collective Memory*, 32.

and administrative status as part of the Tel Aviv municipal boundaries, Salama remained "uncharted territory". Somewhere at the south-eastern edges of Shapira neighbourhood, as it draws near to the Ayalon watercourse (known previously by its Arab name, Wadi Musrara), streets ceased to bear names. As appears in the first street-map of greater Tel Aviv – drawn only three months after the official declaration of the city's new municipal borders (Figure 4.2) – all the streets beyond that point remain unnamed: Shekhunat Hatikva, Shekhunat Ezra and Salama are mentioned on the map, but, devoid of street names, appear more as geometrical abstractions or unrealised sketches of future neighbourhoods.

If "Street names reflect and manifest a certain political identity",[58] what identity is manifested in unnamed streets? What political engagement is implied in spaces that remain as blanks on the map? From the official statements of the Tel Aviv Municipality, it is the winding shape and "disorderly fashion" of the streets in the Arab neighbourhoods that prevented their proper demarcation. This explanation, however, falls short of accounting for the situation revealed in the map: Shekhunat Hatikva, with its grid-like street plan, is not dissimilar to Yad Eliyahu to its north, a neighbourhood that by that time had already partially been granted an assortment of street names and numbers. The shape of streets therefore only partly resolves the problem. Following the methodological and theoretical premises presented in Chapter 2, the map's emptiness and the absence of names must be understood as part of a broader negotiation through which physical and symbolic spatial forms are produced.

Not often are we able to find visual documentation that captures not just the blank spaces of the map, but the more intricate early stages of expansion and the incorporation of vast Arab sections of the city. In this sense, this map exposes the primary moment of encounter. The specific historical and political circumstances set this process apart from the more familiar examples of American or European urban sprawl. Instead, it provides critical insights into the ambivalence, almost reluctance, to blur the dividing lines that separate urban centres from their periphery in a state of settler-colonial, ethno-national conflict. This spatial history of expansion exposes some of the obstacles that hinder a smooth, uninterrupted accumulation of territory and some of the practices implemented in overcoming them.

---

[58] Azaryahu, "Street Names and Political Identity", 581.

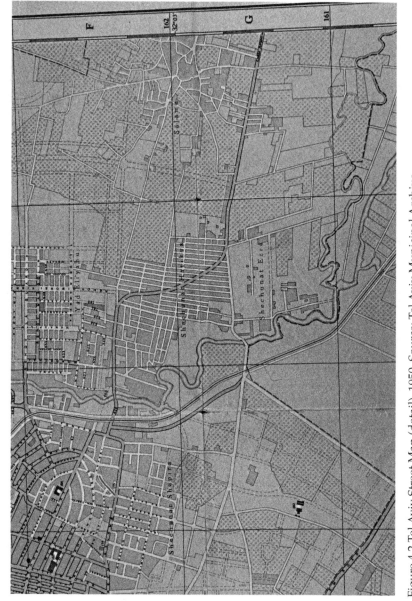

Figure 4.2 Tel Aviv Street Map (detail), 1950. Source: Tel Aviv Municipal Archive.

As Maoz Azaryahu shows, throughout its formative years in the 1920s and 1930s, Tel Aviv saw itself as a "European oasis in the midst of the Asian desert".[59] Using fantastic imagery that illustrated how "beyond the gates of Tel Aviv a black night is clinging to the soil of ancient Arabia",[60] Tel Aviv sought to actualise the threatening Orientalist "beyond" and solidify a sense of a cohesive identity through the negation of the others that existing outside. In this process, the actualisation of borders was of utmost importance. While Jaffa to the south and the Mediterranean Sea to the west could easily be associated with the historical negotiation of Tel Aviv's borders,[61] the south-east perimeters provided no clear feature that could determine the differentiating limit. In this sense, Salama provided Tel Aviv with the image of the threatening "ancient Arabia". The village's size and location just north of the main highway leading from Tel Aviv and Jaffa to the eastern hinterland, actualised the sense that Tel Aviv was encircled and under the threat of being overcome by a "black night".

For this reason, the establishment of the Jewish neighbourhood of Shekhunat Hatikva in 1935 – between Tel Aviv and Salama – was seen to provide Tel Aviv with a "buffer" that would stave off the threat from the east, and at the same time separate Jaffa from its Arab periphery. Despite its function in separating Tel Aviv from Salama, Shekhunat Hatikva was administratively included in Tel Aviv's municipal boundaries only after 1950, along with Salama and Ezra, another nearby Jewish neighbourhood. However, during this process the Tel Aviv municipal authorities discovered that both the Arab village and the Jewish neighbourhoods surrounding it presented similar features that were not aligned with the desired spatial order of the city. A report prepared by the governmental Borders Committee determined that

---

[59] Azaryahu, *Tel Aviv*, 58–60.
[60] Avraham Wissotzky 1928, quoted in ibid., 58.
[61] Several accounts in recent years have discussed this issue. Hannan Hever analyses the sea as a central trope in the Israeli and Zionist literary canon. Hever charts the changes that this trope undergoes, from its perception by 1920s and 1930s writers as a space of transition to the homeland, and then, in the 1950s and 1960s, as a site that is scorned and dismissed. Barbara Mann dedicates a chapter in her book to the "edges" of Tel Aviv and closely reads the manner by which these edges were constructed in the cultural imagination of the city. Mann focuses on the way borders were constructed and represented in literature, in painting, and through the assignment of street names. Maoz Azaryahu illustrates the way boundaries dictated the manner by which Tel Aviv constructed its mythography, and yet again concentrates on the literary, poetic, journalistic and other written expressions that take part in the composition of this mythography. Sharon Rotbard follows a more heterogeneous methodology by incorporating source material from both spatial and literary archives. See: Rotbard, *White City, Black City*; Mann, *A Place in History*; Azaryahu, *Tel Aviv*; Hever, *Toward the Longed-For Shore*.

the neighbourhoods of Ezra and Hatikva and the borders of Salama evolved in terms of construction without any engineering supervision and without any urban planning intervention ... Even if the efforts to restrain these construction violations succeed, many years will pass before the distortion can be fixed and these neighbourhoods are rebuilt according to an approved urban-planning scheme.[62]

The change in the legal status of the borders of Tel Aviv – which now included what was previously assumed to be an external border-territory that sets apart urban from rural, Jews from Arabs, order from disorder – also demanded that the authorities act to incorporate these ambivalent spaces into the text and texture of the city. The emptiness of the streets in Salama and Shekhunat Hatikva suggested not only their status as newly acquired space but also their availability to be inscribed into the symbolic space of the new entity "Tel Aviv – Jaffa". It is at this moment that the city encounters the frontier: while the border was easily shifted through swift legal amendments, the spatial qualities of the frontier disappear ever-more slowly. The Border Committee suggested, for example, that drastic changes take place in the physical planning and construction of the neighbourhoods. But these lengthy procedures and the substantial resources they required could be accompanied, if not surpassed altogether, by the symbolic gesture of street naming – which actualises the presence of the new cultural and political order. The following analysis of the process through which street names were assigned in Salama/Kfar Shalem presents, on the one hand, the imposition of symbolic sovereignty; but on the other, the limits of symbolic power and the ways spatial phenomena subvert the projection of external orders.

Dead-End Streets

Unlike the Arab houses of Salama, which were populated almost overnight, filling the emptiness of street names was a gradual process. In Salama, municipal authorities initially assigned Hebrew letters to mark street names, thus following the same logic that led to the numbering of other streets in Jaffa. The Municipal Names Committee explained that

In the deserted [Arab] neighbourhoods and villages in Tel Aviv's areas, the streets are narrow and unpaved and are intended for demolition according

---

[62] Governmental Borders Committee, "Borders Committee Report on the Jurisdiction of Tel Aviv, Ramat Gan, Bne Brak and Givatayim", 73.

to the Town Planning Scheme. No commemorative names will therefore be assigned to these streets out of respect.[63]

In this sense, Salama was still perceived as a temporary space that was destined to undergo substantial changes and should not, therefore, be fixed through the assignment of names.

In Shekhunat Hatikva the naming procedure seems, at first sight at least, to have taken a more determined course. By 1954 the Municipal Names Committee was able to assign new names to the streets throughout most of the neighbourhood, although it was stated that some of these were to be "temporary and mundane, to be replaced at any time by specific names".[64] What exactly counted as a "specific" name remains vague. However, the list of names assigned to Shekhunat Hatikva suggests that at least on a symbolic level, the neighbourhood was successfully incorporated into the dominant Zionist-Israeli imagination: in addition to biblical names, several main streets were provided with names relating to the 1948 War, such as *Hanitzakhon* ("victory") or commemorating Israeli military forces like the Haganah ("defence"), *Shiryon* ("armour") and *Kiryati* (the brigade that fought in the area during the war). For a neighbourhood that was placed at the margins of the grand urban mythography, this act was a gesture that signalled a redrawing of the administrative and symbolic borders. As time went by, though, the benevolent gesture proved insufficient in eradicating old borders that retained their persistent presence. In a novel set in Shekhunat Hatikva during the 1970s, Dudu Busi captures the lingering sense of isolation and detachment felt by those growing up on the "wrong" side of the Ayalon watercourse (or Wadi Musrara as it was known at the time). In one scene, the first-person narrator and a friend stand near the filthy creek and look at the moon's reflection:

A green full moon peeped at us from the piles of construction waste and the torn-up tyres that were scattered in the shallow water. "Look at the moon", Sasson said and pointed at the green stain that floated in the water, "look how crappy it looks in the wadi, like cats' shit".

"It's because it's stuck where we're stuck", I said pulling my nose, "in stagnant stinky water, in the juice of the garbage".[65]

Long after the official borders of Tel Aviv were altered to include the south-east periphery, those who lived and grew up in Shekhunat Hatikva, Salama and Shekhunat Ezra continued to experience the

[63] Ben-Yishai, "New Names for the Streets of Tel Aviv", 25.
[64] Ibid.
[65] Busi, *The Moon Goes Green in the Wadi*, 86.

concrete divides that marked their existence at the margins of, if not completely outside, the city.

The persistence of borders works both ways, though, as the authorities were to discover. The first attempt to reorganise Salama's "disorderly" streets and reconstruct the village according to the planning norms and architectural forms of the time was presented a decade-and-a-half after Salama was seized and repopulated. A 1963 master plan for the neighbourhood, known as Plan 460, sought to thoroughly redesign the area and placed specific focus on the formation of an orthogonal road grid that would cater for the transportation needs of the housing projects built in the area since the late 1950s. In accordance with the modernist planning conventions that imagined space as a clean slate on which lines can be drawn *ex nihilo* (as will be discussed at length in the following chapter), Plan 460 was based on two circular roads crossed by a horizontal artery that dissects the new neighbourhood. In addition to its physical aspects, the Plan also allowed for a thorough reorganisation of the symbolic landscape of the neighbourhood through an extensive programme of street naming that would replace the number system that had designated most streets until then.

The main horizontal road of Plan 460 cuts through the centre of the village in order to connect Shekhunat Hatikva, on the west, and the neighbourhoods built east of Salama. The road ran parallel to an existing artery which was historically used for transportation from Jaffa to the Arab town of Lydda (Lod). The new road, however, was designated to cross over a densely populated area south of the village centre. Despite its approval by the Tel Aviv Municipality and the Ministry of Housing, the Plan was never fully realised, primarily because it inevitably required a large-scale reorganisation of the space of the village and mass evictions of residents, an obstacle that could have been easily avoided by retracing and adapting it to the existing spatial logic of Salama.

In this collision, the symbolic power of names was of little use. The road was designated as Mahal Street, a Hebrew abbreviation for "volunteers from abroad" – commemorating those who came from around the world to join the Israeli army during the 1948 War.[66] The nationalistic allusion of the name illustrates the planners' hope that that act would not only reshape physical space but intervene in the "routinized practices and traditional relations between ordinary people and their habitat".[67] This simultaneous operation of spatial practice and meaning

---

[66] Padan, *Guide to Tel Aviv-Jaffa Streets*, 274.
[67] Azaryahu, "The Power of Commemorative Street Names", 317.

forms what Edward Soja described as "nodal points" which "twin together collective activities around … relatively fixed settings".[68] Referring to Soja's notion, John Noyes importantly added that "the transformations associated with nodal points have effects not only in geo-political space, but also in subjective and signifying space".[69]

In the case of Mahal Street, routine collective activities (like shared vocabulary and orientation ability) are supplemented by historical knowledge, which results in two complementary effects. First, historical narratives are inserted into, and thus gain permanence as part of subjective experience which already corresponds with existing cultural and political conventions, and therefore take part in a broader "regime of nodal hierarchies".[70] In addition, the act of writing introduces meaning into a "spatial void" (literally, as suggested by Figure 4.2), and therefore "produces it" according to a desired image.

But Salama was not a void, and roads in particular played an important role in the village's historical evolution. Schematically, Salama is constructed on a star-shaped road system, whose centre lies at the village core. These main arteries, which led from the village to Jaffa in the west, Tel Aviv in the north-west, and the main Jaffa-Jerusalem railroad in the south, also determined the pattern of building in the village: in addition to dividing each section in the village between extended families, inner footpaths were used to distinguish between private and public zones and between individually owned units. Furthermore, private and public spaces were mutually dependent: paths had to take into consideration cultivated plots, just as private houses could not be built without concern for the public's ability to access their surroundings. The physical street layout in the village therefore reflected social norms and routine practices that dictated the formation of an intricate spatial *logic*, not simply the arbitrary and senseless shape seen by the Israeli planners and authorities. Superimposing the new road system on Salama's existing spatial order illustrates the inevitable clash between the two – although similarly to other cases documented in this project, what was deemed old and foreign showed surprising resilience.

To this day, Mahal Street remains incomplete: as the double-lane road enters the neighbourhood it abruptly narrows and turns into a small winding street that makes its way between houses, bypassing back yards and splitting into small alleyways. In the eastern part of the neighbourhood the street makes a sharp turn to circumvent a

[68] Soja, *Postmodern Geographies*, 151.
[69] Noyes, *Colonial Space*, 107.
[70] Ibid.

synagogue situated in one of Salama's Arab houses. The resilience of the Arab spatial order blocks the completion of Mahal Street and other main roads that were part of Plan 460. The anecdote about the road that winds between the "ghost villages" I noted in Chapter 2, appears here in actual form as Salama is maintained as a stubborn presence in space, hindering the realisation of modernist projections that seek to tame the "chaos" and "disorder" of the Arab village. Yet it is exactly the fallacy of this latter perception, and the fact that the Arab space is a well-organised system, deeply situated in social orders and corresponding to cultural traditions, that makes its erasure such a laborious task.

What is illustrated here should not be confused with critical celebrations of "resistance" of some sort, since spatial history is rooted in rather more modest terms. What is created here is spatiality as a form of negotiation between the old and the new: on the one hand one finds the forces of centralised planning that seek to increase efficiency of movement and maximise economic value while adhering to the national convention of urban mythography; while on the other, there is life as it is organised by accumulated practices and daily routines. The spatial reality of Kfar Shalem suggests that what is ostensibly an unequal encounter in terms of political power and economic resources is nonetheless an undetermined negotiation: the "small and winding streets" remain present 60 years after Salama's depopulation and over four decades after concentrated effort began to physically reshape and symbolically reinscribe it.

Salama in Parenthesis: Some Thoughts on Patterns of Containment

From the street sign on Derekh Salama, to the impasses of Plan 460, this chapter illustrates how the formation of a controlled, homogeneous space remains mostly an unfulfilled aspiration. Instead of the smooth reinscription of blank and empty spaces, and the selective erasure of disturbing histories in favour of narratives that will abide by dominant imperatives, one often finds evidence of unfinished labour. Both the multiplicity of names and the inability to fully realise ambitious planning schemes suggest that the analogy between space in the city and the space of writing is an imperfect one: acts of writing on the material surface of the city are subjected to pre-existing as well as reactive forces that contextualise, supplement and direct human experience in ways that broaden its potential to be altered and manipulated in form and meaning. The mere fact that city-texts are produced and practised on

a mass scale and by a heterogeneous mass of addressees, makes closing and controlling their meaning a nearly impossible task. Street-level
inquiry of spatial history constantly confronts us with what Massey
defines as "the event of place", situations where "something which
might be called there and then is implicated in the here and now. 'Here'
is an intertwining of histories in which the spatiality of those histories
(their then as well as their here) is inescapably entangled."[71]

In this regard, spaces that have been subject to a powerful web of political and ideological forces are not devoid of this spatial quality. Rewriting
spatial forms and meaning does not occur instantaneously and abstractly,
but over time and in space, in what Hever and Shenhav describe as the
"spatial volume" in which cultural (re)signification is negotiated and
articulated.[72] To understand the "de-Arabisation" of space one has to
constantly move between projected desires and the contingent conditions in which they (literally) take place in search of protracted negotiations and incomplete compromises. As Bhabha reminds us,

Such a syntax of deferral must not merely be recognized as a theoretical object,
the deferral of the space of writing – the sign under erasure – but acknowledged as a specific colonial temporality and textuality of that space between
enunciation and address.[73]

Importantly, if we consider enunciations and addresses as inseparable
components in the negotiated production of space and its meanings,
we also maintain the potential for an alternative politics of space.

However, the pattern that emerges out of the ambiguity of names in
Derekh Salama, or in the incompletion of Mahal Street, indicates that
the official mechanisms responsible for the transformation of space
are themselves highly adaptable. In both cases, once attempts to completely redesign the Arab space prove unsuccessful, the emphasis shifts
to methods of *containment*: if the Arab sign refuses to disappear, it will at
least be forced to reside within clearly defined borders, in parentheses.
On the one hand, these rhetorical or physical boundaries demonstrate
the persistent presence of all that remains, spatial forms and meanings that cannot be simply brushed aside. These are not insignificant
remainders – incidental leftovers do not require policing and imposed
constraints. However, this "space in parentheses" is also a dynamic
environment that accommodates unsettled and disturbing negotiations
between people, physical surroundings and those responsible for the
governance of these spaces.

[71] Massey, *For Space*, 139.
[72] Hever and Shenhav, "Arab Jews – A Genealogy of a Term".
[73] Bhabha, *The Location of Culture*, 135.

There is a real risk in presenting these sites of containment as reified spaces of resistance or celebrations of otherness. Several critical efforts have helpfully harnessed the conceptual power of "third-spaces" and "third-places" to explore sites where hybridised identities problematise hegemonic socio-political impositions and the paralysing binarism of either/or frameworks.[74] This "thirding", however, is limited both conceptually and politically. First, this critical prism is almost exclusively concerned with the hybridisation of specific ethnic communities, subaltern groups and cultures, most notably the spaces and places inhabited by Arab-Jews. Conversely, the centres of power, the mechanisms of governmentality, and the institutions of governance are rarely implicated in, or contaminated by, this process. As the analysis above shows, ambiguity and "incomplete signification" are inherent to the colonising political authority, not external or antagonistic to it. While the postcolonial corpus contains numerous articulations of this latter critique, it remains largely overlooked in Israeli spatial analysis. Rather than confine the investigation to the (social, ethnic or urban) hybridities of the margins, the critical lens proposed here focuses on the unstable heart of the colonising process, its primary administrators, and its principal agents. Second, the focus on the emancipatory virtues of this postcolonial third-place (as opposed to Bhabha's abstract, discursive space) too easily glosses over its close relation to processes of ghettoisation and segregation that "permit" such alternatives to emerge as long as they do so in well-confined places – as it were, in parentheses. The challenge here is not only to remain cognisant of the distributive rights of those who inhabit these spaces[75]; it is to critically ask whether place-oriented "third-spacing" inadvertently replicates a liberal logic that tolerates difference by confining it to clearly defined enclaves.

The roadside spatial history presented throughout this chapter illuminates, in fact, the ambivalent, incongruous interplay between freedom and control, which results in alternate – not simply "counter" or transgressive – social and spatial ordering.[76] The following chapter further examines this pattern of containment, highlighting the price it exerts from those who are fixed by it and the political horizons of engagement and action it opens.

---

[74] Benjamin, " 'Present-Absent' "; Yacobi, *The Jewish-Arab City*; Yiftachel and Tzfadia, "Between Periphery and 'Third Space' ".

[75] Yacobi, "From State-Imposed Urban Planning to Israeli Diasporic Place", 78.

[76] In a parallel discussion of heterotopias, Hetherington notes how these sites function as laboratories of modernity and sites in which alternative social order emerges, though not always in diametrical opposition to existing social and cultural conventions. Hetherington, *The Badlands of Modernity*, chapter 3.

5   Housing Complex: Between Arab Houses and Public Tenements

Avshalom Ben-David has a clear view about the tenement blocks built around Kfar Shalem. "They built these tenements to suffocate the village", he said while we sat in his living room one sweltering afternoon in the spring of 2009. Ben-David lives in one of the Arab houses of Salama and is proud to maintain the small congregation that gathered around his grandfather, a prominent Yemenite rabbi who was settled in the village in 1950. "Before they built the blocks", he continued, "you could stand here and get the best summer breeze. Now we are enclosed." For Ben-David, the purpose of these tenements is unmistakable: "It's because they want to kill the village."[1] This statement falls short of clarifying who "they" are, or why they intend to "kill"; what remains evident though, is the role of the tenements in an ongoing spatial struggle and the apparent antagonism they evoke.

From his humble house overlooking the southern part of Kfar Shalem, the spatial battlefield of the neighbourhood appears unequally divided between dominating rows of housing blocks with their imposing verticality and serial recurrence, on the one hand, and on the other, the clusters of makeshift dwellings – Arab houses that underwent modifications and alterations in the past 60 years to accommodate their Jewish residents. But the inclination to adopt a simple bipolarity, placing the tenement and the Arab house in a binary relation, is likely to overlook the spatial and historical processes and forces that brought about this multifaceted urban environment, which continues to sustain diverse, perhaps conflicting, elements. Highlighting the spatial, architectural and material aspects of the historical interrogation, we are able to observe a complex relationship between these radically different urban forms, a relationship that exposes a decades-long struggle over housing rights, civil equality and access to socio-political resources.

---

[1] Ben-David, Interview with the author.

The first housing blocks in Kfar Shalem did not make an exceptional mark on the architectural corpus of public housing in Israel.[2]
These humble three- and four-storey buildings, built by the semi-
governmental Labourers' Housing Corporation in the late 1950s, were
not celebrated as "pioneering endeavours" like those built in peripheral new towns in Negev or Galilee, regions that were only scarcely
populated with Jews until that time. In the years that followed the
establishment of the state, the grandiose statements that presented the
public housing block as a key instrument in the geopolitical conquest
of the national territory slowly faded; slogans and celebrations made
way for the laborious handling of the challenges that arose from mass
immigration and state-building processes. It is at this point of relative
stabilisation of the post-war period that the tenements built in Kfar
Shalem acquire their special significance, not just as pragmatic solutions to housing needs, but as markers of another, more intricate stage
in the attempt to fuse nation and territory. If the Arab house and the
transit camp were the epitome of the emergency period, the housing
block typifies the years that followed, with their collective ideals and
their specific breakdowns. In this space of encounter, this chapter identifies the seeds of social disillusionment and the articulation of contesting visions about space, society and politics.

The Housing Block: Morphology and Ideology

A seemingly innocuous sketch stored in the National Zionist Archives,
depicts two red rectangular shapes. It is a 1959 construction plan of
two tenement blocks built that year at the south-east edges of Kfar
Shalem.[3] The intentionally schematic nature of these plans creates an
almost abstract geometry that has no mention of existing buildings or
features around it. The only elements that situate the roughly outlined
blocks in a concrete environment are the vague contours of the streets,
along which these tenements are located. The floating appearance of
the blocks are not incidental. In the period between the aftermath of
the 1948 War to the late 1960s, the housing block became the dominant

---

[2] Few references can be found, and none discuss in any detail the role these tenements
played in the attempts to absorb the village into the urban fabric of Tel Aviv. For example, Sharon Rotbard suggests that Kfar Shalem presents an "anthology of public housing
from the 1960s and 70s" while Zvi Efrat, in his historical research of Israeli architecture
includes two diagrams of housing blocks built in the neighbourhood. Rotbard, *White
City, Black City*, 198; Efrat, *The Israeli Project*, 585.
[3] Jewish National Fund Central Bureau, "Salama C Construction Plan", NZA KKL5/
25149.

feature of Israel's emerging cityscapes: from the peripheral towns in the north and south, to the new suburban neighbourhoods built at the edges of major cities, the housing block became the generic form of Israeli urban vistas. In the eyes of its planners, and the policymakers who embraced it, the housing block's morphology was understood to capture and manifest an underlying logic, one which advocated uniformity and conformity, repetition and functionality. "On the face of it", writes Israeli architectural historian Zvi Efrat,

sketching a plan of a block cluster is an especially simple task. Oftentimes, it involves a new beginning, a clean slate of paper unsoiled by footprints of existing construction, on which rectangular marks can be placed, identical or similar, according to more or less precise rules of density, direction, distance between facades and gaps between access ways. There is no style, no habit, no experience, no historical conditioning, no irregularities of existing patterns, no "spirit of place", no view, no topography, no time. There is only a raw composition that needs to construct, again and again, each time slightly different, not the image of the buildings themselves, but their background – the empty surface on which they were placed, their liberating detachment from origin and place, their ability to produce a wide range of imprints, outlines, figures, names, without losing anything from their similarity, generality and serial quality.[4]

From the early 1950s to the late 1960s, the hegemony of the housing block was unchallenged, dominating the physical landscape and manifesting the social, geopolitical and ideological aspirations of the country's leadership. The supposed simplicity of placing a series of "rectangular marks", without having to acknowledge existing spatial conditions, appealed to those who wished to imagine the new territory as an unspoiled, clean slate. There were, however, more concrete agendas that dictated settlement and housing policies. Israel's chief architect, Arieh Sharon, a leading figure behind Israel's first master plan and one of the first to explicitly tie the government's social and geopolitical agendas with architectural and planning procedures, explained that decisions on settlement construction "must be based on economic, social and on national-defence considerations".[5] These three aspects dictated the location of new settlements as well as the actual shape they took, with the tenement emerging as the central pillar of the new urban vision. The first two functions stand at the focus of a large critical corpus, one which examines the various ways Israel's socioeconomic, political and ethnic divides coincide with and are expressed by the evolution of the state's

[4] Efrat, *The Israeli Project*, 172.
[5] Sharon, "Planning in Israel", 66.

housing policy.[6] The use of housing tenements for social engineering was inspired by European modernist traditions,[7] most notably by the conviction that cities must be regularised in order to maintain their viability as advanced human environments.[8] This included the development of new forms of housing that would provide for the massive demographic changes that overtook major urban centres around the world during the nineteenth and early twentieth century.[9]

Beyond its general association with European modernism, two historical influences joined to shape the immense public housing project in Israel. The first regards the European experience of extensive housing shortages and the challenge of reconstructing major urban areas that suffered immense damage during World War II.[10] In Israel during the 1950s, as in post-war Europe, emphasis was placed on an orchestrated effort to deal with the immediate aftermath of a period of emergency, armed conflict and the mass movement of a population.[11] In addition to the dramatic growth in Israel's population in the first years of independence, and the need to provide appropriate housing for 170,474 people who were still residing in immigrant camps between 1952 and 1954,[12] the housing block provided the country's leadership with a "unifying mechanism" for an extremely diverse society, an archetypal housing model in which "conventional" people lead "standardised" lives. According to one government economist, the civilising mission of the housing block was unambiguous: "To educate [the immigrants] to the general housing standard which is acceptable ... [because] there are habits one

---

[6] There is a growing body of research which addresses this issue. See, for example, Klaff, "Residence and Integration in Israel"; Gonen and Hasson, "Public Housing as a Geo-Political Instrument"; Law Yone and Kallus, "The Dynamics of Ethnic Segregation"; Yacobi, "Architecture, Orientalism and Identity".

[7] The decisive influence of the modernist movement on Israeli architects and planners has been thoroughly discussed in numerous accounts, with special attention given to the influence of the International Style and the Bauhaus movement on the formation of Tel Aviv. See, for example: Kamp-Bandau, Nerdinger and Goldman, *Tel Aviv Modern Architecture, 1930–1939*; Efrat, *The Israeli Project*; LeVine, *Overthrowing Geography*; Rotbard, *White City, Black City*. For criticism of this assumption, see Monk, "Autonomy Agreements"; Nitzan-Shiftan, "Contested Zionism – Alternative Modernism".

[8] Frampton, *Modern Architecture*, 20–8.

[9] Choay, *The Modern City*; Home, *Of Planting and Planning*; Frampton, *Modern Architecture*.

[10] Balchin, *Housing Policy in Europe*; Pawley, *Architecture Versus Housing*.

[11] For instance, the dilemma of the quality of construction, its design and architectural virtues, versus the need to supply mass housing in a relatively short period of time, appears both in post-World War II Britain and in Israel after the 1948 War. Similarly, in both cases policymakers were faced with a post-war emergency period that forced the replacement of initial plans for permanent housing construction with ad hoc temporary solutions. Compare Bullock, *Building the Post-War World*, 9, with Darin-Drabkin, *Housing in Israel: Economic and Sociological Aspects*.

[12] Hacohen, *Immigrants in Turmoil*, 270.

cannot tolerate, and it is obligatory to educate the tenant to dispose of."[13] However, the gap between an ideal spatial socialisation and the reality of life in the housing block became apparent after a short while:

Often one can find in small apartments in development towns, that the lavatory rooms have been turned into laundry rooms or an extension of the kitchen, as the residents are not used to using a lavatory placed inside the apartment.[14]

The dissonance between the prescribed, ideal habitation of the housing block and its eventual function is a telling one, suggesting that the space between the drawing board and the lived environment produces unpredictable variations and distortions. Moreover, it invites us to question whether the "liberating detachment from origin and place" Zvi Efrat describes with regard to the sketching of the housing block, is perhaps not fully liberating and only partially detached from the environment in which it is located. It is this dissonance that I wish to develop throughout this chapter.

When discussing urban history in Israel, it is also important to remember that the ideals of European modernism were implemented in a non-European, settler-colonial environment. The history of colonial cities therefore provides an important addition to the historical corpus against which the evolution of Israel's urban space can be evaluated. As stated above, metropolitan trends of urban thought and praxis had considerable influence on Israeli urban planning and were, accordingly, placed at the centre of numerous analytical accounts of its history. However, and this is an issue that rests at the foundation of this book in general, once European modernism is practised in a colonial or postcolonial setting, it must be viewed with an awareness of the inevitable adaptations, modifications and variations it undergoes as it traverses from the metropole. Its operation in a non-European environment brings about a unique set of interactions and counteractions that result in a polysemic space, combining external elements with pre-existing ones. If intellectual and ideological forms travelling from Europe are bound to mutate in the non-European environment, then there are sound reasons to suspect that spatial and architectural forms – influenced by, or resulting from these intellectual trends – will undergo similar transformations. While the housing block is indeed an explicit marker of a modernist spatial legacy, its specific appearance in Israel should be considered with acute awareness of the "constant slippage between intentions and effects"[15] that form an integral part of its history.

[13] Darin-Drabkin, *Housing and Absorption in Israel*, 80.
[14] Ibid.
[15] Yeoh, *Contesting Space*, 167.

As noted above, several scholars have scrutinised the housing block and its role in Israel's social and urban history. In one of the most theoretically informed analyses, Haim Yacobi suggests that the construction of housing blocks was an instrument for the "creative destruction" of the Arab built environment and a mechanism through which a colonising society established its superiority over indigenous space. Yacobi does not suggest that the Israeli housing block was simply a symbol of the destructive transition from Arab to Jewish space and identity. On the contrary, in the housing estates he identifies the formation of a "third-place" in which *Mizrahi* Jews are able to disrupt the homogenous and unifying mechanisms that were prominent in the ethno-national architectural discourse of the time. Modifications to the apartments, "were considered 'illegal', 'ugly', 'disregarding the public space' ... [and] by doing so, the housing block challenges the purifying power of the national logic".[16]

Yacobi opens a challenging horizon for the reconceptualisation of the housing block and its relation to social, ethnic and cultural power struggles. Nevertheless, his discussion presupposes that the transition between the spatial forms he describes – the Arab house, the housing blocks and the private detached houses constructed after 1977 – is linear, with one form replacing the other. In Yacobi's critique, the "co-contamination" exists in stylistic gestures, the use or abuse of architectural motifs which undermine the hegemonic pretence to achieve a centralised, stylistically homogenous and ideologically conformed architectural discourse. As such, amendments made to the housing block or detached houses, using arches and decorations borrowed from "Arab" architecture, are perceived as disruptions to the imposed aesthetic-spatial order. This is a welcome challenge to the predominance of the binarism that still governs many of the critical histories of Israeli-Arab space. But the fact that these radically different housing forms may actually *share the same space*, has little significance in Yacobi's analysis. In some of the built Arab regions seized during the war, the construction of housing blocks occurred in close proximity to Arab houses, at times sharing intimate adjacency without the latter being simultaneously razed. Although this was the case in numerous places throughout the country, this spatial heterogeneity and simultaneous existence remains mostly overlooked and under-theorised.

---

[16] Yacobi, "'The Third Place'", 73.

The following analysis seeks to "provincialise" the housing block from its rigid European origins,[17] and turn the focus to the encounter between the housing block and the Arab environment. This encounter opens a specific set of questions: what is the relation between the Arab house and the tenement block that would go beyond mutual exclusion? Does this co-presence also establish a new social and spatial order? What are the horizons – political, social and theoretical – that are opened by these spatial coexistences? Through this encounter, I would argue, we witness yet another articulation of a critical process that underlies this book as a whole; namely, the way state violence against the Arab space morphs into violence directed inward, at the Jewish communities that came to inhabit these places.

Blocking the Border: Tenements and the Formation of an Urban Frontier

Approximately ten years passed until the encounter between Salama's village-houses and the housing blocks took place. The neighbourhood of Neve Zahal, a collection of 24 tenements constructed to house the families of military personnel, was built in 1958–9 by governmental housing firms. Prior to the construction of these blocks, agricultural lands owned by Salama's Arab residents were handed to governmental housing firms that constructed in the mid-1950s two Jewish neighbourhoods north-east of the village. The housing blocks built at the edges of the neighbourhood, along the main road that encircles Kfar Shalem from south-east to north-west, created a perimeter that surrounds and clearly delineates the end of one spatial order and the commencement of another. This visual encapsulation shows how the housing block's morphology and serial positioning operates with relation to the existing built environment of Salama. In this case, the visual effect is suggestive of the official Israeli planning policy that aspired to eliminate the ad hoc temporary housing devised in the emergency period, and replace it with a permanent residential environment that abides by a nationally prescribed order.

The relative decline of immigration rates between 1952 and 1959[18] enabled the planning and construction authorities to begin the implementation of the country's first master plan – the so-called Physical Planning in Israel. Two main objectives topped the planners' agenda;

---

[17] I refer here to Dipesh Chakrabarty's interrogation of Eurocentric epistemological convictions that govern historical research, by infusing them with contradictory, plural and heterogeneous struggles. Chakrabarty, *Provincializing Europe*.

[18] In those years, 272,446 immigrants arrived in Israel, compared to 687,624 who arrived between 1948 and 1951. Central Bureau of Statistics, "Immigrants, by period of immigration (1948–2007)", 4.

namely, the dispersal of people into regions scarcely populated with Jews, and the utilisation of planning tools for social-cultural engineering. Salama was unlikely to prominently feature in this plan. In the grand scheme of things, the construction of housing blocks was mostly affected by what were considered to be "military needs". First, tenements were built in cities and towns that still retained some of their Arab populations, then in cities that were located in regions containing a significant Arab population, and, finally, in places that had no Arab population at all.[19] This policy partly explains why the construction of housing blocks in and around Kfar Shalem, which was completely devoid of an Arab population, began only in the mid-1950s – though given the dire conditions of the population residing in the village, they were clearly urgently needed. Perceived as an instrument of national security, the block was first to appear in places like the eastern parts of Katamon and Musrara neighbourhoods in Jerusalem, which bordered parts of the city that were under Jordanian rule until 1967. Utilising its morphological qualities, the block became a spatial buffering object that earned its name not only through its shape but also through its function.

The circumstances through which the housing blocks were built in and around Kfar Shalem mark another phase in this process, which reflects the integration of a national collective into a national territory. It is useful to consider this social, cultural and spatial process through Oren Yiftachel's conceptualisation of the "internal frontier", in which "frontier strategies are put into practice ... when minority dominance of key regions threatens the territorial integrity of the state, and subsequently the effectiveness of its state-building project".[20] One of the key instruments through which the majority group asserts its presence in, and domination of, an ethnically mixed frontier, is through the operation of state-initiated planning apparatuses. Spatial policies can be used in these regions to contain the territorial expansion of such minorities, typically by "imposing restrictions on minority land ownership, restricting the expansion of minority settlements, and settling members of the majority group within the minority region for control and surveillance".[21] Frontier strategies usually take place as part of the *nation*-building process that precedes the formation of a formal state structure.[22] The internal frontier, meanwhile, emerges in the later *state*-building phase, during which practices that "are associated with

---

[19] Sharon, "Planners, the State, and the Shaping of National Space in the 1950s", 124; Yacobi, "The Daily Life in Lod", 63.
[20] Yiftachel, "The Internal Frontier", 44.
[21] Ibid., 48.
[22] Turner, *The Frontier in American History*.

colonizing external frontiers, are combined to generate pressures of penetration into hostile or alien areas *within* the new state ... regardless of the changing geographical-political context".[23]

The case analysed here importantly expands this definition of the internal frontier. First, Yiftachel develops this term in order to refer to spaces inhabited by ethno-national minorities, like the Arab-Palestinian or Bedouin communities in Israel.[24] In the period discussed here, namely from the early 1950s, Salama/Kfar Shalem housed only Jewish residents, presumably members of the majority group. What, then, is the role of frontier strategies in spatial constellations that do not relate directly or explicitly to a Jewish-Arab binary? The analysis below first follows the role of the housing block in the enclosure of Salama's Arab space. In this act, I argue, we find the roots of disillusionment and discontent as a *Jewish* community that saw itself as part of the Zionist mainstream found itself subjected to acts of containment and segregation primarily because of the space it inhabited.

Containment

The construction of housing blocks from the second half of the 1950s marked the transition of Israeli planning policies from the first years of uncertainty, to a period during which vast housing projects were carried out throughout the country. The initial period began in 1951 with high expectations of constructing 30,000 permanent apartments; but as then Labour Minister Golda Meir later confessed, the plan was submitted and authorised by the Israeli parliament without the funding sources for its implementation having being put in place. As Zvi Efrat rightly comments, Meir's vision of the houses in her plan "can compete with any manifesto of minimalist living":[25]

What we want to do is to give each family a luxurious apartment of one room; one room which we will build out of concrete blocks. We won't even plaster the walls. We will build roofs, but no ceilings. What we hope is that as these people will be learning a trade as they build their houses, they will finish them, and eventually, one day, add another room. In the meantime, we will be happy, and they will be happy, even though it means putting a family of two, three, four or five into one room. But this is better than putting two or three families into one tent.[26]

---

[23] Yiftachel, "The Internal Frontier", 42, emphasis added.
[24] Haim Yacobi's work on the Israeli city of Lod investigates the applicability in an urban environment of Yiftachel's ethnocratic model, which relies partly on this earlier conceptualisation. Yacobi, *The Jewish-Arab City*; Yiftachel, *Ethnocracy*.
[25] Efrat, *The Israeli Project*, 519.
[26] Meir, *My Life*, 218.

Meir was not being facetious. The official policy that aspired to abolish at all cost all temporary housing built in the emergency period by the end of the 1950s, required extreme measures; asking two or more families to share an apartment in unfinished tenement blocks was not perceived to be exceptional under the circumstances. However, by 1955 the government was still dealing with 88,000 people who were living in temporary housing.[27]

Despite the housing shortages, Salama saw little government effort to replace the emergency housing at that time. Although the Israel National Fund agreed to transfer the village's lands into the hands of public housing firms, no housing project was actually implemented in the first years, mostly due to bureaucratic disputes.[28] Despite the delays, some housing projects succeeded in replacing temporary housing with tenement blocks. The neighbourhood of Ramat Hashikma, located east of Kfar Shalem, was constructed in 1954 to house residents of three transit camps nearby which were then demolished; and as mentioned above, additional housing blocks were built between Shekhunat Hatikva and Kfar Shalem in 1958–9 for army personnel. The effect of these constructions was not, however, the abolition of Salama's Arab houses, but the gradual creation of a *contained zone* in which they continued to exist. Interestingly enough, through its morphological qualities and serial positioning, the housing block became the instrument through which this containment was achieved.

I have already dealt with the way Salama's spatial features are contained through the creation of the new urban order around it. The analysis in Chapter 4 showed how this spatial containment isolates the village from its urban surroundings, yet allows for the formation of a spatial enclave in which a "foreign" order prevails. It is important, however, to distinguish the dynamic of containment in a settler-colonial context as discussed here, from its application in the management of post-Fordist urban sprawl.[29] Emerging out of the spatial contestation between an indigenous and a settler society, containment consists of a range of physical-material, discursive and legal measures that are applied to restrict the presence of the indigenous sign. In previous chapters, we have already seen several practices that serve this function – from the parentheses enclosing Arab place-names, to "temporary groves", both of which are illustrative of the pervasiveness and longevity of efforts to hold the Arab sign/space at bay. At the same time, this prevalence

[27] Hacohen, *Immigrants in Turmoil*.
[28] Golan, "From Abandoned Village to Urban Neighbourhood", 80–1.
[29] Dawkins, Nelson and Sanchez, *The Social Impacts of Urban Containment*.

of containment also indicates the resilience of the object that is being contained – Arab spatiality – and the endurance of its perceived threat, the instigating factor for this containment in the first place.

The duality of containment, creating a location of simultaneous negotiation and confrontation between two dissimilar spatial orders, reiterates the duality found in the frontier – a region that represents strict separation by linear borders, and a site of encounters, juxtapositions and interconnections.[30] Viewed through this prism of frontier containment, the housing blocks that surround Salama do not simply float on "the empty surface on which they were placed" and do not simply celebrate "their liberating detachment from origin and place" (as they are described in the opening of this chapter). Instead, they mark the encounter with the former Arab village's built environment and respond to it by presenting an oppositional spatial order that manifests the conviction that this new built environment marks "improvement" and "development". The underlying assumption here is twofold. First, it suggests that the Arab built environment is inherently flawed, either by what it contains or by what it lacks, and must therefore be improved. Additionally, the people destined to live in former Arab spaces are in some way in need of being rectified.

A powerful portrayal of the spatial opposition between the tenements and the existing Arab houses is depicted in a small leaflet (Figure 5.1) published by Halamish, the national municipal housing company formed in 1961 and mandated to deal with the reconstruction of slum areas in the Tel Aviv region.[31] The leaflet, *It is time to change your apartment*, invites residents in Kfar Shalem to exchange their house for one of the apartments provided by the company in a nearby tenement project. The leaflet's text and images provide a characteristic narrative through which one environment is juxtaposed with the other. Visually, what seems to be an Arab house in a state of dilapidation – partly ruined and partly improvised – is set against the image of a street lined with housing blocks on both sides. The latter image presents what planners hoped would become a quintessential Israeli neighbourhood with street lighting, pavements and open spaces between buildings.

Much like the images, the pamphlet's text is deeply Manichean, and offers important insights into the logic of its authors. The text begins on the right hand side, above the image of the Arab house:

[30] Kemp, "Border Space and National Identity".
[31] Halamish, Municipal-Governmental Company for Housing in Gush Dan, *It is time to change your apartment!*

Figure 5.1 Pamphlet prompting residents to relocate to housing tenements. Tel Aviv Municipal Archive.

Dear tenant,

For many years you have been living in harsh conditions, your undersized and tight-measured apartment preventing you and your children the little privacy and convenience sought by any person in their house.

Your house is rickety, the walls cracked, the plaster falling, the ceiling dripping, the kitchen and the restrooms remote from the house.

These living conditions threaten your health and the health of your family.

Your children grow up in conditions of filth and neglect and are educated in the streets.

At least on the material level, the description of living conditions in Kfar Shalem was not far from the truth. Many of the houses in the neighbourhood were indeed in dire condition. Since the inhabitation of the village by Jews in 1948, residents had called on the authorities to take action and improve the sanitary and hygienic state of the neighbourhood which, as one complaint noted, "resembles remote villages or tiny towns in eastern Europe during the last century".[32] The writer goes on to describe in detail how, due to the lack of proper sanitary facilities, residents are forced to relieve themselves in the streets or in open spaces in and around the neighbourhood. However, this complaint letter is also clear to point out those it sees responsible for the situation: "it is extremely saddening that today, after seven years of the neighbourhood's existence *as part of the city*, no real and serious step has been made to change the situation".[33] By stating that the neighbourhood was "part of the city", the writer refers to Salama's inclusion in the municipal boundaries of Tel Aviv, part of the council's jurisdiction and, subsequently, its responsibility. It seems to me, however, that the issue here exceeds bureaucratic negligence, and that the association of Kfar Shalem with eastern European towns is hardy incidental. In fact, it relates the neighbourhood's containment to a longer historical legacy in which hygiene and sanitation served as potent cultural mechanisms for the formation of national, ethnic and class divisions, as well as the construction of physical barriers.

Looking at the history of sanitation and hygiene in inter-war Tel Aviv, Anat Helman observes that in the discourse of the time these terms were used to demarcate the borders of identity for the emerging Hebrew city.[34] The discourse of sanitation and hygiene "served to define Jewish national borders vis-à-vis Palestine's Arab population",[35] although Helman clearly shows that the conviction that Tel Aviv – the new, modern, cosmopolitan city – was hygienically superior to Jaffa is

---

[32] Halodnivicz, "Letter to Tel Aviv Mayor Haim Levanon".
[33] Ibid., emphasis added.
[34] Helman, "Cleanliness and Squalor in Inter-War Tel-Aviv".
[35] Ibid., 95.

highly contestable. At the same time, this discourse was used to prevent Tel Aviv from being associated with Jewish traditions that were perceived to represent the characteristics of diasporic degradation. Most notably, this was directed at the typical Jewish town in eastern Europe, the *Stetl*. The "double negation" of the "East", at once associated with the Arab orient and with diasporic Jewish life in eastern Europe, obviously made its mark on the collective imagination since both continue to surface 30 and 40 years after Tel Aviv's establishment. The conflation of a former Arab village housing mostly Yemenite Jews with an eastern European town seems out of place at first, blurring two evidently different environments by virtue of open sewage. But the discursive function of this conflation does not change in essence. As in the case of Tel Aviv, which sought to isolate itself from Jaffa, the highlighting of poor conditions of sanitation and hygiene in Kfar Shalem alludes to a potential contamination of the urban environment, and consequently raises the need for the isolation, or containment, of the space at hand.

The sanitary discourse provided the key justification for the replanning of urban centres around the world. Indeed, the most instructive parallels can be found in historical examples that have mostly remained outside the purview of urban history discourse in Israel. James Cobban, for example, traces the Dutch colonial authorities' response to the development of Indonesian *Kampungs*, residential areas located discontinuously within or in the periphery of large cities, which housed mostly indigenous and non-European residents. Hygiene, sanitation and measures to prevent the spread of contagious disease dominated housing policies in colonial Indonesia during the first decades of the twentieth century. However, documentation from the First National Housing Congress in 1922 that discussed housing solutions in Indonesia suggests that officials were also aware that

City planning could benefit housing in the colony so long as it adapted European ideas to the Indies climate and to the ethnic and economic diversity … rather than the outright adoption of concepts developed for conditions in a north temperate climate and for cities with ethnic homogeneity.[36]

Such acknowledgement of the limits of European models of planning (at least on a declarative level)[37] was often the exception. More often, notes Anthony King,

[36] Cobban, "Public Housing in Colonial Indonesia", 882.

[37] Nihal Perera importantly reminds us that architectural modernism often "recognized only climatic difference in relation to the [well balanced] temperate Europe". By placing non-European environments as a "Climatic Other", planners and architects could engage with the new environment in a scientific, rationalised and impersonal manner

indigenous definitions of health states, the means for achieving them and the environments in which they existed were replaced by those of the incoming power in a total ecological transformation. Thus ... historically and socially derived concepts of "over-crowding" developed in metropolitan society are applied to the indigenous environment, irrespective of cultural context or the larger economic and political situation. In the interest of "health", new environments are created ... surrounded by "light and air", "open space", gardens and recreational areas in total disregard of the religious, social, symbolic or political meaning of built environments as expressed in indigenous villages and towns.[38]

Other examples throughout the colonial world in the first decades of the twentieth century present the "overriding, even obsessive, concern with health"[39] that guided colonial preoccupation with modifying the built form of urban environments. Following the precedence of slum clearance in Bombay in 1898, other cities – from Calcutta to Singapore, Lagos and Rangoon[40] – saw the emergence of colonial trusts that led the clearance projects in the name of public health. These actions included not only demolition of slum areas, but also their replacement by new forms of housing that were assumed to be more suitably equipped to provide for public health, sanitation and hygiene. From the 1920s, the Trusts of Bombay and Calcutta began constructing three-, four- and five-storey buildings called "new style" chawls, which formed an early prototype for what would later emerge in other colonial cities.[41] The shortcomings of these new forms of housing solutions were, however, soon exposed, as one Captain Richards – stationed in Calcutta – noted in 1914:

Block-dwellings are not productive of good citizens ... The present new chawls of Calcutta are a disgrace to any city ... the author is no advocate for this type of housing, and much prefers single-family dwellings or cottage flats built on such suburban areas as are suitable.[42]

The improvement of sanitary conditions, we learn, is not the motivating force behind the construction of colonial tenements; the ultimate goal is political socialisation, the production of "good" citizens. Similar sentiments were expressed by Golda Meir[43] decades later when she stated that "good citizenship, a real sense of belonging, the beginning of

while completely disregarding it as a "Cultural Other" with its own belief and culture system. See Perera, "Indigenising the Colonial City", 78, 118; See also Perera, "Contesting Visions", 190.

[38] King, "Exporting Planning", 210.
[39] Yeoh, *Contesting Space*, 167.
[40] Home, *Of Planning and Planning*, 80.
[41] Ibid., 100–13.
[42] Quoted ibid., 113.
[43] Meir, *My Life*, 217.

integration – in other words, the creation of a good society – depended to an overwhelming degree on how people lived".[44] The British critique of the "block-dwellings" and its preference for suburban cottages also seems to prophesise the decline of the Israeli housing blocks and the rise of the detached suburban house in the 1970s. But during the early years, the housing block project in Kfar Shalem was presented with celebratory tones and promises of a better, healthier future. The public housing leaflet continues:

> For years you have been complaining about this [the dilapidated state of the village], but in the years of the great immigration, the government and the council could not invest efforts in rehabilitating the dwellings in Tel Aviv. Now we made the efforts and recruited the resources to help you replace your current apartment with a modern one.
>
> If you look through your window, you can see how close the new tenements of "Halamish" are to your current place of residency.
>
> In the new neighbourhood you and your children will enjoy all the services and conveniences of a modern residential area.
>
> At your disposal you will have a new and modern shopping centre, cultural centre, primary and secondary schools, playgrounds and gardens.
>
> And most of all, a new and modern apartment.[45]

Serving the obvious purpose of luring residents to relocate from their old homes, the Halamish leaflet relies on a series of rather unsophisticated binaries: the Arab environment is old, dilapidated, filthy, unhealthy and lacks privacy or convenience; the new environment offered to the residents is new, convenient and has all the facilities and services one needs. Most of all, the new neighbourhood promises to be "modern", an adjective used more than any other in the text. Visually and textually, the leaflet is unambiguous in its intention to replace one built environment with another, and the housing block is juxtaposed with the Arab house as its ultimate antithesis. This juxtaposition gained such prominence that one can easily find its traces in contemporary critical analyses of urban history in Israel, in which the housing block replaces the built Arab environment in a process of

---

[44] In both examples, specific spatial forms of habitation are construed as a central mechanism that produces political subjectivity, thus bringing to mind notions of Althusserian interpellation on the one hand; and the utilisation of space as an arena of power-knowledge relations – often associated with Foucault's late work – on the other. While it is important to note that both importantly inform this discourse, the complexities of the subject matter require a more gradual construction of the epistemological framework in a way that leaves room for contingent subjectivities and the formation of cracks in the power-knowledge structure.

[45] Halamish, Municipal-Governmental Company for Housing in Gush Dan, *It is time to change your apartment!.*

"physical demolition validated by capitalist reason and the moderni-zation enterprise".[46]

In the case of Kfar Shalem, however, the process of "sanitising" the built environment proved to be considerably more ambiguous, paved with conflict and negotiations. In order to understand this, it is important to briefly note the institution of Halamish, the municipal-governmental housing company established in 1961 with responsibility for the Tel Aviv region. Halamish was one of several housing compa-nies established at the time to implement urban redevelopment pro-grammes,[47] and for that purpose received 673 dunams of Salama's land that were administered by the State of Israel.[48] The company began its operation in Kfar Shalem in 1962 by providing alternative housing for those residents who wished to relocate to purpose-built tenements nearby. In line with the perception of the housing block as the remedy for social and medical "urban illnesses" which were supposedly to be found in Kfar Shalem, the tenement was intended to provide an alter-native to a situation in which "most houses are scattered in the perim-eter without any *logical order*, along three main arteries and winding allies".[49] In the battle against the "illogical disorder" of the Arab built environment, the housing block was a primary weapon, though its suc-cess highly questionable.

Three decades after the seizure of Salama by Israeli forces, and 25 years after it was included in Tel Aviv's municipal borders, Kfar Shalem was far from presenting an unambiguous image of urban homogeneity. During the 1950s the urban landscape of the neighbour-hood and its surroundings was rapidly changing, but these changes did not result in the eradication of the Arab built environment by the "logical order" of housing blocks. Instead, a pattern of containment was formed around the village: first on the outer circle, then gradually

---

[46] Yacobi, "Architecture, Orientalism and Identity", 101.

[47] Several works in recent years have dealt with this period and the operation of these firms. Arnon Golan's seminal work on the incorporation of Arab lands after the 1948 War is the most expansive of these accounts in its depiction of public housing and construction firms during the first decades of the state. Other noteworthy works have mostly dealt with specific historical case studies or with issues of social justice. Yfaat Weiss's work on Wadi Salib, one of Haifa's Arab neighbourhoods settled with Jews, provides the most elaborate example of these micro-histories. Again, Haim Yacobi's analysis of the city of Lod stands out as it engages with the political and social hori-zons that are opened by specific discrepancies, and by doing so presents a complex picture of the flow of power and distribution of authority in the city. Golan, *Wartime Spatial Changes*; Weiss, *A Confiscated Memory*; Yacobi, *The Jewish-Arab City*.

[48] Halamish, Municipal-Governmental Company for Housing in Gush Dan, "Kfar Shalem Survey. The Construction and Eviction of Development Areas", 27.

[49] Ibid., 29.

surrounding the margins of the built sections by making use of open spaces previously used for agriculture. Despite the additional construction and the changing trends of architectural designs,[50] the spatial effect of containment, isolation and encapsulation of the Arab built environment did not change. In this sense, it reinforced a line of division – a boundary – between one spatial form and another. But the creation of a boundary was not part of the authorities' initial intention, at least not explicitly; as mentioned before, their actions relied on the "founding assumption of the demolition of the village's houses and the construction of a modern residential area that will become an organic part of the city's development in the future".[51] The spatial standoff between the two built environments opens two related directions of inquiry: the first places emphasis on the preserving powers that enabled the resilience of the Arab built environment, while the second considers the various ways this juxtaposition was used to demarcate cultural, ethnic and socioeconomic differences. The following considers both to reveal the heavy social and cultural toll that containment had on those enclosed by it.

Blocked In: Segregation and Disillusionment

One of the critical moments documented throughout this book is the moment when the state's policies seeking the destruction of the Arab space are turned against the Jews who inhabit it. This inverted violence becomes a profound experience for those subjected to it, shattering the sense of collective identification and political cohesion. The containment processes described thus far provide a striking illustration of this inverted violence. As the construction of housing blocks completes the restrictive enclosure of Salama's remaining Arab buildings, the disillusionment of those "blocked in" continues to mount. For the latter, the third-space provides little solace. Instead, we witness an effort to forge a space of equal civil engagement to oppose the spatial constellation that deems them deviant or external to the legitimate civil or national space solely by virtue of their residence in former Arab homes.

Despite an official policy presented in the early 1950s – both on the national and urban levels – to bring about the termination of temporary housing areas, a large portion of residents in Kfar Shalem were

---

[50] The frugal aesthetics of the 1950s, during which construction was financially limited to the very basics while leaving aside almost any decorative element, later made way for stylistic additions and attention to design. Efrat, *The Israeli Project*, chapter 14.

[51] Halamish, Municipal-Governmental Company for Housing in Gush Dan, "Kfar Shalem Survey. The Construction and Eviction of Development Areas", 1.

not provided with viable housing alternatives and were left to seek solutions through other means. Those who could afford the initial down-payment could join the government-initiated Popular Housing Scheme, which offered housing solutions that were between 40 per cent and 50 per cent cheaper than those built by private housing companies at the time.[52] The majority of the residents were not, however, able to afford even the initial sum needed and had to hold on to their existing houses, which provided them only with the most basic conditions: In 50 per cent of the households, three people or more were sharing a room; 55 per cent of the houses did not include fundamental utilities such as bathrooms, lavatories or a kitchen for the sole use of the occupants; while the average house size did not differ substantially from the Tel Aviv average – two rooms per house on average compared to 2.1 in Tel Aviv – the average size of a family in the neighbourhood was one-and-a-half times the regional average.[53]

Problems with the redevelopment project emerged during the first years of its implementation, due to two processes that highlighted the fundamental flaw in the perception that the housing block could provide a viable alternative to the Arab environment of the village. Relying on the general housing policy of the time, the authorities assumed that families wishing to relocate would be able to take advantage of government-subsidised loans that would assist them in purchasing flats in Halamish tenements. This financial scheme, put in place during the 1960s, was designed mostly for the benefit of large families relocating to the new housing blocks[54] in the hope of replacing the relatively small spaces of the Arab houses with the "new, modern apartment" that was promised in the Halamish leaflet. However, many of the families that chose this option – ahead of the possibility of using a small compensation grant to relocate to other suburbs in the area – struggled to pay off their loans.[55] By 1969, soon after the initial stage of the project was completed, another problem became apparent – one that depended specifically on the gap between the ideals associated with the block and the daily reality of its residents. An official survey conducted in the neighbourhood at the time notes that the blocks suffered from "low standards of housing, excess

---

[52] Darin-Drabkin, *Housing in Israel*, 67.
[53] Halamish, Municipal-Governmental Company for Housing in Gush Dan, "Kfar Shalem Survey. The Construction and Eviction of Development Areas", 32.
[54] Ibid., 9.
[55] According to figures provided by the bank managing the finance of the relocation scheme, only 6.5 per cent of the new residents were able to successfully manage their loan and mortgage repayments, compared to the 37.5 per cent who did not pay any of their financial obligation from the time of occupancy, and the 56 per cent whose payments were delayed for a period ranging from four months to two years. See ibid., 64.

of large families in high-rise buildings and over concentration of problematic families ... [which] caused a situation of neglect and a negative image of these tenements in the eyes of the tenants".[56] Despite the mounting challenges of the tenement project, the authorities continued to focus their rehabilitation efforts at the 726 families still residing in the Arab houses and in makeshift structures built around them; this population was seen to represent the "characteristic features of the population in impoverished areas (*in the neighbourhoods of abandoned property that were populated in 1948)*".[57]

But the apparent failure of the public housing blocks that were constructed near Kfar Shalem was expressed not only in terms of the financial difficulties that many of the new residents found themselves in. The incompatibility of the apartments in the tenements to the needs and abilities of the new occupants became evident to official surveyors only five years after the new buildings were first occupied. The surveyors described the "neglect and forlorn image of the houses", and a report went on to point out that

In fact, signs of deterioration and the formation of a *new slum* are already apparent ... The developments that were inserted into the blocks, despite improving living conditions in the neighbourhood, did little to improve the negative image of the regeneration activities.[58]

Even in the eyes of those who administered the project it became clear that the spatial legacy formed in the village since 1948 could not be easily replaced. The fact was that socioeconomic difficulties and cultural differences did not disappear once people were replanted into a new environment that was supposed to possess the virtues of modern order. Reading this national project with an attention to the material and spatial details suggests that "solutions" soon presented new, yet familiar, "problems"; "slum clearance" resulted in slum appearance.

To prevent the complete collapse of the redevelopment project, which came to almost a standstill by the end of the 1960s, Halamish resorted to operating in accordance with "The Eviction-Construction Law – 1965". Despite its applicability to numerous sites around the country, Kfar Shalem was the first neighbourhood in which the law was implemented, four years after its official enactment. The law stipulated that the authorities could order compulsory eviction from

[56] Ibid., 8.
[57] Ibid., 31, emphasis added.
[58] Ibid., 65–6, emphasis added.

a property in exchange for offering an equivalent property elsewhere. Implementing the law in Kfar Shalem meant that once eviction orders were issued, residents were then obliged to leave their former properties and relocate to public housing apartments in the residential blocks. Faced with government-supported legal procedures that would lead to removal from their homes, an outcry among Kfar Shalem residents soon followed:

For many years, Kfar Shalem housed people that were frontier-refugees, natives and veterans of the land, that in the War of Independence were relocated here for security reasons; the aforementioned law disregards completely their rights and its implementation may bring about their discrimination and abandonment in temporary housing … In addition, there are many large families without means; widows and helpless elderly people; many young people out of military service and soldiers about to be released that will find themselves homeless, or [dealing] with the large debt of their families.[59]

This appeal against the implementation of the law exposes an important undertone that recurs in much of the correspondence between the residents of Kfar Shalem and the authorities; namely, their insistence to remain *part of* the national collective and to be acknowledged as such. This demand is especially pertinent because it exposes the way spatial struggles in the village became instruments that determined one's access to the national community and consequently, one's access to civil and political rights.

The growing sense that the legal battle against the relocation to housing blocks was in fact a struggle to remain an equal and legitimate part of the national space became increasingly apparent once Halamish began legal procedures against residents who were unwilling to relocate to public housing blocks. To overcome the clauses restricting eviction until proper housing alternatives were provided, legal procedures were launched against residents who "trespassed" onto state lands by building extensions on land adjacent to their homes. Originally, these places were designated for use as allotments; over time, however, some people extended the initial Arab structures onto these lands and were therefore exposed to state-initiated lawsuits. These proceedings dealt with relatively small areas around the existing houses that could in no way be used for the construction of new tenements. Instead, this was an attempt to replicate, on ever-smaller scales, the pattern of containment formed around the neighbourhood, by preventing those still living in Arab houses from transgressing into the areas around them.

---

[59] Kfar Shalem Residents, "Objection to the Promulgation of 'Renewal Project'", 150.

In addition to their rejection of the authorities' attempts to outlaw the state of affairs that was acceptable – *de facto*, if not de jure[60] – until then, residents claimed that the official bodies responsible for the maintenance of the neighbourhood were deliberately neglecting their official obligations. In a petition published in the late 1970s, Kfar Shalem's council presented a strong indictment against those who had been given a mandate to assist residents in the first place: "As part of the psychological warfare against the residents, the [housing] companies impose ... personal pressure on families by reducing the quality of life of a neighbourhood"; this deliberate negligence is intended "to *set the neighbourhood's residents against the place*".[61] The feeling that there was an intentional attempt to alienate people from their environment through deliberate institutional neglect resonates with Ford's claim that

> Race-neutral policies, set against an historical backdrop of state action in the service of racial segregation and thus against a contemporary backdrop of racially identified space – physical space primarily associated with and occupied by a particular racial group – predictably reproduce and entrench racial segregation and the racial-caste system that accompanies it.[62]

In the case of Kfar Shalem, socioeconomic and ethnic segregation of the Jewish population was fused with the ethno-nationally motivated effort to eradicate their built environment; namely, the Arab homes they inhabit.

The appeals and organised actions of the residents from the late 1960s reflect, in form and content, contemporaneous social and cultural protest movements that emerged in Israel. Perhaps the most well known of these were the Israeli Black Panthers, a group formed in the Musrara neighbourhood of Jerusalem in 1971 by young Mizrahi Jews protesting against institutional discrimination by the Ashkenazi-dominated establishment.[63] Indeed, the spectre of the Black Panthers is traceable in

---

[60] In his verdict in the case of *The State of Israel v. Shimon Hamami*, Justice A. Gershoni suggested that the possession of land adjacent to the houses in question, over a long period of time, must have been known to the authorities: "There can be no doubt that the owners of the land, namely, the Custodian for Absentees' Property and the Development Authority following it, knew about the possession of the land ... and one should see this behaviour as an agreement to the defendant's possession of the land ... the defendant should therefore be seen as authorised-possessor."

[61] Kfar Shalem Residents' Council, "Public Petition", emphasis added.

[62] Meir, *My Life*, 1845.

[63] The movement gained a prominent status in the history of social struggle and ethnic protest in Israel, evident, for example, in an online historical archive documenting material related to the group's activities, documentary films and exhibitions dedicated to their activity. The group has also gained prominence in the literature documenting

appeals written by Kfar Shalem residents in the early 1970s, as a potentially explosive threat that might materialise if the conflict between the
authorities and residents was not appropriately addressed. In one of
these letters, for example, the warning is clearly stated:

> The perpetuation of these injustices will give birth to "Panthers" in action or
> intention, [and] will bring about distrust and friction in the nation. Anyone in
> their right mind can imagine what our soldier-sons feel when they return home
> and find out what the state they are serving is perpetrating. Is there not justice
> in the claim that ... oriental-Jews are discriminated against? Appropriate hous-
> ing is the foundation for any healthy society.[64]

Even when the threat to initiate action against the political establishment is sounded, it is launched with careful attention to its position on
the cusp of the imagined national community. The writers are treading
a fine line: while conscious of their marginal position on the physical
and social perimeters of Israeli society, their call is addressed inwards
at the gatekeepers who control access to the centres of socioeconomic
and political power.

Even more so, the statement above challenges the epistemological
authority that defines the terms and boundaries of socio-political discourse. Every sentence in it is an expression of ambiguity, at one and
the same time reaffirming the speakers' belonging to and alienation
from defining features of Israeli mainstream society in the 1970s: the
threatening rise of "Panthers" and a concern for national integrity; the
sacrifice of the residents through their participation in military service
against a backdrop of state neglect; and perhaps most strikingly, an
insistence to challenge, reclaim and redefine what a "healthy society"
means, despite explicit discrimination. The last aspect goes beyond a
typical complaint about municipal services to present a collective concern for the defining characteristics of Israeli society as a whole. The
counter-hegemonic tones of this petition were clearly heard by officials
in the Tel Aviv Municipality. One advisor claimed that "the complaints
here are launched against the state and its representatives", while
another highlighted the section in the petition "in which the people of
the village claim that the state is their adversary".[65]

---

and analysing social protest, ethnic and socioeconomic stratification, and cultural
conflicts in Israel. See, for example: "The Black Panthers in Israel Archive"; Bernstein,
"Conflict and Protest in Israeli Society"; Chetrit, *The Mizrahi Struggle in Israel*; Hasson,
Urban Social Movements in Jerusalem.
[64] Kfar Shalem Council, "Public Petition".
[65] Virshuvski, "Internal Memo to Mayor Rabinowitz"; "Unsigned Memo to Mordechai
Vershuvski".

Yet this complex and carefully crafted challenge is motivated by, and directed against, a concrete object – the housing block, described in the petition first as a "modern ghetto" and then as a "matchbox". By 1978 the block was already identified as a "modern transit camp on pillars",[66] symbolising the complete erosion of the social, economic and aesthetic ideals that it had stood for earlier on.

Yet not all of the housing block's original functions were lost. In the eyes of the planning authorities, its role as a spatial boundary continued to prevail: the block was a marker of the authorised, legitimate and recognised space, which was *set against* the precariousness of the Arab houses of Salama. The perimeters created by the construction of tenements around the village were not ethnic boundaries per se, because they did not separate two distinctly recognised ethnic communities. Most of those residing in the Arab houses have traditionally been Jews of North African or Arab decent, some immigrants from the former Soviet Union who arrived in the 1970s and 1990s, and a small number of migrant workers; the ethnic composition of those living in the housing blocks is not substantially different. Reading this process through a spatial-historical prism, segregation as "stratification … enforced by public policy and the rule of law"[67] is carried out against *spaces* that are perceived as a threat to the cohesiveness of the national territory and the symbolic meanings it is expected to present. Long after its social and economic ideals have been eradicated, the block preserved its status as a frontline tool in the struggle against the "perils" of the Arab space. In this clash, the Jewish residents were dismissed, their rights compromised, and their demands delegitimised because of the houses they inhabited. This by no means dismisses the importance of the institutional discrimination of Arab-Jews in the struggle between the residents of Kfar Shalem and the authorities. It merely poses a historical framework in which the marginalisation of Arab-Jews is *spatially* linked to the ostracised status of the Arab built environment.

Conclusion

The juxtaposition of the humble, makeshift houses of Salama and the rows of tenements that encircle them is a striking one, visually narrating the obvious imbalance in resources and access to institutional patronage. And yet, the massive institutional efforts to establish the

[66] Kfar Shalem Residents' Council, "Public Petition".
[67] Meir, *My Life*, 1844.

tenement as the dominant form of Israel's urban environment, one that will remedy the maladies of pre-existing Arab settings, already establishes the fact that the remnants of an Arab village could not be simply disregarded. In the eyes of state bodies responsible for the design of "appropriate" urban environments, Salama's houses were more than an eyesore; they were, and still are, a disrupting obstacle in the modernising mission that aspires to create an "organic", homogenous urban space which abides by a pre-given set of rules and conventions.

What is first at stake here is the very ability to stabilise and mend the fractures which appear in the ideologically constructed notion of "the Modern" once it is put into practice and exposed to the corrosive power of spatial context and human intervention. If the notion of the "modern space" is no longer a stable and ideal category, but rather a contested vision that is open to scrutiny and negotiation, the juxtaposition of the tenements and the Arab houses is not "just" an obvious layering of different historical strata. It is, rather, a testimony of the conflicted nature of the foundational categories that inform the imagined and physical "Israeli" space. It obliges us to replace "European Modernism" – itself a problematic category that demands to be treated with suspicion – with a local idea of modernity that is informed by European elements, yet always supposes their exposure to forced manipulation and transformation.[68]

This proposition of "localised modernity"[69] consequently reinserts a degree of uncertainty to the presupposed results of settler-colonial spatial encounters; at the very least it enables contesting articulations of hegemonic ideals like the notion of "healthy society". It is from these spaces of undetermined interaction and contesting epistemology that new forms of social, cultural and political action can be forged. As Homi Bhabha notes,

If the effect of colonial power is seen to be the production of hybridization rather than the noisy command of colonialist authority or the silent repression of native traditions, then an important change of perspective occurs. The ambivalence at the source of traditional discourses on authority enables a form of subversion, founded on the undecidability that turns the discursive conditions of dominance into the grounds of intervention.[70]

---

[68] Nihal Perera's eye-opening interrogation of Chandigarh's planning history and his elaboration on Nehru's notion of "Indian modernity" provided me with important cornerstones for this conceptualisation. See Perera, "Contesting Visions", 180–1.

[69] The shift from "modernism" to "modernity" broadens the scope of the discussion beyond the aesthetic and cultural expressions to critically reflect on conceptual foundations of modernity, from progress and development to history and freedom.

[70] Bhabha, The Location of Culture, 112.

On the face of it, this conclusion reiterates a point already made by Haim Yacobi[71] who, following Bhabha, identifies concrete "third-places" that accommodate a process of subversive negotiation of dominant identities and hegemonic power relations. Yacobi is aware that the "third-space" may provide grounds for subversion and challenge, but at the same time "preserve the cartography of power" by limiting subversion to clearly defined boundaries.[72] In this tension I wish to err on the side of caution, mostly because a celebration of subversive alterity – a conflation of resilience and resistance – ignores the very appeals made by the residents of Kfar Shalem's Arab houses in the face of the blocks that surround them; namely, to be recognised as an integral part of the legitimate (and legal) Israeli space. This expresses a subtle yet important difference from a critical focus on third-places of opposition and resistance. It draws on Bhabha's rather humble notion of "intervention", which positively lacks the boldness of "resistance". Importantly, by refusing to associate Salama/Kfar Shalem as yet another "third-place" I wish to refrain from discursively replicating the physical pattern of containment and segregation that was formed around the village over the last six decades.

The alternative is not a return to the old polarities that set the housing block as the binary opposition of the Arab house, but a restored search for the unique historical and spatial dialogue that takes place between them, and the emergence of alternative social and political action triggered by it. The unsettled spatial history of Salama/Kfar Shalem exemplifies what Chatterjee describes as a heterogeneous and unevenly dense temporality that does not automatically pave the way for historicist imaginings of identity, nationhood and progress – cornerstones of the modernising project of the nation-state.[73] The space that opens, literally and theoretically, between the Arab house and the tenement block, exposes the fallacy of politics that inhabits the utopia of empty homogeneous time, idly detached from spatial and physical contingencies. Furthermore, the political potential of what has been forming in Kfar Shalem over the last four decades is intriguing exactly because it does not retreat to the havens of identity politics or "soothe the liberal bad conscience with the balm of multiculturalism".[74] It is not an outright rejection of modernity, nationhood or capitalism, but rather an effort by a disenfranchised group to engage, as equals, in

[71] Yacobi, "Architecture, Orientalism and Identity".
[72] Ibid., 115.
[73] Chatterjee, "Anderson's Utopia".
[74] Ibid., 130.

the process through which these terms and their implementation are determined. The shift from the empty homogeneous time of modernity to the heterogeneous actualities of space encapsulates a political engagement – Bhabha's "intervention" – that articulates broad social and economic agendas on the foundations of concrete spatial histories and experiences.

In quite the same way that the housing blocks and the Arab houses in Kfar Shalem remain far from their idealised forms – neither an Orientalist fantasy nor a purely functional "living machine" – the political horizons that emerge in their midst do not adhere to the conventions that continue to guide Israel's political mainstream or its detractors. This issue will surface again in the coming chapters.

6   Sacred: The Making and Unmaking of a Holy Place

The Shalom Synagogue, a humble building that is carefully maintained by a small and aging congregation, is one of about a dozen synagogues and religious seminaries densely packed along approximately 100m of Kfar Shalem's main street, many of which have been established in former Arab cafés, shops and houses. Above the entrance door to the synagogue, several plaques have been embedded in the wall – a typical ornamentation found in community synagogues of this kind (Figure 6.1): The Ten Commandments, a list of the synagogue's founding members and a plaque stating "Shalom Synagogue for Greek immigrants, Kfar Shalem (Salama) in the year 1953". Another plaque, however, stands out in form and content. Written in Greek, the sign reads "Israelites Temple Synagogue"; underneath it, a smaller plaque states that the sign was originally placed over the entrance gate to the Jewish synagogue in the Greek Island of Zakynthos at the order of the Nazi occupiers "to mark the place of the community's concentration". The plaque was brought to Israel by one of the community members after the synagogue collapsed in the 1953 earthquake that caused widespread destruction around the Greek islands.

This entrance intriguingly juxtaposes historical allusions: it evokes the presence of the old community synagogue alongside commemorations from recent years, but also captures a familiar form of material stratification, calling to mind the relation between the sign of the Greek synagogue, the Arab café that existed in the building before 1948, and the current Shalom Synagogue. Again, as in all other cases discussed throughout this book, the synagogue is an example of the residual appearances that dot the Israeli landscape in varying forms and for various functions. However, unlike other spatial transformations examined here, the spatial history of the synagogue expresses and results from a qualitatively different shift, from the realm of the profane to the sacred. This transition draws our attention to the operation of theology, religion, tradition and myth in the evolution of spatial meaning and the relation between people and place.

158

Figure 6.1 Entrance to the Shalom Synagogue, Kfar Shalem.
Photo by the author.

At the opposite end of Salama's main street stands Masjid Salama, the
village mosque and shrine of Salama bin Hashem, one of the Prophet's
companions, who, according to Arab-Palestinian traditions, is believed
to be buried there. Although the mosque is currently fenced off and has
fallen into disuse, it is perhaps the most prominent feature that evokes
the Arab history of Salama; no other element brings to mind the former
life of the village and its absence in such a stark manner. Between 1948
and 1981, the mosque was used as a youth centre for the children of
the neighbourhood, its yard was often turned into a makeshift football
field, and the prayer hall was divided into rooms where children would
spend their after-school hours. The transformation of the mosque presents a mirror process to that of the Shalom Synagogue: while the latter was formed through the transition from the profane to the sacred,
the former presents a reverse process in which secular, mundane practices of space replace religious rites. Although consecration practices
have been decisive in enabling the Shalom Synagogue to reside in an
Arab café, it is worth consciously suspending the inclination to identify the process that occurred in the mosque simply as desecration, a
term that implies a rather unambiguous value judgement and blurs

the contingent site-specific history of the place. Indeed, the historical events that surround the mosque reveal that the ongoing interaction between the place and the residents of Kfar Shalem included iconoclastic expressions, generated by fear, and culminating in outright violence. However, these came as part of an intricate historical process, a process that reveals perils, pain and promise.

This chapter illustrates the role of social-religious practice in the transformation of post-conflict space. It suggests that these practices allow for subtle interactions between past and present, even when historically these have been presented as diametrically opposed. Furthermore, the argument posits that without such practical engagement, these spaces are isolated and alienated from the daily lives of people, potentially instigating a highly volatile process of confrontation and violence. To comprehend the multiplicity of forces that operate in the formation and transformation of sacred space, the analysis invokes Jewish and Muslim attitudes toward the sacred, consecration and worship traditions of Mizrahi Jews, and the implicit social and cultural tensions that are inseparable from these traditions in Israel.

Synagogues: Consecration and the Rituals of Space

The plate brought from the ruins of the Greek synagogue and placed above the entrance door of the Shalom Synagogue in Kfar Shalem did not significantly alter the Arab building. Moreover, the religious significance of the place to the people who made it their house of prayer would not have been undermined if the plate had not been salvaged by Reuven Dalmadigo and embedded into the front wall of the synagogue. Yet this plate represents and articulates fundamental practices through which the Jews who arrived in Salama overcame their inherent foreignness in a new place that still bore the apparent signs of its previous inhabitants. However, closely investigating the cultural and historical forces that were involved in this process of "taking place", indicates that this was by no means an unambiguous act of appropriation. Conflicting notions of destruction and rebuilding, exile and restitution, solidity and transience will have to be incorporated into the analysis if the relationship between the past and the present in Salama/Kfar Shalem is to be brought to light. The Greek plate above the entrance to the Shalom Synagogue is an apt point of departure.

As already mentioned, the Shalom Synagogue in Kfar Shalem is a reincarnation of a Candiot synagogue that bore the same name, and served the small Jewish community of Zakynthos, the third largest of the Ionian islands. First records of Jewish life on the island date back to 1498 when Venetian authorities offered special privileges to those who settled there.[1] During the following centuries the island provided a safe haven to Jews seeking refuge from political turmoil and religious persecution.[2] The bonds formed between Jews and Christians over 500 years also withstood the invasion of Italian and German forces during World War II: when the island's Bishop Chryssostomos and Mayor Loukas Carrer were ordered to come up with a record of all Jews residing on the island, they presented the Germans with a list containing only their own names. The local community sheltered all 275 Jews who lived in Zakynthos and all survived the war without need to relocate. Following the establishment of the State of Israel many emigrated from the island; only 39 Jews lived in Zakynthos by 1953 and all were forced to leave as a result of the devastation caused by that year's earthquake.[3]

The plate commemorating the Greek synagogue, as well as the use of the old name for the synagogue in Kfar Shalem, alludes to the tight bond formed between commemoration and destruction in Jewish tradition, liturgical practices and scriptural narratives. Indeed, it was only after the destruction of the Second Temple in Jerusalem in 70 CE that the synagogue gained its prominence as a central institution in Jewish liturgy.[4] In rabbinic literature, the synagogue is often referred to as "a little sanctuary" or "lesser temple" (מקדש מעט), an expression originating in Ezekiel 11:16, where God's presence is promised to those who were forced into exile in Babylon after the destruction of the First Temple in 597 BC. The rise of synagogues is therefore closely tied not only to the destruction of the Temple but also to the demise of territorial Jewish sovereignty and the emergence of diasporic Jewish life. The transition from temple to synagogue fundamentally decentralised worship practices. Hence, for example, the establishment of a synagogue requires only a quorum of ten, or *minyan*, therefore enabling synagogues to be founded by and cater for small communal or familial groupings. The synagogue marked a new phase in Jewish religious life, providing a rather more intimate space in and around which communities organised, even in the absence of territorial sovereignty. Destruction, ruin and exile are thus closely entwined in the cultural genome from which the synagogue emerges.

However, the plate at the entrance to the Shalom Synagogue rearticulates the narrative of destruction and salvation – a pattern that recurs throughout the biblical tales of the Jewish people – at the specific

---

[1] Deutsch and Caimi, "Zante".
[2] Baron, *A Social and Religious History of the Jews*.
[3] Plaut, *Greek Jewry in the Twentieth Century*, 66, 68.
[4] Kunin, *God's Place in the World*, 49.

moment when this narrative permeates from religious traditions into the Israeli national ethos.[5] Although the Shalom Synagogue in Kfar Shalem was established independently by a local community, it coincided with a broader state effort to use religious practices of consecration to transform the historical and religious geography of the newly established state. As several authors[6] point out, a concentrated effort was made by the Israeli Ministry of Religious Affairs (MRA) and its director-general, Shmuel Zanwill Kahana, to "Judeise" holy Muslim sites and recreate the sacred map of the Holy Land in a way that would express the age-old relation between the Jewish people and the territory of the newly established state. While there was little public dispute over the need to reclaim and reinstate this historical link, the specific use of religious traditions and practices was viewed as a defiance of the secular "state religion"[7] that dominated Israel in the first three decades of independence. The MRA and Kahana came under heavy criticism from the academic establishment, in what appeared to be "turf-wars" over the authority to determine the significance of space:[8] according to the dominant political culture of the time, the opinions of geographers, archaeologists, historians and orientalists – all "rational men of science" – held more sway than those of religious figures. The question of whether traditional Arab sites should at all be altered to reflect the ideological aspirations of the new state was never explicitly asked.

Some scholars have suggested that the appropriation of sacred Muslim sites and their transformation into places of Jewish worship was an instrument for establishing what John Noyes terms as a "script of possession", "the marks by which a group of people agree to represent their own experience of history, as related to territoriality".[9] The political and ideological impetus behind these acts is now broadly accepted.[10] However, the relation between consecration and possession of space goes beyond the perimeters of the Israeli-Arab dispute. In his seminal work on the nature and importance of sacred space, the

---

[5] For example: Zertal, *Israel's Holocaust and the Politics of Nationhood*.

[6] Bar, "Reconstructing the Past"; Bilu, "Sanctification of Space in Israel"; Kletter, *Just Past?*

[7] Liebman and Don-Yihya, *Civil Religion in Israel*. Maoz Azaryahu also discusses the emergence and dominance of secular nationalism in that period, which he describes as the "cult of nationalism". See Azaryahu, *State Cults*.

[8] Bar, "Reconstructing the Past", 4.

[9] Noyes, *Colonial Space*, 243.

[10] See, for example: Benvenisti, *Sacred Landscape*, chapter 7; Robin, "The Necropolitics of Homeland"; Falah, "The 1948 Israeli-Palestinian War and Its Aftermath"; Azaryahu and Kellerman, "Symbolic Places of National History and Revival"; Bar, "Reconstructing the Past".

historian of religion, Mircea Eliade, suggests that consecration plays a fundamental role in differentiating between "Cosmos" and "chaos":

At first sight this cleavage in space appears to be due to the opposition between an inhabited and organized – hence cosmicized – territory and the unknown space that extends beyond its frontiers; on one side there is a cosmos, on the other a chaos. But we shall see that if every inhabited territory is cosmos, that is exactly because it was first consecrated … The sacred reveals absolute reality and at the same time makes orientation possible; hence it *founds the world* in the sense that it fixes the limits and establishes the order of the world.[11]

For Eliade, "Cosmos" refers specifically to the world as an orderly, harmonious entirety; the process of consecration transforms fragmented, unstructured, meaningless phenomena into a coherent, structured and meaningful whole.[12] It is exactly this dialectic of Cosmos and chaos that is crucial in the case of the Shalom Synagogue, and at least three expressions of this transition can be retraced here. The first regards the role of the synagogue in general Jewish tradition as an institution that emerges out of the chaos of destruction and exile. The second repetition of this pattern regards the specific history of the Jewish community in Zakynthos, the devastation of the synagogue on the island, and its reinstatement in Salama. The third appearance of consecration as a way of ordering the world can be detected in the encounter between the Jewish immigrants and the Arab surroundings of Salama. On the face of it, then, the establishment of the synagogue merges both the theological-redemptive path that moves from destruction and exile to deliverance in the homeland, and the national-Zionist version of this narrative, in which "the rhythm of exile and return"[13] is delivered by earthly, political instruments. However, to avoid a simplistic perception of what is in fact an intricate negotiation of cultural and historical residues, it is worth further examining the unresolved tensions between destruction and restitution and the way this ambiguous existence manifests itself in the small front wall of the Shalom Synagogue.

The past, and the specific history of Jewish suffering in the diaspora, has been instrumental in shaping the national political community in Israel. Numerous works have examined the ways that state apparatuses in Israel have used the Jewish experience to solidify a sense of communal destiny and national cohesion.[14] However, the plate

---

[11] Eliade, *The Sacred and the Profane*, 29–30, emphasis in the original.
[12] Allen, *Myth and Religion*, 103.
[13] Vital, *The Origins of Zionism*, 5.
[14] This, of course, is not unique to the Israeli case and can perhaps be considered as a common feature in the formation of national imagined communities more broadly.

commemorating the destroyed Greek synagogue does more than resurrect the pain of Jewish suffering in exile and its positive resolution
through national revival. Exile is not simply negated, as in many traditional Zionist accounts, but made present again as a legitimate chapter
in the history of the community. The establishment of the synagogue
was by no means an attempt to turn one's back on the past, nor instrumentalise it, but rather to transplant the memory of the diaspora into a
new environment.

From a present-day perspective, this seems like an act of negligi-
ble significance. Yet this act was carried out at a time when dominant
national institutions sought to unify a heterogeneous society around
consensual narratives of history and national revival. Individual
commemoration that weaves diasporic space into a space of national
renewal was hardly a common sight. For comparison, the construction of two structures using foreign architectural motifs in the 1980s – a
replica of the Brooklyn headquarters of the Ashkenazi ultra-Orthodox
Chabad movement and the grave of the Jewish-Moroccan *tzadik* (saint)
Rabi Yisrael Abuhatzeira – was seen to mark, according to one com-
mentator, "a kind of 'end to Zionism' or, to shift to a different metaphor, an ending of the Zionist hegemony".[15] These claims are obviously
hyperbolic: Zionist hegemony did not lose its dominance merely as a
result of the strengthening of Chabad or the Moroccan religious community in the 1970s. But notably in places like Salama – where the presence of dominant nationalist sentiments would be expected in order to
counter the presence of the Arab space and imprint upon it marks of
national ownership – the subsistence of diasporic memory as part of an
active place-making communal process indicates, at the very least, an
ambivalence toward the sharp binaries that constituted Israel's spatio-
politics at the time.

In this light, the significance of the Shalom Synagogue lies in the way
it fuses two elements that had been sidelined from the commemorative mainstream of Israel in the 1950s. On the one hand, it conveys and
preserves the exilic Jewish existence in the newly established national

It is important to remember, however, that Zionism has always held an ambivalent
relation to the past. On the one hand, the near past – mostly provincial Jewish life in
eastern Europe or the bourgeois Jews of central and western Europe – was deemed
inappropriate as a model for the creation of a new national Jewish figure. On the
other hand, epic episodes from biblical and rabbinic times, as well as the more contemporary tales of early Jewish pioneering in Palestine, were promoted as founding
national myths. See, for example, Almog, *The Sabra*; Gertz, *Myths in Israeli Culture*;
Zertal, *Israel's Holocaust and the Politics of Nationhood*.

[15] Weingrod, "Changing Israeli Landscapes", 377.

space. The ambivalent relation between residents and the state, which was discussed in detail in Chapter 3, is further accentuated as religious spatial practices become the central prism through which the encounter with the new space is conducted. While their influence over the absorption of Salama into the national space must not be dismissed, symbols of secular nationalism remain in the shadow of traditional-religious forms of spatial interaction. In addition to conserving a degree of ambivalence toward the national imperative to break from the diaspora (further discussed in Chapter 2), the synagogue also reflects the negotiation between the new Jewish inhabitants of Salama and the Arab space into which they arrived.

For some years after Jews began residing in Salama, summoning the community's previous life in Greece, Yemen or Iraq, provided reassurance in the face of an unfamiliar, and at times chaotic, new environment. The establishment of the Shalom Synagogue and numerous other synagogues in Kfar Shalem became a way for communities to "found a world", to use Eliade's term, in a place that presented itself as foreign to them. Avshalom Ben-David, whose grandfather established a Yemenite synagogue in the village in 1949, explained that "while people in Tel Aviv went to Habima [the national theatre], we built a synagogue. And just like Habima, the synagogues were the heart of this community."[16] Ben-David's counter-position echoes more than just cultural differences between secular Jews who went to the theatre and religious communities that congregated in synagogues. Decades earlier, in September 1950, members of the North African synagogue in Salama appealed to the authorities for assistance in receiving a permit to construct a synagogue "in the empty lot adjacent to the little room that serves as a temporary synagogue for hundreds of people".[17] While appearing at first as ordinary pleas against an indifferent bureaucracy, the letters sarcastically[18] shed light on the cultural logic of the time. After community leaders encountered calls from the congregation to launch demonstrations against the authorities' negligence, an alternative idea was raised:

Our suggestion [to the crowd] was to ask, instead of a permit for a synagogue – which is too difficult to get from you – for a permit to build a theatre. And we

---

[16] Ben-David, Interview with the author.
[17] North African Synagogue Salama-Tel Aviv, "Letter to the Ministry of Religious Affairs".
[18] An effort was made in the translation of the letters to preserve the tone and the register of the Hebrew, which fuses biblical Hebrew syntax and grammar with more contemporary phrasing. Grammatical or punctuation inconsistencies and errors were therefore left unchanged.

assume that this is an important venture for the development of the *yishuv*[19] and its advancement, and now we are confident that shortly, we will all be employed in the theatre and nobody will speak out.

The proposal was accepted with loud applause and everybody agreed that instead of praying, especially in the approaching Days of Awe [the Jewish High Holy Days], every man will be given a permanent job in the theatre, and that will be the end of it. Please inform us of your opinion on the matter.[20]

In a letter sent to the Ministry of Religious Affairs on the same day, the addressers make sure to clarify – as if such a clarification was at all needed – that the idea for a theatre was "merely a trick to obtain a building permit".[21] The juxtaposition of the theatre and the synagogue was not incidental, deriving from the former's prominent place in Tel Aviv's cultural history. The Habima National Theatre was planned by Oscar Kaufman in a Bauhaus style as a large building with six Greek-style columns around its façade.[22] The neo-Classical gestures echoed Sir Patrick Geddes's 1926 master plan for Tel Aviv, in which the theatre house formed one part of the city's "cultural Acropolis".[23] It would have been difficult for Salama's North African community to remain oblivious to the national status of the theatre building, which was completed and opened only five years earlier.[24] Mockery was not the sole intention of the letter, but merely a way to "set the stage", as it were, for the scathing criticism that followed:

When we were in the diaspora under the Arab government in Northern Africa, there is no village, even a small one that has only two quorums that is 20 Jewish

---

[19] A term used in Hebrew to refer to the body of Jewish residents in Palestine before the establishment of the State of Israel.
[20] North African Synagogue Salama-Tel Aviv, "Letter to the Ministry of Religious Affairs".
[21] Ibid.
[22] Nagid, "Israel".
[23] Biger, "A Scotsman in the First Hebrew City"; Welter, *Biopolis*. In 1958, Kaufman's neo-Classical design was modified, inserting a balcony in between the columns and altering its vertical dimensions into horizontal, modernist ones. This was but one of several changes to the building, the last of which was completed in 2012. During this latest renovation, the building's façade was demolished and for several months the theatre stood in a state of ruin that resembled, according to Israeli critic Itamar Mann, one of Kasper David Friedrich's tragic landscape paintings, reminding "the viewer that all the pleasures of life will not overcome the looming death". Considering the events that took place around Salama Mosque in October 2000, discussed below, this is a striking observation. See Mann, "Think of 'Habima' as a Tragic Landscape Painting".
[24] In the ceremony marking the laying of the building's cornerstone in 1936, Tel Aviv Mayor Meir Diezengoff said, "This beautiful and magnificent building will beautify our city and will forever stay as a memorial for our generation's efforts in the field on culture and art".

men – that does not include a synagogue and all its instruments. A swift thing even a permit is not required. Very simple, you have – or don't have – you'll get – a lot, hire some workers to build, and after a short while the synagogue is built magnificently inside the *Arab* city or village.

Are we in the State of Israel, in an Israeli city, and Israeli village according to the boundary divisions – for heaven's sake – we run from place to place, from office to office, letters moving in the air and on land and no results.[25]

It is interesting to note how the letter suggests that the village was "Israeli" only by virtue of boundary divisions, and presented no immanent feature that would affiliate it with the more obviously national space of Tel Aviv. Furthermore, the writers "dare" to suggest that under Arab rule in North Africa, one was in some ways better off. By doing so, they defy one of the foundational binaries of Zionism; namely, the diametrical opposition between Arab and Jew, and the narrative that sets the Jewish state as a resolution to the inherent plight of diaspora.[26]

The authorities were not oblivious to the problems this marginality – externally imposed, but also used by the residents for their own purposes – might pose to the social and spatial cohesion of the national collective. In a 1953 letter appealing to the Tel Aviv Municipality to prevent the demolition of a synagogue that operated in what was previously an Arab grocery shop, Rabbi Shmuel Greenberg alludes to the situation in former Arab spaces – commonly referred to as abandoned places – and the potential impact these ambiguous spaces have on the identity of those who inhabit them: "Kfar Shalem is among the abandoned places that were inhabited by new immigrants, and the effort of every cultural and religious institution is required in order to shape the spiritual image of the local residents."[27] The ominous prospects of failure are not mentioned, but the gravity of this mission is unmistakable.

Establishing a synagogue and marking the old buildings with familiar symbols of religious and communal significance are rather unremarkable practices in the relation of people to a new environment. But this integration-through-sanctification is significant because it does not require the obliteration of existing spatial features, while providing the necessary mediation of an otherwise unsettling encounter, as discussed at length in Chapter 1. The evocation of sacred forms or figures, Eliade reminds us, is required "for the immediate purpose

---

[25] North African Synagogue Salama-Tel Aviv, "Letter to Tel Aviv Municipality Permits Department", emphasis in the original.

[26] Shenhav, *The Arab Jews*.

[27] Greenberg, "Letter to the Tel Aviv Municipal Sub-Committee for Construction and Urban Development".

of establishing *orientation* in the homogeneity of space. A *sign* is asked, to put an end to the tension and anxiety caused by relativity and disorientation – in short, to reveal an absolute point of support."[28] Reading this, the Greek tablet hung over the entrance to the Shalom Synagogue immediately comes to mind as an instrument through which the new residents recreated a grid of orientation, both temporally – through the evocation of the familiar past in the unfamiliar present – and spatially, through the inscription of one's ethnic and religious signs into a place that retains the marks of its previous life.

Research of Jewish traditions in the Cretan islands situates the Greek tablet in a longer history of commemorative practices and the relocation of historical inscriptions. In his analysis of three inscriptions of Jewish origin in Crete, Zvi Ankori suggests that

> Following a reverent practice of long standing, Jewish communities would not discard broken, displaced or obsolete inscriptions, whether synagogal or heraldic or even sepulchral, but, rather, preserve the pieces within the precincts of a new or renovated synagogue, often immuring them in the courtyard walls.[29]

The Greek-Jewish tradition of preserving inscriptions through their relocation stemmed from the community's relation to, and fear of, the non-Jewish environment around it. The anxiety of passing through non-Jewish neighbourhoods en route to old cemeteries or synagogues located outside the city, and the fear of travelling through unprotected roads, were the motivating force behind the relocation of commemorative tablets to a new synagogue. Similarly, during various times of emergency,

> the dead who had been deprived of regular burial were remembered by way of small-scale *siyyunim*, or memorial tablets. These were not tomb-stones, really, but commemorative plaques which, from the very outset, very likely were immured in, affixed to, or displayed in any other form in the synagogue courtyard.[30]

Pointing out the traditional custom of relocating plaques and tablets is significant because it sheds light on the affective undercurrents that guide spatial practices. The prominence of ethnic and cultural traditions in the consecration and transformation of the Shalom Synagogue are not divorced from the social and cultural politics of space in Israel. As Roger Friedland and Richard Hecht point out, "Sacred spaces are not separate from the powers of the state; they are ... deeply connected

---

[28] Eliade, *The Sacred and the Profane*, 27–8 italics in the original.
[29] Ankori, "The Living and the Dead", 38. Similar Jewish tradition exists with regard to worn or unused religious literature that is deposited in special chambers before being given a proper cemetery burial, known as *genizah*.
[30] Ibid., 44.

to sovereignty or the ability of the state to control its boundaries and the meanings that are given to its important national sites."[31] It is impossible to detach the sacred history of Salama/Kfar Shalem from the intervention and influence of the state and the political-ideological efforts to shape a national landscape that adheres to strict ethno-religious ideals. But the synagogues established in coffee shops, private houses and shops along Salama's main street were more than reaffirmations of state sovereignty over territory and control of spatial meaning. Rather, the process of consecration exposes a deep ambivalence toward the norms and forms that dominated the mainstream of Israeli society in the early 1950s, and some that remain to this day. These ambivalences are worth highlighting because through them one comes closer to understanding how these synagogues preserved the Arab building in which they reside, while buildings used for other purposes were demolished over time. Sanctity, in its socio-cultural manifestations as well as its religious ones, plays a significant role in accommodating the contradictory conjuncture of Jewish life and Arab history, and consequently plays a decisive role in conserving Salama's built environment.

When compared with a quintessential example of national commemorations in Israel during the same period, the uniqueness of the Shalom Synagogue and the spatial history it preserves truly comes to light. In 1951, the heyday of Zionist-socialism in Israel, the sculptor Nathan Rapaport was commissioned to design a monument commemorating Mordecai Anielewicz, one of the leading figures of the Jewish resistance movement in the Warsaw ghetto during World War II, which would be placed in Kibbutz Yad Mordecai. This work fuses two themes that Rapaport had already dealt with in previous works; namely, the Holocaust and the 1948 War.[32] Literally combining elements from both events, an imposing figure of Anielewicz clutching a hand grenade stands in the foreground, while a bullet-ridden water tower, shelled during the 1948 battles on the site, appears behind him (Figure 6.2). Beyond the figure's shoulders, the landscapes of the kibbutz and the adjacent fields open out. The Israeli historian Idith Zertal astutely notes how "contrary to the chronological order of events, the site is constructed so that it appears to the visitor that Anielewicz's statue, representing the earlier event, grows out of the destroyed water tower,

---

[31] Friedland and Hecht, "Sacred Urbanism", 34.
[32] Rapaport's most famous work is his Warsaw ghetto memorial, designed in 1943 and dedicated in 1948. Another monument designed by the artist in 1953, the War of Independence memorial in Kibbutz Negba, earned praise for "the artist's successful efforts to unite all the details making for a concentrated representation of the ideal Israeli hero". Levinger, "Socialist-Zionist Ideology in Israeli War Memorials of the 1950s", 721.

Figure 6.2 The Anielewicz Monument, Yad Mordechai.
Photo by the author.

representing the later event".[33] This visual and spatial anachronism succeeds because it assumes that as an aesthetic and emotive object, the ruin loses its status as a historical signifier, and chronological order or causality are replaced by the symbolic and emotive effect.

Initially, members of Yad Mordechai intended to remove the remains of the destroyed tower altogether, but were persuaded by Rapaport's design. However, this was just one difference in opinion between the artist and the kibbutz. A more substantial discrepancy was exposed with regard to the ultimate priority given to the act of commemoration over the dire physical conditions in which the kibbutz found itself in after the 1948 War:

[Rapaport] relates that when he arrived in the kibbutz to survey sites for the monument, he was shocked to find the kibbutz itself nearly destroyed. "After rebuilding your houses, then maybe you should think about statues," he advised the kibbutz. But they wanted to begin with a monument: that is, they would now refound the kibbutz ... literally around a monument of its namesake.[34]

There is no doubt that for the members of Yad Mordechai, commemoration of Anielewicz was required before any other need of the community could be properly addressed. In the way it enabled, perhaps even conditioned, the establishment of a new Cosmos out of the chaos of war and the calamity of the Holocaust, national commemoration of this sort gained sacred status in the first two decades of Israeli independence. However, a distinction between national and religious consecration is required: like social-Zionism's relation to the role of the past in general, sacred status was often associated with events that could justify, legitimise or motivate the national endeavours of the day, while often preserving its distinction from religious traditions. Commemorative Jewish practices were left outside the national mainstream, making way for the development of a "civil religion" that shaped dominant national attitudes toward Holocaust commemoration, diasporic Jewish life and the formation of a cohesive national community in Israel.[35]

How then does the Shalom Synagogue relate to this state religion differently from the Anielewicz Monument in Yad Mordechai? To begin with, there is nothing physically or symbolically monumental in

---

[33] Zertal, *Israel's Holocaust and the Politics of Nationhood*, 37, fn 78.

[34] Young, *The Texture of Memory*, 233.

[35] In *Civil Religion in Israel*, Liebman and Don Yihya defined the term as a symbol system that provides sacred legitimisation to the social order, and pointed specifically to the political sacralisation and ritualisation of the Holocaust. This critique has become one of the most contentious pillars of the public and academic debate in Israel over the past two decades, as scholars seek to interrogate the political utilisation of the Holocaust. See, for example, Ophir, "On Sanctifying the Holocaust"; Zertal, *Israel's*

the Shalom Synagogue. Despite this, perhaps even because of this, its humble features succeed in presenting a subtle yet significant example of the ability to accommodate several histories without resolving the apparent tension between them. In its form, function and relation to national paradigms of commemoration, the synagogue in Kfar Shalem exemplifies an alternative approach to the past. It stands in contrast to historical narratives that emerge into space *ex nihilo* (the mythic birth of Tel Aviv "out of the sands", for example) or instrumentalise existing spatial features in a way that either ignores completely or blurs beyond recognition their previous meaning (Yad Mordechai's water tower).

Contrary to these dominant trends, the Shalom Synagogue presents a rather more subtle intervention in space. First, this is not the case of manipulation through anachronism: the front wall of the synagogue and the plaques affixed to it do not conflate the community's past and its present. Bringing back the inscription of the old synagogue's name is a symbolic gesture that simultaneously makes present and acknowledges absence; the fragment is not, and does not intend be, a replacement of the whole, but synecdochically illustrates what was and what is gone. As previously noted, this practice emerged out of a real physical *inability* to access sites of old synagogues or cemeteries, and the fragments or inscriptions taken from these sites made them available to the congregation while still maintaining and acknowledging their inapproachability. The Greek tablet was not intended to create a "metonymic transfer" of objects that allow immigrants to generate, as Pnina Werbner has argued in another context, "the illusion of spatial contiguity, a lack of spatial separation" from the homeland left behind.[36] Instead, the plate affixed to the synagogue wall is part of a community's effort to overcome a sense of foreignness in an unfamiliar environment, not by its eradication but through subtler spatial gestures that implant the community's past, unsettled as it is, in its present.[37]

Similar to the way the diasporic past is planted in the Israeli present without nostalgically recreating it, the Jewish present and the Arab

---

Holocaust and the Politics of Nationhood; Shapira, "The Holocaust"; Feldman, *Above the Death Pits, Beneath the Flag*. For a critique of the term and its use in this context, see Yakira, *Post-Zionism, Post-Holocaust*.

[36] Werbner, "Global Pathways", 25–6.

[37] It is remarkable that the sign chosen to act as the reminder of the community's past was, in fact, placed on the Greek synagogue at the order of the Nazi occupiers of Zakynthos and not by the community itself. Is the sign of the perpetrator just a reminder of past suffering that legitimises one's claim for territorial sovereignty? As footnote 34 above suggests, this is an assertion that has been made with regard to

past of the place do not overshadow each other. To be sure, this is not a customary form of commemoration; but the Arab name – Salama – is included in the inscription above the door: "Shalom Synagogue for Greek immigrants, Kfar Shalem (Salama) in the year 1953". In Chapter 2 we encountered the Arab name placed in parenthesis, on a street sign on the main historical artery that led from the city of Jaffa to Salama. In the case of the synagogue, the Arab name was included by the residents themselves as a reminder of the common name used at the time to identify the village, one year after the new Hebrew name was officially assigned. However, conversations with residents in the neighbourhood suggest that beyond the lingering of the name, the history of the place as an Arab village is not dreaded: when asked about the Arab name on the sign, the synagogue's *gabai* (administrative manager) explained simply, "This was an Arab village, you know."[38]

How can we come to terms with this imperturbable acceptance of a past that is closely tied to violent events, a long history of animosity between communities, and conflicting demands over the right to the land? Relying on centuries-old traditions, the sanctification of synagogues did not require the residents to directly confront the symbolic weight of the buildings; through the use of socio-cultural practices, Arab cafés, shops and houses could be dissociated from the disturbing history of their Arab past. As Joan Branham explains, "The religious space of the synagogue is without inherent definition until its character is actualized … Topos and ritual mimesis reciprocally give significance to synagogue space. The moment of 'emplacement' infuses the synagogue with sacrality reminiscent of the Temple."[39] Once the Torah scroll and the *Bimah* – a platform used for the public reading of the scriptures – were placed within the small hall of the building, no other physical modifications were needed for the building to attain religious significance.

The qualitative differentiation of physical sites through communal and individual rites – the transformation of space into place through human practices, in de Certeau's terms[40] – is especially relevant when we consider the sacred as a realm *set apart* from the ordinary. While mostly critical of Durkheim's famous definition of religion as "a unified system of beliefs and practices relative to sacred things, that is to say,

---

the function of Holocaust commemoration in Israel's political culture more generally. However, the cultural history of commemorative plaques complicates this utilitarian perspective and suggests that the Greek tablet functions as an ambivalent object that conveys several, not fully complementary meanings.

[38] Dalmadigo, Interview with the author.

[39] Branham, "Sacred Space Under Erasure", 392.

[40] de Certeau, *The Practice of Everyday Life*, 74.

things set apart and forbidden",[41] Matthew Evans suggests the "set-apart sacred" as a starting point for an evaluation of the sacred that is not directly linked to religion.[42] He asserts that

the feature common to the set-apart sacred is its valuation beyond utility, and that this mental setting-apart of certain things, sometimes accompanied by a literal setting apart, is largely based on non-rational (which is not necessarily to say irrational) features, like their emotional value.[43]

While Evans does not go on to fully explore the specific qualities of this characterisation, it moves us closer to conceptualising the Shalom Synagogue as a space set-apart by a complex cultural process of consecration, rather than solely a religious one. The Greek plate, for example, is not a religious object and the synagogue would retain its significance even in its absence, yet its presence draws attention to cultural and social traditions that are crucial in making the Arab space meaningful for the Jewish residents.

Beyond the specific process of consecration and the various histories it draws together, the question "why there?" still requires a more thorough consideration. At least ten synagogues and religious seminaries are currently situated in the main street of Kfar Shalem, which invites us to ask whether location has a role to play in processes of consecration and spatial transformation in Salama/Kfar Shalem. In most scholarly work on historical, political and social transformation of space in Israel, the public function and practice of space remains rather marginal.[44] Even Doron Bar, who dedicates a recent article to "The Creation of Jewish Sacred Space in the State of Israel, 1948–1967" summarises the "Judaization" of Muslim holy places in rather unambiguous terms:

---

[41] Durkheim, *The Elementary Forms of the Religious Life*, 62.

[42] It is important to note that linguistic traditions suggest that spatial and conceptual differentiations are long connected with the notion of the sacred. In his review of this history, Colpe notes that in the Roman tradition, "*Sacer* and *profanus* were therefore linked to specific and quite distinct locations; one of these, a spot referred to as *sacer*, was either walled off or otherwise set apart – that is to say, *sanctum* – within the other, surrounding space available for profane use." The setting-apart of sacred objects, places or people is a recurring theme that crosses religious and geographical boundaries: the ancient Egyptian word *dsr* was used to denote the creation of distance between sacred and profane spaces. In addition to its meaning as "pure", the Hebrew notion of *qadosh* also defines differentiation; German and Dutch make use of the ancient root *ueik-*, meaning "to set apart" or "to oppose oneself". Colpe, "The Sacred and the Profane".

[43] Evans, "The Sacred", 39.

[44] I refer here to some of the most cited works on the subject. Arnon Golan has been writing on this issue for over a decade-and-a-half, while focusing his analysis on state mechanisms' operation in specific locations and the response of local communities to this intervention. However, only rarely – as in his analysis of Salama/Kfar Shalem and parts in his book on the transformation of Arab land after the 1948 War – does

Figure 6.3 Salama Mosque.
Photo by the author.

In practice, Jewish ownership of these places was made effective by the different associations and individuals that frequented them daily. They held regular prayers, feasts, and special celebrations in those sites and conducted small-scale development projects on-site, gradually reshaping the appearance of the sacred sites and giving them a more Jewish character.[45]

What actually qualifies as "Jewish character" remains unclear, but the above passage suggests that the practices performed by communities and individuals were important in determining the meaning of these sites in the decades that followed the establishment of the State of Israel. Transformation in this case relied heavily on the rather prosaic

he follow the actual use that Jewish inhabitants make of Arab property, and even in those cases the relation between people and space is not factored into the analysis. See Golan, "From Abandoned Village to Urban Neighbourhood"; Golan, *Wartime Spatial Changes*. Other accounts of the appropriation of Arab property have been published in recent years (Ben-Ari and Bilu, *Grasping Land*; Fischbach, *Records of Dispossession*; Forman and Kedar, "From Arab Land to 'Israel Lands'"), yet the description rarely goes beyond the relations between state apparatuses and the Jewish residents of Arab property. The interaction between people and place remains mostly outside the analytical purview. Tamar Berger's *Dionysus at Dizengof Center*, Shlomit Benjamin's "'Present-Absent'", and to a lesser degree Yfaat Weiss's *A Confiscated Memory* are examples of works that also incorporate spatio-physical elements into social, economic and political analyses.
[45] Bar, "Reconstructing the Past", 8.

ability of people to frequent these places, and the latter's ability to maintain their meaning as part of a dynamic public realm. Much like the Arab owners of cafés and shops in Salama's main street, Jewish congregations sought to place their synagogues in a central, accessible and visible place. Again we are confronted by the way Salama's spatial history and the everyday organisation of public space that evolved until 1948, remained relevant long after the first Jewish residents moved in.

In retrospect, however, the sanctification of Arab buildings had an even greater effect, playing a substantial role in the protection of the Arab built environment from destruction. A 1963 map, which charts the location of public buildings in Kfar Shalem, shows how many of the buildings along the main street of the neighbourhood were used for public or commercial purposes. Comparing the street with one of Tel Aviv's most famous nightlife spots, one resident said that this "was the *Diezengoff of the south*".[46] However, by 2008 almost all of the buildings used for private commercial use – a barber shop, a kiosk, a grocery store and a restaurant – had been demolished as part of the council's regeneration plans for the neighbourhood. In fact, the only exception is a Yemenite restaurant that has become a social institution for those who consider themselves "veterans" of the neighbourhood. The only remaining Arab buildings along the main street are those that have been transformed for religious purposes.

It was illustrated earlier how the synagogue in general, and the particular example of the Shalom Synagogue in Kfar Shalem, is closely linked to a history of destruction. However, a spatial history of consecration in Kfar Shalem suggests that this process is similarly tied to the conservation of the Arab built environment. In other words, the Yemenite, Iraqi and Greek communities that pray and study in these buildings have become their custodians, sustaining them against the constant threat of demolition.[47] Inevitably, this assertion opens up a series of highly charged questions: is this "conservation" only an attempt to disguise the fact the Arab owners of this property have been dispossessed? Does physical sustenance also maintain the symbolic and cultural meaning that these places held for their Arab residents, or is this yet another case of erasure of the Arab landscape through its "designification"?[48] Can this notion of spatial conservation qualify as a subtle interaction between Jewish residents and the Arab past of the

---

[46] Ben-David, Interview with the author.
[47] Custodianship is, of course, not an unproblematic term, and in the Israeli context it is laden with political meaning. I return to address this difficulty in the Conclusion.
[48] Falah, "The 1948 Israeli-Palestinian War and its Aftermath", 261.

village, or are these, as Hannan Hever suggests,[49] "spectacles of control" left by the victors to reaffirm their dominance over the defeated?[50]

I address these demanding questions by first looking at Muslim holy
sites in Kfar Shalem and their fate following the 1948 War. A broader
analysis of the spatial history of sacred spaces will show that the relation between the Jewish residents of Kfar Shalem and the Arab past
stored in the physical remains of Salama, is far from unambiguous.
Exploring the boundaries between destruction and conservation will
expose just how volatile and fragile the current spatial status quo is.

Salama Mosque: Deconsecration, Conservation and the Looming Set-Apart

In a website cataloguing prominent architectural landmarks in Tel Aviv
ahead of the city's centennial celebrations, Salama's mosque and shrine
were listed alongside other prominent monuments in Tel Aviv and Jaffa
like the Grand Synagogue and the Hassan Beq Mosque. Yet unlike these
well-known sites, it is highly doubtful that the majority of the city's
residents, let alone occasional visitors who might encounter the website, would be able to identify the building or even locate it on the city
map. Nonetheless, Salama Mosque does stand out as the only mosque
in the former Arab periphery of Tel Aviv–Jaffa that remains fully intact:
mosques and small prayer rooms in Sheikh Muwanis, Jamousin and
Khayriyya did not survive the 1948 War and its aftermath. In Summeil,
a small village located just north of Tel Aviv's Municipality building, a
prayer room remained intact and was transformed into a synagogue
after the war, as did the Mosque of Yazur approximately three miles
south of Salama. According to one figure, only 40 of 140 mosques in
the depopulated villages survived to some extent.[51] In comparison, the
mosque in Kfar Shalem remains surprisingly unharmed and at first
sight shows no apparent sign that it had been altered since it was seized
nearly seven decades ago.

Although the building is surrounded by a tall wall, it still retains an
imposing presence, located at the top of a small hill and surrounded
by few single-story buildings. With two domes and bare-stone walls,
the building is identified in oral histories and Palestinian village books

---

[49] Hever, *Producing the Modern Hebrew Canon*, 207.

[50] Hever's main concern is with the role of the Arab in Hebrew canonical literature.
The Arab figure, Hever insists, is not erased from the pages of mainstream Israeli
literature, but is placed in a position that solidifies a paradigmatic inferiority in the
encounter with the Jew, as part of a spectacle of control.

[51] Benvenisti, *Sacred Landscape*, figure 16.

as the burial place of Salama bin Hashem, one of the companions of the Prophet Muhammad who died in battle near Jerusalem.[52] However, despite the obvious visual contrast between the mosque and its surroundings, it is unclear why it was chosen to be included in the official centennial architecture list, when other, perhaps more prominent sites, were left out.[53] A possible answer may be found on the webpage dedicated to the Salama Mosque, which states that, "the abandoned mosque of Salama village is the only remnant of the thriving village that once existed there".[54] This short text is fascinating for two reasons: first, it suggests that the architecture students of the Bezalel Art Academy, who were responsible for the research and documentation of the project, remained oblivious to a wide variety of Arab remnants that can still be found in the village, including buildings and spatial formations to which I allude throughout this book. It is not incidental that the prominent visibility of the mosque obscures other forms of Arab architecture and landscape that are part of the village's spatial history.

The second aspect regards the status of the mosque as the representation of Arab life in Salama. The text implies a synecdochic relation, in which the mosque stands for the entire array of Arab spatial features that did not survive or do not stand out as such. While the identification of Arab history through the figure of the mosque may be intuitively understandable, the spatial history of Salama Mosque suggests that its meaning was far from static; a multiplicity of factors and forces were involved in its survival and function in and as part of the space of the new neighbourhood. At times, these historical contingencies integrated the mosque into the life of the neighbourhood, while at other times they played a decisive role in producing a sense of antagonism between the fenced-off mosque and the neighbourhood around it. The shifting of meaning – from cohabitation to confrontation – occurs at historically specific points that reorganise spatial practices and redefine socio-cultural patterns; in other words, "the Mosque as a symbol of Arab past" is far from obvious, but rather a highly contingent assumption that emerges out of specific spatial and discursive conditions that need to be brought to light. Following key stages in this historical process will illustrate how the "set-apart sacred" remains a fundamental quality of the space of the mosque, but undergoes important transitions

---

[52] Davis, *Palestinian Village Histories*, 32.
[53] Dan Yahav notes that at present, only two or three mosques remain active out of the ten mosques that served the Muslim communities of Jaffa until 1948. From this list, only two – Hassan Beq Mosque and Mahmoudiyeh Mosque – are included in the centennial list. Yahav, *Yaffo, Bride of the Sea*, 31.
[54] "Kfar Salama Mosque".

that dramatically alter the relation between Jewish residents and the Arab building.

In the period before 1948, the compound containing the mosque and the shrine also included a library and a space for social gatherings for the Arab residents of Salama. In the cultural and architectural history of mosques, the incorporation of multi-purposed spaces in a single compound is not exceptional.[55] Patrick Gaffney reminds us that the first mosque built by Muhammad was the enclosed courtyard of his house in Madinah.[56] Beyond serving as the customary place for the performance of worship, it also served as the effective seat of governance, the centre of civil and military administration, and a place for the hospitality of strangers. In addition to their function as social, religious and political centres, mosques regularly served as schools, often under the tutelage of a local imam. Similarly, the adjacency of the Salama Mosque to a shrine commemorating Salama Ibn Hashem is linked to the Muslim traditional view of the mosque as a multifaceted assortment of spaces representing different spheres of life:

> To deflect the admonitions of the Muslim orthodox that perceived tomb building as irreligious, Arab builders in North Africa, Egypt, the Arabian Peninsula, and the Levant made the mausoleum part of larger religious complexes. The mausoleum is thus often one part of a complex composed of a mosque, madrasa, or religious school, and sometimes a hospital or khanqa (residence of a Sufi leader).[57]

The fluidity between sacred and profane spaces has its roots in the theological foundations of Islam. Traditionally, mosques possess certain features that are distinctly related to rituals of worship like the *mihrab*, a niche in the wall indicating the direction of Mecca; or the *minbar*, the pulpit from which the imam addresses the congregation. However, it is important to remember that to the Muslim believer, all things and spaces are equally subject to the will of God, and therefore the sharper Christian differentiation between sacred and profane does not apply. The consequences of this process are significant for the understanding of the social and spatial function of mosques: "In many respects, therefore, besides its religious role, the range of activities traditionally associated with the mosque was comparable to those previously associated with the Greek Agora or the Roman forum."[58] Modern mosques

---

[55] Yahav, *Yaffo, Bride of the Sea*, 48.
[56] Gaffney, "Masjid", 437–8.
[57] Kavuri-Bauer, "Architecture", 74.
[58] Frishman, *The Mosque*, 32.

in Israel still reflect this tradition, often using different storeys in the building for commerce, education, social events and religious practice.[59]

Like many other mosques in Arab towns and villages occupied during the 1948 War and resettled with Jewish residents, Salama Mosque was used for purposes other than prayer: the building was transformed into a local youth club operated by the municipality's welfare department.[60] Children from the neighbourhood would arrive at the club after school, do their homework and play in the yard. The club was the only facility for such purposes in the vicinity and served children from other neighbourhoods for after-school and summer activities. For many in an area with very limited financial means, this was a highly significant space.

Perhaps more than any other spatial feature, Arab sites of religious and symbolic significance like mosques, graves of local sheiks, shrines and cemeteries, evoke strong reactions against their appropriation in the post-1948 period. These sites convey the cultural codes that link a society to its territory and their appropriation by another is perceived and an intentional act that humiliates, as well as disinherits, the defeated population. This spectrum of sites, graves, cemeteries and shrines erected in the memory of religious figures or local communal leaders, obtain a special status because they form a "script of blood"[61] that testifies to one's ancestral connection to the earth.[62] In his analysis of native grave sites in south-west Africa, John Noyes explains that the grave obtains its exceptional status because it forms "the [material] marking of the earth and the marking of subjective affective economy: a script on the earth and script in the heart".[63] Given the way grave sites provide a space that links emotional and historical ties between people and place, the harsh reactions that their appropriation and reuse incites are only natural. During an academic symposium in Jerusalem, for example, Israeli-Arab architectural scholar Yosef Jabareen expressed the deep sensitivities to the non-religious use of former Palestinian spaces of worship, when he described the transformation of Salama Mosque as an act that had a "torturing" effect.[64]

It is noteworthy that this sense of direct embodied pain is expressed specifically with regard to a building that still remains standing,

---

[59] A'araff, Interview with the author.
[60] Kfar Shalem Neighbourhood Council, "Letter to Tel Aviv Mayor Shlomo Lahat".
[61] Noyes, *Colonial Space*, 258.
[62] See for example Falah, "The 1948 Israeli-Palestinian War and its Aftermath"; Benvenisti, *Sacred Landscape*.
[63] Noyes, *Colonial Space*, 258.
[64] Jabareen, "Response to 'Memory and Planning: Uses and Abuses'".

relatively intact and unharmed. In contrast, the two cemeteries that were situated just north and north-east of the mosque did not attract such an impassioned response. The first village cemetery that served the Palestinian residents of Salama until the 1920s is currently used as a small playground; the second cemetery, which was active until 1948, was demolished for the construction of a tenement block in the mid-1990s. Unlike the mosque, the cemeteries' subterranean nature makes them far less perceptible, and less ingrained into the practices of everyday life. The presence of the mosque sets it apart from the seemingly serene playground built on the old cemetery and the rubble that can still be identified on the site of the demolished newer one. Jabareen's reaction suggests that more than six decades after the occupation of the village, and after extensive changes have taken place throughout and around it – some which have altered its appearance altogether – the structure of the mosque and the shrine continues to carry distinctly identifiable features that mark it as the quintessentially Arab relic of Salama. This anger is directed at the desecration of the sacred space, at the same time as it protests against the perceived erasure of the cultural and historical meaning of the place – what Salman Abu Sitta describes as the "collective amnesia" that plagues the Jewish public in Israel. The political indifference and disrespect involved in the transformation of a mosque are intrinsically linked to the eradication of historical meaning of Palestinian life in Salama and in Israel-Palestine more broadly.

Transformation of the mosque started shortly after the occupation of the village. While the mosque also served non-religious purposes before the village's conquest in 1948, the new functions of the building resulted in its practical deconsecration. Physically, some parts of the building were altered to accommodate the new functions: the main hall, for example, was divided into smaller, classroom-sized spaces. Most of the features that identify the building as an Arab-Muslim site remain largely unchanged, externally and internally; even the *mihrab*, the traditional niche indicating the direction of prayer, is still clearly intact to this day. Nonetheless, the new function of the building appears to have largely disregarded its past as a sacred site, at least in the sense that it omits any explicit recognition of the place's cultural and religious significance.

Yet turning the former religious building into an integral part of the mundane routine of Kfar Shalem may have also contributed to its eventual survival. My thesis here suggests that the deconsecration of Salama Mosque, and the highly contentious abolition of its separation from the profane, daily routines of the new inhabitants, directly assisted in physically sustaining it and sublimating the antagonisms between the Jewish community of Kfar Shalem and the Arab past of the village.

Walid Khalidi's monumental study of the depopulated Arab-Palestinian villages in Israel was aptly titled *All that Remains*, alluding to the enormity of destruction of Arab space in Palestine.[65] Yet this title can also prompt us to seriously consider "all that remains" – the little that still stands – resisting powerful spatio-political mechanisms as well as sheer neglect and indifference. When numerous other mosques, shrines and grave sites were either intentionally demolished by the Israeli authorities during or shortly after the 1948 War, or left desolate and gradually crumbling into decay, the material endurance of Salama Mosque cannot be taken for granted. Some examples suggest that even sites of this sort which were used by Jews after 1948 did not survive natural erosion: in Kfar Gvirol, a Jewish neighbourhood established in the depopulated Arab village of Qubeiba, the mosque was used as a synagogue by Yemenite immigrants until it collapsed following a rain storm.[66] Investment of money and labour was required in order to sustain the structure and carry out the transformation of Salama Mosque, and these would not have been available without the intervention of official state and municipal bodies – the Welfare Ministry at first, and later the municipal Education Department.[67] To be sure, the authorities were not maintaining the building because of its symbolic value as a site of Muslim religious significance; if at all, the work was done in spite of this. However, in actual terms, this resulted in the physical conservation of one of the clearest sites of Salama's Arab spatial history, in and as part of Kfar Shalem.

By describing the physical maintenance of the mosque as a process of conservation, as opposed to preservation, I wish to point out a qualitative difference between these two related notions. Despite their etymological proximity, preservation and conservation are not homonymous: while sharing a similar root, *servō*, meaning to save or rescue, each prefix points out an inherently different approach to the performance of spatial history. The Latin prefix of the former, *pre* or *prae*, designates previous, beforehand and prior, and thus can be read as "to keep in a previous state". This definition emphasises the effort to maintain the object in a static form and supposes a clear historical referent that provides a model toward which one should aspire. *Conservation*, on the other hand, presents a fundamentally different relation to the

[65]   Khalidi, *All That Remains*.
[66]   Benjamin, " 'Present-Absent' ".
[67]   Rabinowitz, "Club on 16 Righteous Street in Kfar Shalem".

past. The prefix *con* means "together; of sympathy, union ... mutually". It therefore assigns a wholly different imperative through which *servō* is carried out, one which does not rely on the temporal dimensions of before and after, but rather on a spatial relation of proximity and simultaneity. It is through a shared existence that saving or maintaining can happen; unlike what we may describe as a "preservationist" approach, conservation does not imply that evolution and change are inherently a threat to the past. Instead, another relation between past and present is suggested, where each is reliant on, and is facilitated by, the other.

In addition to the physical maintenance of the building, the activity of the youth club opened the mosque to the social and practical networks that took part in the formation of Kfar Shalem's spatial history. To further explore this process, we can focus on two aspects of Lefebvre's triad of spatial production;[68] while leaving aside those aspects of space that are produced through abstractions of science or politics, we can shift our attention to the way the mosque was conserved as part of the daily practices of people and the impact this had on its meaning and significance.[69] In terms of spatial practices, the transformation of the mosque most notably altered its status as a set-apart sacred space, a site that is distinguished from its surroundings by symbolic significance. The special meaning associated with the set-apart sacred does not necessarily imply its exclusion from the general public space, but assumes more complex social and cultural criteria that condition and limit access. Needless to say, access into a youth club does not require ablution or spiritual intent. Without disregarding the moral and political contentions involved, in practical terms deconsecration meant that the building was frequented and incorporated into a broader network of paths and routes that formed public space of Salama/Kfar Shalem after 1948.

Spatial practice is also closely linked to the representational aspects of space; namely, the meaning and significance associated with spatial objects and forms. Lefebvre posits that what he terms "lived" environments, defined by physical use and practice, are often changed and appropriated through imagination and representation. Representational

---

[68] Lefebvre, *The Production of Space*.

[69] This is of course a methodological suspension that takes on Alon Confino's critique of prevalent trends in cultural history and memory research, which often subordinate specific practices of reception and contestation to an overarching story of construction. Confino, "Collective Memory and Cultural History", 1395–9. Lefebvre himself notes that "conceptualized space", space that emerges from "technocratic subdividers and social engineers ... is the dominant space in any society" – which again rearticulated the need to critically reconsider this subjugation. See Lefebvre, *The Production of Space*, 38–9.

space overlays physical space, making symbolic use of its objects.[70] In other words, images and symbols can take priority over the materiality and physical presence of things. However, as we have seen throughout this analysis, the superimposition of symbolic meaning on physical space is never hermetic, and previous histories, which are embedded in that space, are not simply blocked out. When discussing a site that exhibits distinct features like the domed building of Salama Mosque, the question becomes even more pressing: did the significant change of function also blur the historical meaning of the place and bring about a selective amnesia regarding its Muslim and Arab past? Archival evidence suggests that this was not the case. The building's identification as "the mosque" continues to appear in official correspondences, conversations and mundane references decades after it ceased serving this purpose.[71] The idiosyncratic appearance of the building established it as a central landmark with relation to which, for example, directions are given; "The mosque", not "the youth club", acted as the central orientation reference in Kfar Shalem.

Undoubtedly, these are prosaic examples that may well be dismissed as anecdotal. Debates about post-war transformation often blur the difference between historical knowledge and its political utilisation, between "ordinary" people's ability to identify the signs of previous stratum around them, and the lack of a "proper" ethical, moral or political response. In a book which emerges, according to its author, from recent critical trends of spatial and historical writing in Israel, Noga Kadman suggests that the depopulated Palestinian villages were relegated from the Israeli discourse and contends that "the dispossession of the Palestinians by Jewish communities established on depopulated villages" was never followed by a meaningful engagement "with their history, the circumstances of their depopulation and the moral question of making use of their houses and property".[72] Kadman adopts a broader critical position that views the space of the former Arab villages as fundamentally a "space of representation" in Lefebvre's terms, mediated through maps, signs and pamphlets produced by official Israeli bodies like the Jewish National Fund or the Israel Nature and National Parks Protection Authority. To be sure, Kadman's analysis of official mediation of space and the construction of authoritative narratives is a valid one, providing important insights

[70] Lefebvre, *The Production of Space*, 39.
[71] See for example: Halamish, Municipal-Governmental Company for Housing in Gush Dan, "Kefar Shalem Survey. The Construction and Eviction of Development Areas", 30; Rabinowitz, "Club on 16 Righteous Street in Kefar Shalem"; Kefar Shalem Neighbourhood Council, "Letter to Tel Aviv Mayor Shlomo Lahat".
[72] Kadman, *Erased from Space and Consciousness*, 14.

into the ideological and political production of spatial power relations. The problem emerges when official signs and state publications are seen to be the only sources through which space becomes historically intelligible. My concern here, and in the analysis of spatial phenomena throughout this book, is that unless we broaden the analytical prism to include other, more prosaic expressions of spatial knowledge, space and history are reduced to narrow political constructs. As Alon Confino rightly notes,

one unfortunate side effect of treating memory as a symptom of politics is the lack of explorations of power in areas that are not politically evident. Consequently, a search for memory traces is made mostly among visible places and familiar names, where memory construction is explicit and its meaning palpably manipulated, while in fact we should look for memory where it is implied rather than said, blurred rather than clear, in the realm of collective mentality. We miss a whole world of human activities that cannot be immediately recognized (and categorized) as political, although they are decisive to the way people construct and contest images of the past.[73]

In all certainty, the historical preoccupation with the Arab history of Israel remains outside the mainstream public debate in Israel. As Kadman and others note, only in recent years have we seen the rise of small critical groups that attempt to reinsert these historical chapters into public discourse. Also from the margins, but from the spatial periphery of Tel Aviv and not the critical margins of Israeli academic and activist discourse, Aharon Maduel, a resident of Kfar Shalem, provides a challenging articulation of the encounter between the Jewish residents and the Arab village of Salama. His narrative is historically informed and politically infused, though it refrains from the kind of moral apologetics that are often implicit in similar narratives:

People tell that there were pots on kerosene burners, the Arabs left equipment, houses that were breathing and were expelled from them. There was an aqueduct in the garden, a well, trees that Arabs planted, a cemetery. After the [1967] Six Day War, Palestinians from the territories came for a few visits to see their houses. They were well received and workers from Gaza also lived in rented apartments in the village. In general, I feel we are refugees like them, we left Arab countries, we left property, houses, our parents suffered because of the War of Independence here.[74]

Maduel, the son of Yemenite immigrants, was not yet born when his parents arrived in the village. But for this reason, his account gives

[73] Confino, "Collective Memory and Cultural History", 1394–5.
[74] Quoted in Baruch, "Operation Bi'ur Hametz", 86.

evidence not only of the depopulation of Salama but also of communal traditions that circulate and convey the historical knowledge of the village. Oral transmission of the encounter between the new residents and the Arab village is one source that is alluded to in this process. But no less significant is the way physical, spatial and material elements play a central role in informing this narrative. Maduel is not oblivious to the past of the village, and the significance of the Arab spaces he refers to – houses, cemetery and garden – is neither silenced nor meaningless. Furthermore, this historical narrative uses the space of the neighbourhood to tie together some of the most contentious issues of Israeli and Zionist history: from Jewish-Arab relations in the Muslim world to the occupation of the Gaza Strip and the West Bank in 1967 and recent conflicts between Arab residents of Jaffa and real-estate developers.[75] Although Maduel is an active political figure in the neighbourhood and the city, his knowledge is not the exception. When asked what he knows about Salama Mosque, a young man in a kiosk across the street from the mosque corrected me: "This is actually a Muslim grave, not just a mosque", he said.

The practical conservation of Salama Mosque and its inclusion within and as part of the daily life of Kfar Shalem, enabled it to convey a multilayered history in a mundane, even intimate, fashion. However, despite, and perhaps because of this unique quality of conservation, it also poses a highly complex and demanding challenge. The heterogeneity of space not only holds liberating implications of different pasts lived mutually, it also acknowledges the ability of contradicting and contesting histories to share a single space, without assuming that these conflicts have been fully resolved. Some critics have suggested that these

residues from earlier time have become important sites of pleasure ... because these fragments reawaken forgotten memories that have long been dormant, or because their original function and purpose have been erased, allowing the viewer to substitute invented traditions and imaginary narrations.[76]

But pleasure is only one of an array of responses that can arise from an encounter between past and present. At the same time this endeavour

---

[75] In the interview, Maduel states: "Because of Zionism here, Arab Jews also suffered ... We are refugees without rights on the land since 1948, because in [19]60 my parents were prevented from purchasing our lands, not like with the *kibbutzim* and the *moshavim* [cooperative villages]. We were left on suitcases for 60 years ... The dispossession here is like in Jaffa, the same system, get out of your house without compensation." Quoted in ibid.

[76] Boyer, *The City of Collective Memory*, 19.

runs the risk of evoking other emotions that are far less gratifying, bringing back what Freud famously described as a sense of the uncanny; namely, "that species of the frightening that goes back to what was once well known and had long been familiar".[77] The heterogeneous nature of spatial history conserves not only the desired and enjoyable past, but also what may be seen as signs of painful pasts and a threatening present. While the sign may well be the site of "the completely other", as Derrida[78] posits, it is not at all clear whether this otherness is desired or dreaded.

The history of Salama Mosque did not come to an end in April 1981, when the Tel Aviv Municipality decided to close the youth club and refer children to another community centre built north of the neighbourhood.[79] Parents from the neighbourhood petitioned the mayor against the closure, but were told that cuts in municipal education services resulted in the final decision to terminate the activity of the club. Local residents saw the situation differently, suggesting that the closure of the mosque was just another attempt by the Tel Aviv Municipality to "starve the local centre and transfer all the services outside the village".[80] In practical and spatial terms, the closure of the club resulted in the actual division between the building and the neighbourhood's public sphere. If conservation depends on the coexistence of the past in the present, what might be termed as "maintenance by integration", then the detachment of the mosque from the neighbourhood's public life marked a turning point in its relation to its surroundings. In terms of sacred spatiality, the building regained its set-apart status, but in a way that never existed in the past: this was not the re-establishment of a division between the sacred and the profane, with the former set apart by religious rites and restrictions. The building, now fenced and locked, was literally and physically off limits.

Rupture

Exactly 20 years will pass before the process that sees the isolation of the mosque and the growing alienation between it and the socio-spatial reality of Kfar Shalem will reach a crucial point of collision. Following Ariel Sharon's visit to the Temple Mount / Haram esh-Sharif in Jerusalem on 28 September 2000, widespread violence erupted in Israel, the West Bank and Gaza Strip. Violent clashes

---

[77] Freud, *The Uncanny*, 124.
[78] Derrida, *The Gift of Death*, 68.
[79] Rabinowitz, "Club on 16 Righteous Street in Kfar Shalem".
[80] Ben-David, Interview with the author.

between Israeli-Arab protesters and police also spread into mixed cities, where violence erupted between Jewish and Arab residents. In addition to physical assault against individuals, property and businesses, rioters often directed their acts at symbolic sites: in Shfaram, an ancient synagogue was desecrated and in Jaffa and Haifa Molotov cocktails were thrown at synagogues; mosques in Herzeliya, Tiberius and Nazareth Illit were targeted by Jewish rioters; near Haifa, police prevented Jews from attacking the grave site of the prominent Sheikh Izz ad-Din al-Qassam; and the Hassan Beq Mosque between Tel Aviv and Jaffa became a site of recurring clashes between Jewish and Arab groups.[81] These events share a relatively clear common denominator: violence channelled toward sites that hold symbolic significance is in itself a public demoralisation of the opposing group, and almost every ethnic or religious violent conflict includes manifestations of this sort. However, the state commission that investigated the events also noted a less well-known incident that took place on 9 October 2000:

Approximately 200 Jews carrying metal [bars] arrived in Kfar Shalem with the intention of tearing down a sheik's grave in the place. Approximately 20 police officers from the Yiftach precinct armed with clubs surrounded the grave to shield it from the crowd. The rioters were successful in getting close to the mosque and were able to batter it ... After this, the rioters dispersed.[82]

At first, the attack on the Salama Mosque in Kfar Shalem appears to be just one incident in a chain of violent events that occurred during the October 2000 clashes.[83] Yet the attempt to bring down the mosque and shrine in Kfar Shalem stands out from similar actions around the country, because the violence in this case was directed at a site that had not served as an active mosque for more than five decades, and practically stood empty for two.[84] While the building may have stood abandoned

---

[81] Or, Hatib and Shamir, "The Official Commission for the Investigation of Clashes Between the Security Forces and Israeli Citizens in October 2000", vol. 2, chapter 5.

[82] Ibid., n. 193.

[83] During fieldwork conducted in the neighbourhood, I encountered two versions of the story regarding the time of the attack. According to one version, the events described above took place following the suicide terror attack outside the Dolphinarium night club in Tel Aviv on 1 June 2001. Fundamentally, this does not change the basic thesis proposed in this chapter, but it raises a question about the unstable transmission of historical knowledge and the role of rumour as "trigger and mobiliser" of collective political action. See, in this regard, Guha, *Elementary aspects of Peasant Insurgency*, 256.

[84] Only one other disused mosque, Masjid Sayyidna Ali, the burial site of al-Hasan ibn Ali, near Hertzeliya, was reported to have been attacked by Jewish protesters, although its location near one of Israel's most popular public beaches distinguishes it from the relatively unknown Salama Mosque.

and disused, the time that passed did not erode its identification as a container of symbolic meaning; in the eyes of the Jewish protesters there was no doubt that the building was "Arab" or "Muslim", and in any case, a worthy target of anger, aggression and fear.

This incident presents profound questions about the reappearance of dormant historical residues, the function of material and spatial objects in this process, and a relation between terror and territory that goes beyond their suspected etymological proximity. It was suggested above that spatial conservation be understood as the cohabitation of past and present in a mutually dependent relation. The Salama Mosque was conserved by its practical incorporation into people's lives and daily networks; without these, one would not expect Hannah Zohar, a resident of Kfar Shalem, to appeal to the mayor to prevent the closure of a building which she describes as a "kind of home for the children of the neighbourhood".[85] But conservation is not simply the harmonious existence of past and present, and it most certainly does not identify historical meaning solely around sites that may be considered as aesthetically pleasurable (picturesque),[86] financially profitable (gentrified) or historically compliant with a nationally or ethnically cohesive narrative.[87] The histories of war, depopulation, dispossession and marginalisation have sedimented into the physical landscape of Salama/Kfar Shalem, and illustrate more or less explicit expressions of these pasts. Conservation indeed allows for a spatial simultaneity of histories that are often seen as diametrically opposed, but the conflicts that inform these oppositions are not erased. The process that resulted in the 2000 attack on the empty mosque in Kfar Shalem articulates the ambiguity and tension that are integral to conservation as it is described here, and to spatial history more generally.

According to one Israeli security official, the events of October 2000 were the most severe case of public disorder since the establishment of the State of Israel.[88] Former Knesset member Azmi Bishara explained

---

[85] Zohar, "Letter to Tel Aviv Mayor Shlomo Lahat".

[86] Brian Dillon's article on the representation and perception of ruins in art and art history succinctly charts the aesthetic pleasure often associated with ruins and their picturesque quality. Dillon, "Fragments From a History of Ruin". See also Roth, Lyons and Merewether, *Irresistible Decay*.

[87] The gentrification of Arab parts of Jaffa is explored by Mark LeVine through what he describes as the combined force of capitalist and national ideologies. See LeVine, *Overthrowing Geography*, chapter 8. Rotbard, *White City, Black City*, takes a similar approach. In a recent book, Tali Hatuka refines this prism by focusing on the operation of real-estate and capitalism through what she describes as Revisionist Moments that occur around act of violence. See Hatuka, *Revisionist Moments*.

[88] Or, Hatib and Shamir, "The Official Commission for the Investigation of Clashes Between the Security Forces and Israeli Citizens in October 2000", vol. 2, n. 50.

that for Palestinian citizens of Israel, the violence reflected a collective disillusionment, a sense that established political institutions and democratic channels had reached a "dead end" and that "a dynamics between the population and its leadership was created to protest in a more radical way".[89] In the eyes of many Jewish-Israelis, this "dead end" was perceived as an existential threat similar to the dangers faced by the Jewish *yishuv* during the 1948 War. The eruption of explicit and large-scale violent events throughout the country ruptured the traditional division between the frontier and home front in a manner that was not felt even during the terror acts of the 1990s. Furthermore, Israeli media reports blurred the distinction between the violent clashes in Israel and those which took place between Palestinians and the Israeli army in the West Bank and Gaza Strip, therefore accentuating the sense of a combined internal and external threat to the state.[90] On the second day of the violence (2 October), for example, Israel's most popular daily newspaper – *Yedioth Ahronoth* – reported the events under a large headline spread over two pages which read, "War of Independence?" The open question alludes to the Palestinian demand for independence from Israel's occupation and, simultaneously, to the Jewish sense that the State of Israel was itself once again fighting for its independence. Following the same logic, the photograph accompanying the report was appropriately entitled "Battle without Boundaries".

The collapse of boundaries and the potential emergence of limitless violence are crucial for understanding the attack against the empty Salama Mosque. For Jewish residents in Kfar Shalem and Shekhunat Hatikva, the collapse of spatial distinctions and temporal sequences – the threat that is omnipresent and always in-the-present – triggered the reappearance of the Arab village of Salama. In other words, replaying "1948" literally resulted in the re-emergence of former Arab spaces that were, like Freud's concept of the uncanny, "well known and had long been familiar".

As a foundational event, "1948" continues to run through the cultural bloodstream of Israel: when filtered through state mechanisms, it is transmuted through social practices and symbols, which organise and structure it into commemorative narratives that "glue" the social bonds of the imagined community.[91] But underneath this seemingly structured façade of history narrated orally, graphically or through practices and rituals,[92] "1948" also inscribed itself into the spatial history of Israel,

[89] Quoted in ibid., vol. 2, n. 149.
[90] Neiger, Zandberg and Abu-Ra'iyeh, "Civil or Ethnic Media?", 8–9.
[91] Sivan, "To Remember Is to Forget"; Azaryahu, *State Cults*.
[92] Obviously, this historical narration itself never achieves stasis: it remains very much in flux, conserving within it the contradictions and inconsistencies that attest to the

those "spatial *forms and fantasies* through which a society declares its presence".[93] If we are to seriously consider Carter's thesis, then the spatial archive may well contain declarations not only of the dominant societal currents but of conflicting and contrasting trends as well.

The attack on the empty mosque was aimed against a declaration of presence, which articulated itself spatially and materially but was nonetheless clearly comprehensible. Those who set out to demolish the empty building did not identify it as the former neighbourhood youth club or an empty space vacant of human activity and therefore of meaning. Instead, it was identified as the quintessential symbol of Salama, the Arab village from which an attack was launched on Shekhunat Hatikva in December 1947, and against which Israeli paramilitary forces operated during the first months of the 1948 War. What I have described as the resurfacing of 1948 into the Israeli present is in fact a re-encounter with physical and historical residues that had always been there. More than the recurring identification of the Arab village, what is striking is the uncanny repetition of Jewish reaction against empty Arab spaces. The torching of empty Arab houses in Salama by a mob from Shekhunat Hatikva in the very first days after the Arab residents of the village were forced to flee their homes[94] comes to mind in this respect. The 2000 attack suggests that historical matter and meaning in Salama/Kfar Shalem were not completely eroded, despite extensive social and spatial processes of change that took place in and around it. Like the ethnic wars in the former Yugoslavia, and the Northern Irish troubles, the 2000 events signify an extraordinary reluctance to forget the past alongside obvious difficulties of coming to terms with its unresolved rootedness in the present.

So far, I have charted the relation of the attack on Salama Mosque to the macro-historical sphere of national politics and ethnic conflict in Israel. However, these events must also be understood in light of the site-specific process through which the set-apart sacredness of the mosque was replaced by the profane space of the youth club. While this act may well be interpreted as a malicious desecration, it also conserved the mosque and maintained its place as part of the public space of the neighbourhood. In terms of practical engagement, the site retained a set-apart quality once it was closed and sealed off in 1981, but this was

---

ongoing struggle for stability. Hannan Hever traces these tensions in his analysis of Hebrew literature in the twentieth century; the collection *50 to 48* follows similar critical ruptures during the first 50 years of the State of Israel while focusing on social, cultural and political aspects. Ophir, *50 to 48*.

[93] Carter, *The Road to Botany Bay*, xxii, italics added.

[94] "Unsigned Logbook Entry".

a state of limbo: the mosque was not used, but nonetheless it remained part of the visible landscape of the neighbourhood. Without the social and practical ties to its surroundings, the mosque regained the status of a monument, "no longer quite life, not yet death, like shells on the shore when the sea of living memory has receded".[95] Setting-apart also meant that since its closure, the identification of the site as "the youth club (in the mosque)", a phrase that recurs in archival documentation until 1981, is reversed: "the mosque" becomes the main point of reference and the youth club appears only as an afterthought, if at all. The eruption of nationwide violence in October 2000 was only the eventual trigger that set the Arab past and Jewish present in Salama/Kfar Shalem on a destructive collision course.

Aftermaths

The police report on the events of 9 October 2000 suggests that the riots around the mosque were over once the protesters dispersed. The report does not, however, mention that protesters fractured one of the domes of the building and created a hole that remains visible to this day. More than a decade after the attack we are confronted with another layer of events that left their mark on the spatial history of Salama/Kfar Shalem.

In a recent study of violent events in Tel Aviv, Tali Hatuka suggests that violent terror attacks in the city are often followed by an effort to reassert a sense of order and stability.[96] What she describes as Revisionist Moments are the combined operation of official state branches and private stakeholders, groups and individuals, to recuperate the physical and symbolic fracturing of space caused by the violent act. Yet restoring a sense of order in the aftermath of a violent event is not a simple clean-up operation, as it is closely linked to physical and symbolic spheres of life. The problem becomes ever more acute when the violent act is perpetrated not by a foreigner who can be forced out, but by and toward that which is close and familiar; when it is unclear how one delineates the boundaries between inside and outside and when a clear-cut distinction between perpetrators and victims is hard to make. Furthermore, if the attack on the mosque indeed occurred during a "War without Borders", how does one delineate the beginning and end of the Revisionist Moment, both in terms of its temporal duration (when and for how long?), its spatial occurrence (where?) and objective (for or against what?).

---

[95] Nora, "Between Memory and History", 11.
[96] Hatuka, *Revisionist Moments*.

The notion of revision – as a form of recuperative act that follows moments of violence – is insufficient if we are to fully come to terms with the relations between the spatial, social and political realms in Israel, and if we are fully to grasp the way the riots around the mosque testify to a deeper and more complex relation between time and space. Even before the riots, the space of the village was not governed by conventional divisions that compartmentalise and organise relations between past and present. As a result, the hope that some form of *a posteriori* correction will take place in its aftermath seems wishful thinking.

In an interview with a right-wing news website prior to the Tel Aviv local elections in November 2008, Arnon Giladi, an outspoken political figure in the city, announced that he intended to reopen the mosque for the operation of a youth club "without delay":

> It is well known that Muslims do not sanctify their graves like Jews … Only when Jews try to build and operate a youth club – [then] there are Jewish and Arab extremists that use the opportunity for political propaganda against Jews. I am not interested in all that. I only want to create a cultural centre for youth and young people in a place that already served that purpose. If anyone from the extreme left wants to explicitly act against the concerns of the youth in the neighbourhoods of Tel Aviv – he will encounter a very determined stance by myself and the sane voices in the municipality.[97]

It is easy to dismiss Giladi's idea as a populist, pre-election provocation. However, it presents a noteworthy challenge on two accounts. First, it questions the validity of the assumption that convalescence and equilibrium are actual objectives that are pursued after a violent rupture of stability. The period that followed the attack in Kfar Shalem did not bring about any revision in the form of a discursive or practical engagement with the event, its grounds or repercussions. The hole in the dome of the mosque was never fully fixed and remains visible as a testimony to the impact of the violent collision between the Arab space and the Jewish residents. An "open hole" also exists in people's willingness or ability to speak about the events. Avshalom Ben-David was open to discuss at length almost any question that regarded the history of the village. However, when asked about the October 2000 events, he replied: "Forget about it. It is not important. I really don't understand why people keep bringing this up."[98] Ben-David does, nonetheless, have a solid opinion about the reopening of the mosque to the residents:

---

[97] Ezra, " 'We will renew the operation of the club at all cost' ".
[98] Ben-David, Interview with the author.

I think it's a good idea. Why not? Since they sold the *Histadrut* House [trade union club], there is nowhere for us to meet. During the 1990s, when we organised a demonstration against house demolition, we met in one of the synagogues to discuss the action and left from there ... We no longer do that. It's not respectful to turn the synagogues into a political place. So when they came to demolish the houses on [the street corner of] Mahal-Moshe Dayan and we had no place to meet and organise people, I told Arnon [Giladi]: "Let's break the lock, and use the mosque as our meeting place."

The attack on the mosque was only one point in a longer process of Salama/Kfar Shalem's spatial history, in which the Arab presence is negotiated as part of the lives of those who encounter it on a daily basis; namely, the neighbourhood's Jewish residents. For both Ben-David and Giladi, this presence is not merely symbolic or metaphoric. On separate occasions, both suggested that the reopening of the youth club in the mosque would be a preventive measure to counter a perceived threat of Arab-Palestinian claims. Giladi noted that "Muslims visit the grave with students to show them: 'which parts of the city used to be owned by them in the past'".[99] Ben-David went further: for him, reopening the mosque would establish "facts on the ground", equating this act to the "outposts built by settlers in the West Bank", which concretise claims over a disputed land. Whether these analogies are historically founded is of lesser significance. Instead, it is important to note how the mosque's reappearance takes place at crucial moments when the fusion between people and place is seen to be questioned or challenged, first through the threat of house demolition and forced eviction, and second by the possibility that "Arabs" or "Muslims" will reclaim their rights and ownership over property. As shown above, the nationwide violence in October 2000 was perceived as a similar threat, only on a larger scale. In all cases, opening the mosque – as a proposition or in violent action – is a performative act that reinstates the Jewish residents' sense of possession over the entire space of the neighbourhood, especially those spaces that have drifted away from the practised public space.

There is obviously less comfort in seeing the attack on Salama Mosque in October 2000 not as an isolated incident of disorder, nor as a culmination of a process, but as an extreme expression of the unresolved tensions between past and present, between Jewish Israelis and the Arab spaces they inhabit. This view does not offer the (real or imagined) relief one senses in the Revisionist Moment that supposedly takes place in the aftermath of the terror attack. At least in Kfar Shalem, no official body took it upon itself to mend the hole in the dome, and there is

---

[99] Ezra, "'We will renew the operation of the club at all cost'".

little enthusiasm to air the grievances that triggered the incident in the public realm. Instead of catharsis, there is anticipation of the next event that will challenge the seclusion of the mosque, and break in through the locked gate or through the fractured dome. The various proposals to reopen the Salama Mosque challenge the assumption that political violence is necessarily followed by an effort to restore stability and reinstate a sense of order. "Order", in this case, only conceals the fear and anxiety that are still expressed in the face of the empty mosque.

However, the plan – or threat – to reopen the youth club in Salama Mosque also presents a potential weakness of the thesis presented in this chapter, in that it highlights the way conservation can be appropriated into a populist and chauvinist discourse. Conservation as the mutual reliance between past and present – which highlights practical engagement as a form of pragmatic sustenance that avoids the monumentalisation of the past – can easily be seen as rhetorical manoeuvering that neutralises and depoliticises highly controversial acts.[100] This is a valid critique that needs to be carefully considered. In the case of Salama Mosque, even if we ignore the insidious tone of Giladi's proposal, reopening the youth club while ignoring two decades during which the building was sealed is a highly selective and limited use of conservation. It ignores the severity of events that preceded the mosque's transformation in the first place, and disregards the fact that the events that have occurred since 1981 cannot be ignored or undone: the building is (once again) identified as "the mosque". In 1948, transforming a mosque into a youth club resulted from a set of cataclysmic events, from a major war and the depopulation of entire regions, to severe socioeconomic plight. Although there is no reason to suspect that events of such magnitude are likely to recur any time soon, examples from Israel and around the world provide stark reminders of the violent potential of such attempts to turn back the wheels of time.[101]

---

[100] I am grateful to Susan Slyomovics for pointing this out during a round table discussion at the Van Leer Jerusalem Institute, December 2006.

[101] The Great Mosque in the southern Israeli city of Beersheba is an exemplary case. The municipality intends to reopen the Negev Museum which operated in the building from 1953 to 1991. In February 2002, local Muslim groups petitioned the Supreme Court to prevent the municipality from renovating and reopening the museum in the building. The petition also called for the reopening of the Great Mosque for Muslim prayer. Individual attempts to pray in the building resulted in clashes with police and violent confrontations with Jewish groups. See: Mousa, "Beer el-Sabe Municipality Refuses to Allow Muslim Residents". See also the Israeli High Court motion H.C. 7311/02, *Association for Support and Defense of Bedouin Rights in Israel, et. al. v. The Municipality of Beer Sheva, et. al.,* (case pending). The dispute between Muslims and Christians in Nazareth over a plot near the Basilica of the Annunciation,

It would be naïve to suggest that conservation, as a spatial practice that highlights the mutual dependency between past and present layers, can overcome the historical and political conflicts that plague the Israeli space. Like other formulations that try to delineate alternative forms of practice, it is limited in time and space, emerging from site-specific conditions and historical contingencies. As the recent voices calling for the reopening of the mosque indicate, it is prone to be used to justify or excuse actions that seek to capitalise on the reappropriation of the Arab-Muslim sign. There is therefore a sense of irony in the fact that specifically these views, which provoke and antagonise, are responsible for keeping the mosque alive in the public sphere. Without these, the mosque would certainly be drawn back into the silence that surrounds it before and after each eruption. The conservation of the mosque cannot exist without its exposure to the public sphere, even when this runs the risk of revealing the sensitivities, fears and grievances that are still deeply felt by Arabs and Jews who are forced to live within this conflicted spatial history.

Sacred spaces in present-day Kfar Shalem point to two differing results of conservation: while the synagogues built in Arab shops, cafés and houses present surprising resilience that conserves historical layers with unassuming subtlety, the mosque illustrates the opposite end of the spectrum, as a site of confrontation and alienation. The social, cultural and spatial qualities associated with the scared do not, in themselves, guarantee the intricate coexistence and interdependency of the Arab past and the Jewish present. In other words, setting apart does not defuse the historical tensions that materialise in space. For that to happen, a shift is required in the conventions through which history is acknowledged in spatial and material terms. At present, acknowledgement of past events requires some form of tangible spatial representation – a monument, a commemorative garden – and its accompaniment by text that will explicate its significance beyond the visual and the functional. It is this narration that stands at the core of the memorialisation act; without it, the site is perceived as devoid of symbolic or historic importance. This signifying act sets the memorial apart from its

---

which resulted in physical confrontations in the city in April 1999, is another case that exhibits the explosive potential of spatial transformation. See Gal, "Big Bang in Nazareth". The violence that erupted following the destruction of the Babri Mosque in Ayodhya, India, is but one, albeit extreme example of the consequences of spatial transformation in an ethnically charged environment. The 1992 demolition of the mosque by Hindu nationalists resulted in the death of 2,000 people in riots that consequently broke out throughout India. Oza, "The Geography of Hindu Right-Wing Violence in India".

surroundings, and through this process it acquires quasi-sacred quali-ties:[102] while in the public realm, it is regarded as having exceptional status, at times providing a stage for the performance of commemora-tive rituals. Without this declarative text which sets it apart, the site's history is presumed silent or muted, and therefore forgotten.[103]

Within these conventions, there is something almost heretical in the suggestion that some forms of narration are better left outside the still highly-charged engagement between the Jewish residents of Kfar Shalem today, and the Arab history of Salama. As the examples in this chapter show, instances of spatial survival often require a much more profound deconsecration of conventional norms of memory, allow-ing for practical and pragmatic engagement to form the basis through which contentious histories can coincide. Nevertheless, it is impossible to ignore the personal sensitivities, ethical considerations and politi-cal implications that are invoked by this shift toward pragmatic spa-tial conservation. The concluding chapter of this book addressed these issues at length and situates spatial practices of conservation in the broader context of memory politics in Israel.

[102] Though these, in turn, are open to contestation and practical incorporation that may ignore or subvert its exceptional status.

[103] In some cases, this silence is read as the sign of trauma, as the inability or unwilling-ness to recognise the painful events that are associated with the place. As a result, commemoration is understood to be part of a social and cultural healing process. The Centre for the Study of Violence and Reconciliation in South Africa provides a succinct expression of this view: "Memory, as perpetuated through processes such as memorialization seen in national monuments, re-naming of streets, commemorative celebrations etc., can assist divided societies to re-write the narratives of the past; rec-ognise and assist survivors of human rights violations to begin the process of healing; and assist the previously divided society in processes of reconciliation."

Conclusion: Histories of the Rough and Charmless

> The cataclysm has happened, we are among the ruins, we start to build up new little habitats, to have new little hopes. It is rather hard work: there is now no smooth road into the future: but we go round, or scramble over the obstacles. We've got to live, no matter how many skies have fallen.
>
> – *Lady Chatterley's Lover*, D.H. Lawrence

This book began with a conundrum: the steadfast presence of Arab material and cultural history in Israel, and its ability to survive the cataclysmic events of war, ethnic depopulation and destruction, and overcome powerful ideological mechanisms that operate to alter its meaning. Under these conditions, the resilience of space is itself far from obvious, pointing to specific qualities that record and maintain the traces of the past in physical form and in cultural representation. However, this is not a fascination with relics or remainders. Instead I sought to trace the effects this presence continues to have on the individuals and communities who inhabit Israel's former Arab space, the official bodies that govern these spaces, and the cultural mechanisms that mediate historical identities and political allegiances. As such, this project shares a concern for the present as much as it has an interest in the past.[1] Spatial history, it posits, provides a powerful analytical instrument to account for the distinct qualities of space as a repository of present pasts, relating knowledge of past events and offering an insight into their concrete reverberations in the present.

My return to history as it unfolds in space takes place in opposition to two seemingly distinct schools of thought that have shaped the relation between spatiality and historical knowledge in Israel, although each is deeply rooted in broader scholarly and political trends. The first may be described as the "grand spatiality" which harnessed space for the realisation of Zionist aspirations and its national-ideological interests. From

---

[1] Foucault's method of "writing a history of the present" has clear resonance here. Foucault, *Discipline and Punish*; see also, Garland, "What is a 'History of the Present'?"

198

the days of its inception, Zionism has relentlessly invested its political, financial and ideological resources in moulding space as the breed-
ing ground for a national community and for the historical revival of
Jewish sovereignty. In this grand scheme, space has a pivotal role to
play as the container of historical roots that convey the programmatic
bond between people and land, as well as providing the stage on which
national revival can be realised. It was a powerful narrative that took
on hegemonic features, most notably in the three decades that followed
the establishment of the State of Israel as it dominated the physical formation of the national territory and the range of cultural-ideological
meanings it was supposed to convey. Through it, the teleological transition from exile to national revival, from destruction to redemption,
and from diasporic existence to territorial independence, could all be
embodied and experienced in concrete cultural forms, physical sites
and social practices.

Against the dominance of this hegemonic conception of space, a second school of thought promoted what may be described as "counter-
spatiality" that sought to re-present groups and narratives that have
been left out of the mainstream of the Israeli space, or suppressed and
negated in the process of its production. Furthermore, this critical effort
was directed at exposing the collaboration between existing forms of
knowledge production and the prevailing mechanisms of the state.[2]
Israeli space no longer contained just the homogenous ethno-national
narratives, but was gradually populated with histories of the destruction of Palestinian life, the marginalisation of Arab-Jewish communities
and the calculated effort to neutralise and disguise its ethno-national
ideological bias.

Countering the Zionist hegemony of space entailed a critique of
its ideological predispositions, the physical and cultural practices
employed in its production, and the mechanisms that enabled its perseverance. Yet the deep structures on which Zionist spatial logic was
founded remained remarkably uncontested. In particular, this critique
failed to notice or challenge the entrenched perception of space as a
passive platform that could be perfectly moulded to serve ideological

---

[2] In the 1991 introduction to the first issue of the journal *Teoryah Uvikoret* [Theory and
Criticism] – one of the leading arenas for the development of critical discourse in Israel
– the editors note that "in the present state, the academic system [in Israel] contributes
to the production and the preservation of dominant representations of reality more
than to the decoding and exposure of their ideological function, or the creation of alternative representations ... Academia disseminates, together with the media and through
it, instruments for the organisation of the new and the unknown into the familiar coor-
dinate system of the old order, and in the easily digestible terms of a dominant lexicon."
"Introduction", 1.

and political functions. Despite staunch political and ideological divisions, both adherents of Zionism and their critics adopted the textual metaphor of space, which equates the space on the earth with the space of a page and assumes that either can be written, erased and rewritten at will,[3] as long as one possesses sufficient power to impose dominant inscriptions on the land. While Zionist ideologues used this metaphor to create an imagined *tabula rasa* on which national aspirations could be inscribed, their detractors focused their critique on the heavy toll exerted from those who were deemed as the "Others" of this new spatial order. The actuality of the *tabula rasa* – the complete erasure of indigenous and "dissident spaces" and the formation of a homogenous, empty time from which the nation-state can emerge – was only rarely questioned outright.[4]

Yet in the intermittent process of spatial production, the imperfect results of physical and cultural intervention and the signs of the unfinished negotiation that takes place in the encounter between people and space, are evident throughout Israel and coded into the vast corpus of its cultural representation. To fully account for this multifaceted spatial reality, a different analytical approach is required, one which does not presuppose the submission of spatial forms to a prescribed ideological programme, be it in the name of the nation-state or its others. It is at this point that spatial history provides an important addition to our knowledge regarding the processes of historical transformation and the intricate web of relations that constitutes the encounter between people and space.

This shift, however, could not have taken place as an abstract exercise. From my very first visits to Salama/Kfar Shalem in the summer of 2005, I was confronted by phenomena that rejected clear compartmentalisation into defined conventions of spatial transformation. The neighbourhood presented an environment that did not adhere to the conventions of Zionist urbanism, but neither was it a blunt example of an orchestrated process of spatial annihilation. The confusing amalgamation of Arab village houses inhabited by Jews and engulfed by the sprawling suburbs of Tel Aviv required a more complex account of the spatial process that has occurred since 1948 and the ways these reorient our perception of spatial transformation, political alliances and the constitution of collective identities. In other words, space was presenting a history that could not be contained by existing grand- or

---

[3] In *The Practice of Everyday Life*, de Certeau presents this argument at length.
[4] Hever, "Map of Sand", 416; Ram, "Ways of Forgetting".

counter-narratives; space was relating a story that demanded to be acknowledged on its own terms.

In this critical endeavour, this book joins a small corpus that called attention to all that remains, to the myriad of Arab histories that continue to claim their place in the Israeli present. Building on and refining the theoretical prisms proposed by these scholars and discussed throughout the analysis, this book seeks to present a broader critical framework through which these small histories can be reconsidered, not as anecdotal or enclosed in the confines of a third-space, but as the Israeli spatial condition *par excellence*.

Conjoining Pasts and the Challenge of Space

Borrowing Doreen Massey's terminology, I posited in Chapter 1 that the spatial history of Salama/Kfar Shalem presents a concrete example of space as "a simultaneity of stories-so-far".[5] It captures, in material and cultural forms, the possibility that Jewish and Arab spaces may not be mutually exclusive, but mutually reliant. In the context of the conflictual history through which the Israeli space has been produced, this statement may seem utopian at first, detached from physical and political realities of segregation, violence and ethno-national chauvinism. Yet its strength lies in its actual presence in space and in the social and political reverberations such spatialisation creates. Throughout this book, I have rejected the reduction of space to a passive stage on which human actions are played out, precisely because by doing so we are able to suspend the assumption that the encounter between people and place is always already ideologically, politically or culturally predetermined. Instead, I have illustrated how space continues to retain heterogeneous and conflicting facets even under the pressure of blunt attempts to shape and control its form and meaning. The key to this resilience lies in the open-ended negotiation that takes place between people and the environments they inhabit, in the perception of "space as a sphere of relations, of contemporaneous multiplicity, and as always under construction".[6]

This model of co-constructive relations allowed for a thorough reconsideration of the spatial processes that have shaped Salama/ Kfar Shalem, and, for that matter, Israeli space more broadly. In the same manner that the depopulation of Salama and its repopulation by Jews made its mark on the physical and material face of the village,

[5] Massey, *For Space*, 9.
[6] Ibid., 148.

the encounter with Arab space had a profound impact on those who inhabited it. As Massey points out, places "change us, not through some visceral belonging (some barely changing rootedness, as so many would have it) but through the *practicing* of place, the negotiation of intersecting trajectories; place is an arena where negotiation is forced upon us".[7] This is an argument with far-reaching implications. Taking this relation to its full extent means that the "Israeli space" is necessarily always already an Arab-Jewish space, as it facilitates the encounter and the unavoidable negotiation between people and place. Time and again throughout the book, we have seen how this open-ended negotiation forced radical changes on a range of issues and spheres, from norms of urban planning and social engineering, and the administrative and legal organisation of the urban environment, to the intimate practices and religious rituals through which space is made meaningful for individuals and communities.

However, viewing Kfar Shalem as a dynamic sphere of relations that links Arab past and Jewish present in a mutually dependent fashion should not be confused with a harmonious resolution of the conflicts that are inherent to the production and evolution of this space. The formation of an Arab-Jewish space remains in contradiction to the official perception of that space, be it the desire to create a homogeneous space that adheres to ethno-national and modernist-European ideals of urban planning or the later dominant logic that seeks to exert and maximise economic profit by limiting "intrusive" elements that "obstruct" the realisation of capital gain. Contrary to other accounts of similar spaces, which have tended to celebrate the defiance of hegemonic spatial logic,[8] this book highlights how these conflicts result in a rather more ambiguous spatial reality. Rather than a history of victors and victims, this book sheds light on Jewish-Israelis who find themselves as the unlikely custodians of an unwanted past. The pattern of containment described in the fourth and fifth chapters – which saw the gradual encapsulation of the village by the public tenement blocks – illustrated how the accentuation of spatial difference also manifested social stigmatisation, economic and infrastructural disenfranchisement, and a personal sense of strangulation.

As noted in specific discussions throughout, the notion of containment as a political strategy includes acts of separation and segregation, but is not limited to a strict defining mechanism of social or political polarities (us v. them). Contrary to more explicit forms of spatial

---

[7] Ibid., 154.
[8] Nuriely, "Strangers in a National Space"; Benjamin, " 'Present-Absent' ".

partitioning, which have become a common feature in contemporary social and political climates, containment is a process that takes place over a long period of time, and through a diverse set of spatial means and cultural practices that are anyway already provisional and therefore require constant maintenance and repetition. The residual effects of this process go beyond the physical erection of walls, fences and earth mounds. Most importantly, it points our attention to the unfinished production of space and to what it actually means "to take place" – to what Massey identifies as the "myriad of practices of quotidian negotiation and contestation" through which places become meaningful and where individual and communal identities may be formed and transformed.[9] Unlike blunt forms of partition, containment allows us to carefully untangle the spatial and historical contingencies of social or ethnic antagonisms.

In this sense, for example, the construction of an "acoustic barrier" between the Arab village of Jisr a-Zarqa and the affluent Jewish-Israeli town of Caesarea is an expression of socioeconomic segregation, the adoption of the "gated community" mentality in an ethno-capitalist society. But it is impossible to fully grasp the intricacies of this situation without taking into account the fact that this village is one of a handful of Palestinian-Arab villages that were not depopulated in 1948. In one article documenting the proliferation of physical barriers of this sort, residents of the Arab village infer that the large earthen embankment was put up because "we are stuck like a bone in the throat of the country as the only Arab locale to remain along the shore after all the rest were cleared out in 1948".[10] Without losing sight of the local motivations that guided the construction of the embankment, the political scope of this act is significantly broadened when we consider it in a wide spatio-historical context. Furthermore, only in this way will we be able to remain sensitive to the dynamic and ambivalent discourse that takes place in Jisr a-Zarqa and the wider community of Israel's Palestinian citizens with regard to their affiliation with, or rejection of, the Israeli polity.

Kfar Shalem presents a concrete example of the spatial coexistence of Arab past and Jewish present in defiance of dominant ideological and political antagonisms. Yet we must avoid a simplistic celebration of resistance. The residents of the neighbourhood refuse to take upon themselves the role of a political opposition, at least not along

[9] Massey, *For Space*, 154.
[10] Galili, "Long Division".

traditional political dividing lines. An anecdotal example illustrates this point. In almost every Arab house around the neighbourhood, one finds an abundance of Israeli flags hung on hedges, across back yards, or flying from rooftops. This practice performs the most common identification with the state and the national community, marking the house and those who inhabit it as a legitimate part of the "Israeli space". The residents had a concrete precedent to follow: A photograph taken in Salama shortly after its occupation depicts an Arab house that was used for the army's regional command (Figure 7.1). A flag tied to one of the corners of the roof marks the building with the symbol of the new power that now controls it and governs its surroundings. For the current residents of the Arab houses in Kfar Shalem, who have been deemed as dissidents or illicit "intruders", flags are a visual expression of a demand to be recognised and legitimised, a sentiment that has been recorded in numerous examples throughout this book.

Time and again, residents reject the categorisation of the neighbourhood as a third-space or place,[11] which implies, once again, its dissociation from the "legitimate" space of the social and cultural mainstream. In its various iterations, the "thirding" of space importantly sought to break from the binaries that dominate dialectical meta-narratives of progression or class exploitation. It is a new space in which negotiation of meaning and representation can take place, which can enable the scripting of new histories, new cultural expressions and a new politics of hybridity and resistance. Yet at what price? What is one required to surrender when consigned to such "thirding-as-othering"?

The demand repeatedly issued by residents of Kfar Shalem is infinitely more radical, pointing to the fact that what has happened in Salama from 1948 is an inherent act of state, not its "other". By insisting on the village's inseparability from the state, the residents invoke an ethical-political liability to the past and responsibility to the present. All that happened in Salama/Kfar Shalem – from depopulation and repopulation to cultural segregation and socioeconomic plight – was part of the Israeli national project and ought to be considered as such. The demand to recognise and legitimise the Arab-Jewish space *as part* of the Israeli space is the truly challenging prospect illustrated in this spatial history.

In Tel Aviv's 2008 municipal elections, this challenge took on a concrete political form. In the run-up to the elections, a group of residents

---

[11] Rutherford, "The Third Space: Interview with Homi Bhabha"; Yacobi, "'The Third Place'"; Soja, *Thirdspace* (1996); Soja, "Thirdspace" (2008).

Figure 7.1 Salama, shortly after the Israeli occupation, probably early May 1948.
Photographer: Zoltan Kruger, Israel National Archive.

from Kfar Shalem joined forces with activists from Jaffa and other neighbourhoods in southern Tel Aviv to form "City for All", an urban political movement that sought to garner broad electoral support under a social-environmental agenda. Dov Khenin, a member of the non-Zionist communist *Hadash* party, was chosen as the movement's mayoral candidate. The movement was guided by the belief that the city provided a unique sphere for political action that does not conform to traditional ethno-national divisions. First signs that this political agenda was bearing fruit became apparent in the demonstrations that took place in late 2007, when several houses were demolished in Kfar Shalem. The protest attracted eclectic political support from Arab civil rights groups from Jaffa, Israeli NGOs working against house demolition in the Palestinian West Bank, as well as local residents who were self-proclaimed supporters of right-wing and Jewish-religious parties. In the elections, City for All received the largest amount of votes and gained five seats on the municipal council. Khenin, though, lost the mayoral race and stepped down from the movement's leadership to participate in the country's general elections. Aharon Maduel, a resident of Kfar Shalem, consequently became the movement's leading figure.

Maduel refuses to be compartmentalised into familiar political or ethnic identities: he takes pride in being a member of the right-wing Likud party while identifying himself as "a social left-winger". At the same time as he highlights his Yemenite origins, Maduel preferred not to personally present a motion in the City Council that suggested that a traditionally Yemenite neighbourhood – Kerem Hateymanim – preceded Tel Aviv and should be recognised as such, "to prevent the motion from being discredited on ethnic grounds".[12] Maduel's elusive political allegiances have made him a target of attacks from both sides of the political spectrum, but at the same time allowed him to tie the situation in Kfar Shalem with the evictions of Arab families in Jaffa and the state of Arab-Bedouin communities living in "unrecognised" villages without fundamental infrastructure. The form of political activism supported by Maduel and others in City for All uses the spatial reality of Kfar Shalem as an instrument through which new political potentialities can be imagined, while averting the pitfalls of trenchant ethno-national political conventions that govern Israel's political discourse. Imagining a political coalition of Arabs and Jews, secular and religious, united by material concerns and economic interests, was previously part of the utopian vocabulary of the fringes of the Israeli left. In a fittingly humble, pragmatic and unpretentious manner, Kfar Shalem provided the grounds for a short-lived political realisation of this vision.

Yet beyond the explicitly political aspects, Maduel admits that his motivations are found closer to home. "You see these? The trees in my yard were here when we moved in and are from the Arabs' time" he told me in his home, a small Arab house he and his wife bought from an elderly Yemenite woman in the early 1960s. "When my brother added a room to his house next door, he made sure not to damage this big pecan

---

[12] Maduel, Interview with the author.

tree. We care for this place."[13] The intimate relation iterated here goes beyond wistful nostalgia or claims of authenticity. If Maduel is a custodian of the Arab space he inhabits, he does so not through traditional forms of commemoration but through the accumulation of experience and the practical familiarity he and others form with this environment. What is invoked here is spatiality as the sphere of humble politics, where radical horizons are expressed in the most mundane fashion of fences, footpaths and trees, in the practicalities of living, and in the interrelations formed between spatiality and its subjective experience.[14]

It is impossible to consider this form of custodianship without invoking the term's more sinister history, most prominently expressed in the Israeli Custodian of Absentee Property, which oversaw the legal and administrative appropriation of Arab lands and real-estate seized in 1948.[15] Maduel and others who inhabited Salama are guardians who prevent the disappearance of this environment, at the same time as they are part of a history that saw the disinheritance of the village's previous population. This custodianship harbours the unresolved tension of "complicity" so astutely discussed by Mark Sanders in his analysis of intellectuals' response to Apartheid South Africa.[16] "To be complicit" is not the simple vilification that is often pejoratively associated with the term, but a careful consideration of the responsibility that emerges out of one's awareness of her or his relation to their surroundings:

> Complicity ... is thus at one with the basic folded-together-ness of being, of human-being, of self and other. Such foldedness (in contradistinction to the apartness fostered by apartheid) is the condition of possibility of all particular affiliations, loyalties, and commitments.[17]

Sanders' discussion is of particular importance because he insists on the inseparability of opposition from complicity, rejecting the assumption that the former is possible without the latter. From this point of view, he reminds us, it is no longer enough to proclaim opposition: complicity is to be acknowledged and responsibility assumed, not as an act of self-flagellation, but as the point from which a conscious political intervention can commence.

---

[13] Ibid.
[14] Karen Till's notion of a place-based ethics of care is highly pertinent in this regard. Till, "Wounded Cities".
[15] As Louise Bethlehem shows, the notion of custodianship carries a problematic history, appearing in colonial topoi as an expression of cultural and ethnic chauvinism. Bethlehem, *Skin Tight*, 26.
[16] Sanders, *Complicities*.
[17] Ibid., 11.

Following similar ethical concerns, the notion that Salama is *con-served* in and as part of Kfar Shalem, which I discussed at some length in Chapter 6, provides the basis on which physical, social and discursive-political space challenges the separatist logic that sets Jewish and Arab histories and spaces as inherently distinct. As Ariella Azoulay points out, it was this very logic that enabled the Israeli state to produce and maintain the Arab-Palestinian disaster as "a catastrophe from their point of view":

> Its traces remained devoid of context, unconnected to any discourse that could have made them manifest, used them to show the injustice, base on them a claim for redress and for compensating the victims. It was catastrophe that was absent from the many traces it left behind. A catastrophe that left no trace of catastrophe …[18]

Contrary to Azoulay's claim – that all that remains is merely traces devoid of context – what takes place in Kfar Shalem, and in spaces ana-lysed throughout this book, constantly blurs the division line between "their" catastrophe and "ours" and the ideological logic that sets the past completely apart from the present. This is not a case of generalising evil, what the American historian Charles Maier describes as the ever-exonerating "We are all perpetrators; we are all victims."[19] Instead, it is a response to the actuality of spatial histories that are forced together, not as jumbled dead matter, but as active components that shape the conditions of social life and political action.

Yet all too often, Kfar Shalem is understood as a contemporary arena of socio-political struggle that has emerged and evolved with traces of "another" catastrophe in the background. Surprisingly, this separation of the past from the present is replicated not just by the apparatuses of the state, but in critical memory discourse and accounts seeking to challenge hegemonic spatial logic. In order to fully formulate the re-envisioning of spatial history, it is necessary to look at the challenge it poses not only to dominant discourses but also to the critical trends of "counter-spatiality".

Spatial History: Alternative (to) Memory?

The discussion of spatial pasts is as much about meaning as it is about matter, if not more so. Spatial forms are meaningless without a dis-cursive context that mediates knowledge and conveys their historical,

---

[18] Azoulay, "Constituting Violence, 1947–1950", 6.
[19] Maier, "Overcoming the Past?", 296.

social and political significance. However, it is often posited that in quite the same manner that meaning is given, it can be taken away: like other forms of historical representation, a place's past can be selectively told and manipulated, with some aspects highlighted while others are omitted. I have already noted how the critical corpus that reassesses Israel's history and its representation also draws attention to the Zionist use of space, both as a physical territory on which practical interests are realised and as an instrument that expresses and solidifies the historical relation between people and the land. According to this critique, any ambiguity or discrepancy that might "interfere" in the creation of the homogeneous space that will accommodate the (re-)emergence of the Jewish nation is destined to be suppressed. In this regard, both physical destruction and the neutralisation of meaning are seen as dominating practices in the production of space. However, this critique also assumes that a perfect correlation exists between production of space and the formation of collective memory:

> The general picture conveyed to Israelis is that of the dominant Zionist narrative: A Jewish land, with very little Arab heritage, history and geography, whose Arab residents chose to flee – and since then they are no longer of interest to us. The Judeasation project succeeded in leaving its mark both on the country's landscape and demographic composition of the state and on the Israelis' consciousness.[20]

The political dimensions of memory are not a recent discovery in Israel and range well beyond the discussion of space. Yet I am particularly interested in the effect memory discourse has on the perception of space solely as the consequence of political action in its most obvious sense. This restrictive perspective originates from a broader tendency in cultural history to reduce cultural products – space being but one example – to outright political manipulation. In this process, Alon Confino warns, individual and communal memory – the recollection and reconstruction of the past – "becomes a prisoner of political reductionism and functionalism".[21] Historical knowledge about the past, it is claimed, is either mediated by the apparatuses operating directly or indirectly on behalf of the state, or is destined to be suppressed and forgotten. As a cultural vehicle that transmits historical meaning and shapes collective memories, space either conforms to this logic or faces the threat of obliteration. Diagnosing the phenomena of collective denial, Stanley Cohen posits that "Historical skeletons are put in

---

[20] Kadman, *Erased from Space and Consciousness*, 128.
[21] Confino, "Collective Memory and Cultural History", 1395.

cupboards because of the political need to be innocent of a troubling recognition; they remain hidden because of the political absence of an inquiring mind."[22]

To "combat" the manipulation of memory and the silence that is enforced on the Arab-Palestinian past in the Israeli landscape, several groups and individuals have suggested practices that will actively re-present and expose these absent chapters. One Israeli architect, for example, suggested that the 418 depopulated Palestinian villages ought to be recognised as sites of memory and cultural heritage worthy of preservation. This, he claims, will enable a change in Israel's collective discourse and memory in a way that would show respect to all the historical layers of the land, including the Palestinian narrative of the 1948 Nakba – the Palestinian catastrophe of 1948 – and the Arab built heritage.[23] The political and practical improbability of this proposal notwithstanding, it shows a disturbing disinterest in the present. One is left wondering, for example, whether residents of Kfar Shalem living in "heritage" Arab houses would violate the preservation charter if they were to replace a leaking roof or extend a balcony. Salama's built environment did not survive thanks to benevolent preservation and such wistful interventions are unlikely to secure its future.

A more organised and sustained effort to acknowledge the Arab history of Palestine and the disastrous consequence endured by this community following the 1948 War is carried out by Zochrot, an organisation comprising Israeli Jews and Arabs that set itself the goal of "bringing the Nakba into Hebrew" through a wide range of public and educational activities, the operation of an information centre for researchers and students, and the publication of a journal dedicated to the issue of the Nakba and its political, social and cultural repercussions.[24] Zochrot's practice of signposting depopulated Palestinian villages is of specific relevance to this discussion, as it seeks to re-mark former Arab spaces that are perceived to have been emptied of their histories in a deliberate process of designification.[25] This practice presupposes that "As long as razed Palestinian villages remain uncommemorated on the Israeli landscape, their existence in the past and their destruction is repressed." Signposting, on the other hand, is understood as an "action upon the landscape in the hope of rediscovering and remodeling it,

---

[22] Cohen, *States of Denial*, 139.
[23] Groag, "On Conservation and Forgetting".
[24] Lentin, "The Memory of Dispossession, Dispossessing Memory".
[25] Leshem, "Memory Activism".

creating a renewed landscape that will reveal the traces of what has refused to be wiped out, in spite of so many efforts".[26]

There are obvious differences in the practices employed by these two interventions, and their positionality vis-à-vis official bodies of the state. Yet both the proposal to preserve depopulated Palestinian villages as heritage sites, and Zochrot's signposting activity, draw critical strength from the deliberate appropriation of conventional, even hegemonic practices of historical representation in an attempt to present an alternative narrative of the past and potential political horizons. However, there is an even deeper relation here that highlights the prevailing logic shared both by hegemonic and counter-hegemonic currents regarding the *quality* of space. In both cases, the underlying assumption concentrates on material statements and texts *inscribed on* the landscape: both qualify space as the elastic material that is moulded and remoulded in full accordance with the narratives that, as it were, ventriloquise its meaning, past and present. In the process, space is always already secondary to the narratives that represent it, both in the sense of "placing there" what seems to be absent (re-present), and of making a statement on behalf of a person or cause that are otherwise muted.[27] The problem here is not the actual act of representation, but the effects this dominant representational logic has on the ability to identify the multiplicities and heterogeneities that are still there, very much present in space: the Arab place-name on a Hebrew street sign; the prosaic upkeep of an Arab store by an aging Jewish congregation; the fear, shame and confusion of officials assigned to deal with these spaces.

The problem can be formulated in methodological terms: where does one search for spatial history? Furthermore, what form is this history supposed to take? As the cases analysed throughout this book show, a search for coherent narratives, expressed through familiar forms and common practices of communication, is likely to discover little to indicate the simultaneity, multiplicity and heterogeneity I have been pointing to thus far. However, understanding space as a sphere of social and cultural interaction where identity and experience are responsive to the environments they inhabit as much as they shape it, releases both historical investigation and political imagination from the inexorable Manichaean logic that all too often dominates conventional debates about the politics of space and memory in Palestine-Israel, and in

---

[26] Bronstein, "Position Paper".

[27] The double meaning of representation is further elaborated by Gayatri Spivak in the distinction she makes between the German *Vertretung* and *Darstellung*. Spivak, "Can the Subaltern Speak?"

numerous other cases around the world. The spatialisation of experience allows for the identification of multiplicity not only in "the simultaneous coexistence of others with their own trajectories and their own stories to tell",[28] but also in the open-ended negotiation that takes place between people and space and its far-reaching effects. The records of this encounter, which range beyond any limited moment of "discovery", document a complex and ambiguous relation that is laden with uncertainties, fragmentation and slippages. Remaining attentive to the way the means of representation change and adapt in the negotiated encounter in space is not designed to defuse conflicts or alleviate responsibility for historical injustice. Rather, it postulates a more humble recognition of the unfinished histories that maintain a lingering effect on the present.

Spatial history is not an attempt to counter the important assertion that "the project of reparation, remembering, and reconciliation involve the right to tell histories and have them listened to respectively".[29] Instead, it remains wary of the optimism that representing counternarratives through familiar forms of commemoration will pave the way for a future of reconciliation. The violence that erupted around the Salama mosque during the October 2000 riots provides a blunt reminder that residents of Kfar Shalem do not need a plaque to point out the history of their neighbourhood and the affective weight it carries. For them, this contentious past is neither erased nor neutralised. Furthermore, the suggestion that this troubling presence can be overcome or "healed"[30] by an official act of heritage preservation disregards the fact that preservationist isolation was itself the catalyst of alienation between this space and its inhabitants. By highlighting the role of practical engagement and the social functions that tie a site to its human surroundings, spatial history moves away from traditional commemoration discourse: spatial traces of the past are *con*served by their relevance to the lives of people, by the intimate relations formed toward and around them, and by their role in shaping the present. The already precarious state of Salama's Arab spaces, which have survived thanks to this intricate web of relations and despite the challenge they pose to ethno-national spatiality and to capitalist logic, will not be resolved by prosthetic guardianship and ceremonial isolation.

It should be noted, however, that spatial history is not a programmatic policy that seeks to replace political forms of commemorative

---

[28] Massey, *For Space*, 11.
[29] Maier, "Overcoming the Past?", 297.
[30] Groag, "On Conservation and Forgetting".

action, which continue to play a highly important role in shaping the debate about the boundaries of the Israeli imagined community. In March 2011 the Israeli right-wing parliamentary coalition passed a bill authorising the finance minister to reduce state funding or support to an institution if it engages in an "activity that is contrary to the principles of the state". Such activities include "commemorating Independence Day or the day of the establishment of the state as a day of mourning".[31] The bill bluntly illustrates how the events that commemorate the Palestinian Nakba present a concrete challenge to trends of nationalist chauvinism that have been on the rise in Israel recently. These ceremonies, organised by various political movements and groups, increasingly bring together Israeli Jews and Arabs to highlight the price paid by the Arab population of Palestine in the 1948 War, and the establishment of the State of Israel. They provide a rare performative space for Israeli Jews to confront a marginalised historical chapter and its inseparability from the dominant tale of Jewish national revival. Spatial history, which exists in parallel to these commemorative practices, documents another degree or register of engagement, where the encounter between people and space results in forms of historical experience that are largely overlooked and dismissed by the rigid demands of political memory activism. As a method of spatial analysis, it illustrates how engagement with the past proves meaningful even when it does not fall neatly into the categories of memory and forgetfulness.

In a work that has now gained canonical status, Pierre Nora notes that *lieux de mémoire* in fact record the breakdown of memory, for "If we were able to live within memory, we would not have needed to consecrate *lieux de mémoire* in its name".[32] Nora indicates that a *lieu de mémoire* is formed at the moment when it is no longer carried by the vehicles of social practices. Providing memory with a place (*lieu*) – an archive, a library, a monument – is seen as a material prosthesis that substitutes for "natural" communal formations that are responsible for creating the social environment (*milieu*) of memory. There is a sense of nostalgic lament in Nora's view as he posits that while premodern societies used to live within the continuous past as a spontaneous experience, contemporary societies have separated memory from the continuity of social production. As Olick and Robbins put it, "Nora thus contrasts contemporary 'lieux' or places of memory

---

to earlier lived 'milieux'. The former are impoverished versions of the latter".[33]

Spatial history abandons the idea that the past can be summoned back to the present as a perfect reconstruction, be it through social mechanisms or spatial forms; it has no nostalgia for a lost past that can be recollected or recreated as a closed entirety. What is proposed here is an acceptance of the past as part of the present, while acknowledging that it too will have to evolve, change and adapt in order to maintain its place among the living and not only as a remnant of the dead. As a pre-1948 Arab village, Salama will not be resurrected, much like the Shalom Synagogue in Zakynthos or Shimon Yehoshua's house. But all that remains are more than mute traces, devoid of context or contemporary consequence; these and other sites spur political action, mediate experiences of socioeconomic and cultural marginalisation, become symbols of uncommon cultural identities, and illustrate the fragility and volatility of a space that merges past and present. As extensively described in Chapter 2, it is indeed a densely populated emptiness.

"For Life and Action": The Future of Spatial History

In "The Uses and Disadvantages of History for Life", Friedrich Nietzsche famously held that it is impossible to break away from the continual effect of history: "For since we are the products of earlier generations, we are also the products of their aberrations, passions, and errors, and indeed their crimes; it is not possible to wholly free oneself from this chain."[34] Yet recognising this indissoluble relation does not mean that the past becomes the gravedigger of the present. Developing his notion of critical history, Nietzsche explains:

> We need history, certainly, but we need it for reasons different from those for which the idler in the garden of knowledge needs it, even though he may look nobly down on our rough and charmless needs and requirements. We need it, that is to say, for the sake of life and action.[35]

Life and action seldom take place in idyllic sceneries, or, conversely, in landscapes of smoking debris and violent atrocities. A search for spatial histories often leads to places that are "rough and charmless", where the mundane and obvious still accommodate the encounter between

---

[33] Olick and Robbins, "Social Memory Studies", 121.
[34] Nietzsche, *Untimely Meditations*, 76.
[35] Ibid., 59.

people and space. Whether conserved by negligence or by lack of resources, by functionality or necessity, the spaces of the past continue to provide the physical and symbolic environment through which the present is negotiated and the future imagined.

This book has focused on the site-specific analysis of Salama/Kfar Shalem's spatial history, and is specifically concerned with the transition that followed the 1948 War. As such, it does not cover the full range of histories stored in the village itself, and surely has no pretence to present an exhaustive account of Israeli spatial history. Furthermore, the findings identify spatial patterns that may not apply to other sites of spatial transition; it is additionally uncertain that under different social, cultural and political conditions, similar patterns would have produced the same effects. Research of this sort acknowledges that the encounter between people and space always includes unique features that derive from its subjective and contingent nature. Space is not produced in accordance with the strict hierarchical structures and serial logic that dominate the industrial assembly line.

Nonetheless, the spatial history uncovered throughout this book sheds new light on spatial phenomena that have become hallmarks of the Israeli space, from the tenement block to the spatio-legal structure of the state of emergency. The discussion further explores the influence of international trends and ideologies on the shaping of space in the city. It evokes a reconsideration of some of the assumptions about the transformation of space that continue to dominate critical discourse in and about Israel, thus providing not only a critique of space but a sceptical interrogation of the space of critique. Despite being an account of a small place at the edge of town, this work explores some of the aspects that form the spatial, cultural and political genome of Israel, highlighting the concrete shape they take in time and space and the practical impact they have on life and action.

I posited early on that the spatial encounter is inherently open-ended, destabilising fixed projections and prescribed formulations that seek to control and predetermine its outcomes. As such, the future of Salama/ Kfar Shalem remains open, spurring endless questions that would otherwise seem anecdotal. Will Avshalom Ben-David's house, which blocks the completion of Alnekave Street, be demolished to make way for the urban road grid? Will the council's plans to construct a large synagogue for all residents of Kfar Shalem mean the end of the Greek synagogue? Will another round of violence between Arabs and Jews bring about another attack on the mosque that will result in its complete destruction? I have no answer. The resilience of space, which saw the intimate formation of simultaneities and coexistences of past and present, is only the result of its relevance as a space continually practised and experienced; the contingencies of life, rough and charmless as they may seem, yet rich and radical as they are, will also be those which determine its future.

Bibliography

ARCHIVES AND COLLECTIONS

British Library Map Collection, London
Central Zionist Archive Jerusalem (CZA)
Haganah Archives, Tel Aviv (HA)
Hebrew University of Jerusalem Map Collection
Israel State Archives, Jerusalem (ISA)
Tel Aviv Municipality Historical Archive (TAMHA)

LIST OF SOURCES

A'araff, Shukri. Interview with the author. Telephone interview, November 2008.

Abu-Sitta, Salman Hussain. *The Palestinian Nakba 1948: The Register of Depopulated Localities in Palestine*. Occasional Return Centre Studies, 4. London: The Palestinian Return Centre, 2000.

Agamben, Giorgio. *State of Exception*. Chicago: University of Chicago Press, 2005.

Agnon, Shmuel Yosef. *Only Yesterday*. Translated by Barbara Harshav. Princeton, NJ: Princeton University Press, 2000.

Ahad Ha'am (Asher Zvi Ginsburg). "Truth from Eretz Yisrael". Translated by Alan Dowty. *Israel Studies* 5, no. 2 (2000): 160–79.

Allan, Greg. "On Tomason, Or the Flipside of Dame Architecture". 4 February 2008. http://greg.org/archive/2008/02/04/on_tomason_or_the_flipside_of_dame_architecture.html.

Allen, Douglas. *Myth and Religion in Mircea Eliade*. Theorists of Myth, V. 11. New York: Garland Pub., 1998.

Almog, Oz. *The Sabra: The Creation of the New Jew*. Berkeley: University of California Press, 2000.

Anidjar, Gil. *The Jew, the Arab: A History of the Enemy*. Stanford, CA: Stanford University Press, 2003.

Ankori, Zvi. "The Living and the Dead: The Story of Hebrew Inscriptions in Crete". *Proceedings of the American Academy for Jewish Research* 38, no. 71 (1970): 1–100.

Appadurai, Arjun. "Spectral Housing and Urban Cleansing: Notes on Millennial Mumbai". *Public Culture* 12, no. 3 (2001): 627–51.

Asaf, Ami. *The Workers' Community in Israel [Moshve ha-`ovdim be-Yisrael]*. Tel Aviv: Hotsaat `Enot u-Tenu`at ha-moshavim, 1953.

Azaryahu, Maoz. *State Cults: Celebrating and Commemorating the Fallen in Israel, 1948–1956 [Pulhane medinah: hagigot ha-`atsmaut ve-hantsahat ha-noflim be-Yisrael, 1948–1956].* Sedeh-Boker [Beersheba]: Ben-Gurion University of the Negev Press, 1995.

"The Purge of Bismarck and Saladin: The Renaming of Streets in East Berlin and Haifa, a Comparative Study in Cultural-Planning". *Poetics Today* 13, no. 2 (Summer 1992): 351–67.

"Street Names and Political Identity: The Case of East Berlin". *Journal of Contemporary History* 21, no. 4 (October 1992): 581–604.

"The Power of Commemorative Street Names". *Environment and Planning. D, Society & Space* 14, no. 3 (1996): 311–30.

Tel Aviv: Mythography of a City. First edition. Syracuse, NY: Syracuse University Press, 2007.

Azaryahu, Maoz, and Arnon Golan. "(Re)naming the Landscape: The Formation of the Hebrew Map of Israel 1949–1960". *Journal of Historical Geography* 27 (2001): 178–95.

Azaryahu, Maoz, and Aharon Kellerman. "Symbolic Places of National History and Revival: A Study in Zionist Mythical Geography". *Transactions* 24, no. 1 (1999): 109–23.

Azoulay, Ariella. "Who Needs the Truth (in Photography)?" Presented at the Visual Cultures Guest Lecture Series, Goldsmith's College, London, 22 January 2009.

"Asleep in a Sterile Zone". Refugee Watch Online, 29 January 2009. www.refugeewatchonline.blogspot.co.uk/2009/01/sleep-in-sterile-zone.html.

Azoulay, Ariella. "Constituting Violence, 1947–1950: A Visual Genealogy of a Regime and 'a Catastrophe from Their Point of View'". Translated by Charles Kamen. Text for the exhibition, Constituting Violence, 1947–1950. Zochrot Gallery, Tel Aviv, 2009. www://roundtable.kein.org/files/round-table/Azoulay_Eng18-2.pdf.

Azoulay, Ariella. *From Palestine to Israel: A Photographic Record of Destruction and State Formation, 1947–50.* London: Pluto Press, 2011.

Balasi, Dudi. Interview with the author. Audio recording, October 2007.

Balchin, Paul N. *Housing Policy in Europe.* London: Routledge, 1996.

Ballas, Shimon. "Tel-Aviv East". In *Tel-Aviv East: A Trilogy [Tel-Aviv Mizraḥ: Ṭrilogyah].* Tel Aviv: Hakibutz HaMeuchad, 2003.

Outcast. San Francisco, CA: City Lights, 2007.

Bar, Gideon. "Reconstructing the Past: The Creation of Jewish Sacred Space in the State of Israel, 1948–1967". *Israel Studies* 13, no. 3 (2008): 1–21.

Bar-Gal, Yoram. "On the Tribe-Elders, the Successors and the New Ones in the Israeli Geography [Al ziknei ha-shevet, ha-mamshichim, vehahadashim bageographia ha-yisraelit]". *Horizons in Geography* 51 (1999): 7–39.

Baron, Salo W. *A Social and Religious History of the Jews: Late Middle Ages and Era of European Expansion, 1200–1650, Byzantines, Mamelukes, and Maghribians.* Second edition. Vol. 17 (18 vols). New York: Columbia University Press, 1980.

Baruch, Natalie. "'Operation Bi'ur Hametz'. Natalie Baruch interviews Aharon Maduel". *Sedek* 2 (January 2008): 85–9.

Ben-Ari, Eyal, and Yoram Bilu, eds, *Grasping Land: Space and Place in Contemporary Israeli Discourse and Experience*. Albany: State University of New York Press, 1997.

Ben-David, Avshalom. Interview with the author. Audio recording, April 2009.

Ben-Gurion, David. *The War Diary: The War of Independence, 1947–1948 [Yoman ha-Milḥamah: Milḥemet ha-'atsma'ut, 708–709]*, edited by Gershon Rivlin and Elhannan Orren. Tel Aviv: David Ben-Gurion Heritage Centre; Israel Ministry of Defence Press, 1982.

   On Settlement: Collected Writings 1915–1956 [`Al Ha-hityashvut: Kovets Devarim, 1915–1956], edited by Menachem Dorman. *Mekorot*, vol. 3. Tel Aviv: Hakibutz HaMeuchad, 1986.

Ben-Yishai, Aharon Zeev. "The City Council on the Question of Annexation and the Name". *Tel-Aviv Municipality Official Gazette [Yediot iriyat Tel Aviv]* 19, no. 5–6 (1949): 74.

   "The Street Names of Tel Aviv". *Tel Aviv-Jaffa Municipality Official Gazette [Yediot iriyat Tel Aviv-Yaffo]* 22, no. 1–3 (1952): 37–42.

   "New Names for the Streets of Tel Aviv". *Tel Aviv-Jaffa Municipality Official Gazette [Yediot iriyat Tel Aviv-Yaffo]* 23, no. 1–3 (1954): 24–5.

Benjamin, Shlomit. " 'Present-Absent': The Case of Qubeiba/Kfar G'virol". *Teoryah Uvikoret [Theory and Criticism]* 29 (2006): 81–102.

Benjamin, Walter. "Critique of Violence". In *Selected Writings. Volume 1, 1913–1926*, edited by Howard Eiland and Michael William Jennings, 236–52. Cambridge, MA: Belknap Press of Harvard University Press, 2003.

Benvenisti, Meron. *Sacred Landscape: The Buried History of the Holy Land Since 1948*. Berkeley: University of California Press, 2000.

Berger, Tamar. *Dionysus at Dizengof Center [Dionysus ba-senṭer]*. Tel Aviv: Hakibutz HaMeuchad, 1998.

Bernstein, Deborah. "Conflict and Protest in Israeli Society: The Case of the Black Panthers of Israel". *Youth and Society* 16, no. 2 (1984): 129–52.

Bethlehem, Louise. *Skin Tight: Apartheid Literary Culture and its Aftermath*. First edition. Pretoria; Leiden: University of South Africa Press; Koninklijke Brill, 2006.

   "Towards a Different Hybridity". *Teoryah Uvikoret [Theory and Criticism]* 29 (Autumn 2006): 193–204.

Bhabha, Homi. *The Location of Culture*. London; New York: Routledge, 1994.

Biger, Gideon. "A Scotsman in the First Hebrew City: Patrick Geddes and the 1926 Town Plan for Tel Aviv". *Scottish Geographical Magazine* 108, no. 1 (1992): 4–8.

Bilu, Yoram. "Sanctification of Space in Israel: Civil Religion and Folk Judaism". In *Jews in Israel: Contemporary Social and Cultural Patterns*, edited by Uzi Rebhun and Chaim Waxman, 371–93. Tauber Institute for the Study of European Jewry Series. Hanover; Lebanon, NH: Brandeis University Press; Published by University Press of New England, 2004.

Blank, Yishai. "Space, Community, Subject: Reflections on Law and Space". *Din-Udvarim* 19, no. 2 (2005): 19–61.

Boyer, M. Christine. *The City of Collective Memory: Its Historical Imagery and Architectural Entertainments*. Cambridge, MA: MIT Press, 1994.

Branham, Joan R. "Sacred Space Under Erasure in Ancient Synagogues and Early Churches". *The Art Bulletin* 74, no. 3 (September 1992): 375–94.

Brenner, Yosef Haim. *The Writings of Yossef Haim Brenner [Kol kitve Y. Ḥ. Brener]*. Vol. 4 (9 vols). Tel Aviv: Shtibel, 1924.

Bronstein, Eitan. "Restless Park: On the Latrun Villages and Zochrot". Translated by Charles Kamen. *Remembering Imwas, Yalu and Bayt Nuba*, June 2007. www.zochrot.org/images/latrun_booklet_englishsupplement.pdf.

"Position Paper". *Zochrot*. Accessed 22 May 2009. www.zochrot.org/index.php?id=343.

Bulletin of the Israel Exploration Society. "The Sixth Archaeological Conference". 15, nos 3–4 (1950, 1949): 116–31.

Bullock, Nicholas. *Building the Post-War World: Modern Architecture and Reconstruction in Britain*. London: Routledge, 2002.

Bunn, David. "'Our Wattled Cott': Mercantile and Domestic Space in Thomas Pringle's African Landscapes". In *Landscape and Power*, edited by W. J. Thomas Mitchell, 127–74. Chicago: University of Chicago Press, 2002.

Busi, Dudu. *The Moon Goes Green in the Wadi [ha-Yareaḥ yaroḳ ba-yadi]*. Tel Aviv: Am Oved, 2000.

Carr, David. *Interpreting Husserl: Critical and Comparative Studies*. Phaenomenologica 106. Dordrecht [Netherlands]; Boston: Hingham, MA, USA: Kluwer Academic, 1987.

Carter, Paul. *The Road to Botany Bay: An Exploration of Landscape and History*. New York: Knopf, 1987.

   Dark Writing: Geography, Performance, Design. Writing Past Colonialism. Honolulu: University of Hawai'i Press, 2009.

Central Bureau of Statistics. "Immigrants, By Period of Immigration (1948–2007)". Central Bureau of Statistics, 2007. www.cbs.gov.il/hodaot2008n/21_08_028t1.pdf.

Chakrabarty, Dipesh. *Provincializing Europe: Postcolonial Thought and Historical Difference*. Princeton, NJ: Princeton University Press, 2000.

Chatterjee, Partha. "Anderson's Utopia". *Diacritics* 29 (1999): 128–34.

Chetrit, Sami Shalom. *The Mizrahi Struggle in Israel: Between Oppression and Liberation, Between Identification and Alternative [Ha-Ma'avaḳ Ha-Mizraḥi Be-Yiśra'el: Ben Dikui Le-Shiḥrur, Ben Hizdahut Le-Alṭernaṭivah, 1948–2003]*. Tel Aviv: Am Oved, 2004.

Choay, Francoise. *The Modern City: Planning in the 19th Century*. London: Studio Vista, 1977.

Cobban, James L. "Public Housing in Colonial Indonesia 1900–1940". *Modern Asian Studies* 27, no. 4 (1993): 871–96.

Cohen, Hillel. *The Present Absentees: The Palestinian Refugees in Israel After 1948 [ha-Nifḳadim ha-nokheḥim: ha-peliṭim ha-Falesṭinim be-Yiśra'el me-az 1948]*. Jerusalem: The Centre for the Research of the Arab Society in Israel, 2000.

Cohen, Shaul Ephraim. "The Politics of Planting: Israeli-Palestinian Competition for Control of Land in the Jerusalem Periphery". University of Chicago Geography Research Paper, No. 236. Chicago: University of Chicago Press, 1993.

Cohen, Stanley. *States of Denial: Knowing About Atrocities and Suffering*. Cambridge: Polity, 2002.

Colpe, Carsten. "The Sacred and the Profane". In *The Encyclopedia of Religion*. Detroit: Macmillan, 2005.

Confino, Alon. "Collective Memory and Cultural History: Problems of Method". *The American Historical Review* 102, no. 5 (1997): 1386–1403.

Conforti, Yitzhak. *Past Tense: Zionist Historiography and the Shaping of the National Memory [Zeman "avar: ha-hisṭoryografyah ha-Tsiyonit ye-"itsuv ha-zikaron ha-le'umi]*. Jerusalem: Yad Ben-Zvi, 2006.

Custodian Police. "Demolition Order Against Avraham Garame", 23 October 1953. ISA/G/20–3099. Israeli State Archives.

  "Injunction to Halt Construction Against Avraham Garame", 23 October 1953. ISA/G/20–3099. Israeli State Archives.

Dalmadigo, Shelomo. Interview with the author. Audio recording, April 2008.

Darin-Drabkin, Haim. *Housing and Absorption in Israel [Shikun u-ḳeliṭah be-Yiśra'el 1947–1955]*. Tel Aviv: Sifre Gadish, 1955.

Darin-Drabkin, Haim, ed. *Housing in Israel: Economic and Sociological Aspects*. Tel Aviv: Gadish Books, 1957.

Davis, Rochelle. *Palestinian Village Histories: Geographies of the Displaced*. Stanford, CA: Stanford University Press, 2011.

Dawkins, Professor Casey J., Professor Arthur C. Nelson, and Professor Thomas W. Sanchez. *The Social Impacts of Urban Containment*. Aldershot: Ashgate Publishing Ltd., 2012.

de Certeau, Michel. *The Practice of Everyday Life*. Berkeley, CA; London: University of California Press, 1988.

Deleuze, Gilles, and Félix Guattari. *Anti-Oedipus*. Continuum International Publishing Group, 2004.

Derrida, Jacques. *The Gift of Death*. Translated by David Wills. Chicago: University of Chicago Press, 1995.

  "Force of Law: The Mystical Foundation of Authority". In *Acts of Religion*, 228–98. New York: Routledge, 2002.

Deutsch, Gotthard, and M. Caimi. "Zante". In *The Jewish Encyclopaedia*. New York: Funk and Wagnalls, 1910, 1906.

Diken, Bülent, and Carsten B. Laustsen. *The Culture of Exception: Sociology Facing the Camp*. London; New York: Routledge, 2005.

Dillon, Brian. "Fragments From a History of Ruin". *Cabinet* 20 (Winter 2005): 55–60.

Dinur, Ben Zion, Yehuda Slutsky, and Shaul Avigur, eds. *History of the Haganah [Sefer Toldot ha-Haganah]*. Vol. 3. Jerusalem: The Zionist Library, 1954.

Domke, Martin. *Trading with Enemy in World War II*. New York: Central Book Co., 1943.

Dothan, Avraham. "Letter to Yitzhak Eylam, Director-General of the Ministry of Labour", 13 August 1957. ISA/GL/13/44881. Israeli State Archives.

Dowty, Alan. *The Jewish State: A Century Later*. Berkeley; London: University of California Press, 1998.

Durkheim, Émile. *The Elementary Forms of the Religious Life*. Translated by Joseph Ward Swain. New York: Free Press, 1965.

Editorial. "Iran: Lost in Translation". The *Guardian*, 22 April 2009, sec. Comment is Free. www.guardian.co.uk/commentisfree/2009/apr/22/mahmoud-ahmadinejad-iran-farsi-speech.

Efrat, Zvi. *The Israeli Project: Building and Architecture 1948–1973 [ha-Proyekt ha-Yisreeli: beniyah ve-adrikhalut, 1948–1973]*. 2 vols. Tel Aviv: Tel Aviv Art Museum, 2004.

Eisenman, Robert. *Islamic Law in Palestine and Israel: A History of the Survival of Tanzimat and Shari'a in the British Mandate and the Jewish State*. Leiden: Brill, 1978.

Elgazi, Gadi. "Between Man and Place. Review of Tamar Berger's 'Dionysus in Dizengof Center'". *Haaretz*, 6 April 1999, sec. Culture and Literature.

Eliade, Mircea. *The Sacred and the Profane: The Nature of Religion*. San Diego: Harcourt Brace Jovanovich, 1987.

Elon, Avraham. *The Givati Brigade in the War of Independence [Hativat Giv`ati be-milhemet ha-komemiyut]*. Tel Aviv: Maàrakhot, 1959.

Evans, Matthew T. "The Sacred: Differentiating, Clarifying and Extending Concepts". *Review of Religious Research* 45, no. 1 (September 2003): 32–47.

Eyal, Gil. *The Disenchantment of the Orient: Expertise in Arab Affairs and the Israeli State*. Stanford, CA: Stanford University Press, 2006.

Ezra, Hezki. " 'We will renew the operation of the club at all cost' ". Channel 7 website, 24 October 2008. www.inn.co.il/News/News.aspx/180803.

Falah, Ghazi. "The 1948 Israeli-Palestinian War and its Aftermath: The Transformation and De-Signification of Palestine's Cultural Landscape". *Annals of the Association of American Geographers* 86, no. 2 (June 1996): 256–85.

Feldman, Jackie. Interview with the author. Conversation with the author, December 2006.

Above the Death Pits, Beneath the Flag: Youth Voyages to Poland and the Performance of Israeli National Identity. New York: Berghahn Books, 2008.

Felsenstein, Daniel, and Aryeh Shahar. "The Geography of the Ma'abarot". In *Immigrants and Maabarot 1948–1952: Sources, Summaries, Selected Episodes and Additional Material ['Olim u-ma'barot, 1948–1952]*, edited by Mordechay Naor, 87–96. Yerushalayim: Yad Yitshak Ben-Tsevi, 1986.

Fenster, Tovi. "Zikaron, Shayachut Ve-tichnun Merhavi Be-yisrael [Memory, Belonging and Spatial Planning in Israel]". *Teoryah Uvikoret [Theory and Criticism]* 30 (2007): 189–212.

Fischbach, Michael R. *Records of Dispossession: Palestinian Refugee Property and the Arab-Israeli Conflict*. The Institute for Palestine Studies Series. New York: Columbia University Press, 2003.

Fishbein, Anat. "Eviction-Construction: The Story of Shekhuat Ha'argazim". Tel Aviv: The Adva Center, April 2003.

Forman, Geremy, and Alexander Kedar. "From Arab Land to 'Israel Lands': The Legal Dispossession of the Palestinians Displaced by Israel in the Wake of 1948". *Environment and Planning. D, Society & Space* 22, no. 6 (2004): 809–30.

Foucault, Michel. *The Order of Things: An Archaeology of the Human Sciences*. New York: Pantheon Books, 1971.

The Archaeology of Knowledge. New York: Pantheon Books, 1972.

Discipline and Punish: The Birth of the Prison. New York: Pantheon Books, 1977.

"Of Other Spaces". *Diacritics* 16 (Spring 1986), 22–7.

Frampton, Kenneth. *Modern Architecture: A Critical History*. Fourth edition. London; New York: Thames & Hudson, 2007.

Freud, Sigmund. "Civilisation and its Discontents". In *The Future of an Illusion: Civilisation and its Discounters and Other Works (1927–1931)*. Vol. 21. *The Standard Edition of the Complete Psychological Works of Sigmund Freud*. London: Vintage, 2001.

The Uncanny. Translated by David McLintock. Penguin Classics. London: Penguin, 2003.

Friedland, Roger, and Richard D. Hecht. "Sacred Urbanism: Jerusalem Sacrality, Urban Sociology and the History of Religions". In *Jerusalem Across the Disciplines*. Tempe: Arizona State University, 2007.

Frishman, Martin. *The Mosque: History, Architectural Development & Regional Diversity*. New York: Thames and Hudson, 1994.

Fulford, Tim, and Peter J. Kitson. *Romanticism and Colonialism: Writing and Empire, 1780–1830*. Cambridge: Cambridge University Press, 1998.

Gaffney, Patrick D. "Masjid". In *Encyclopaedia of Islam and the Muslim World*, edited by Richard C. Martin. New York: Macmillan Reference USA; Thomson/Gale, 2004.

Gal, Sharon. "Big Bang in Nazareth". *Haaretz*, 19 April 1999, sec. B.

Galili, Lily. "Long Division". *Haaretz*, 18 December 2003. www.haaretz.com/hasen/pages/ShArt.jhtml?itemNo=373698.

Garland, David. "What is a 'History of the Present'? On Foucault's Genealogies and Their Critical Preconditions". *Punishment & Society* 16, no. 4 (1 October 2014): 365–84. doi:10.1177/1462474514541711.

Gelber, Yoav. *Palestine, 1948: War, Escape and the Emergence of the Palestinian Refugee Problem*. Brighton; Portland, OR: Sussex Academic Press, 2001.

Gertz, Nurith. *Myths in Israeli Culture: Captives of a Dream*. London: Vallentine-Mitchell, 2000.

Ginsburg, Shai. "Politics and Letters: On the Rhetoric of the Nation in Pinsker and Ahad Ha-Am". *Prooftexts* 29, no. 2 (2009): 173–205.

Golan, Arnon. "From Abandoned Village to Urban Neighbourhood, Kfar Salama 1948–1950". *Merhavim* 4 (1991): 71–85.

"The Transfer to Jewish Control of Abandoned Arab Lands During the War of Independence". In *Israel: The First Decade of Independence*, edited by Ilan S. Troen and Noah Lucas, 403–40. Albany: State University of New York Press, 1995.

"The Transformation of Abandoned Arab Rural Areas". *Israel Studies* 2, no. 1 (1997): 94–110.

Wartime Spatial Changes: Former Arab Territories Within the State of Israel, 1948–1950 [Shinui Merhavi – totsat Milhamah: Ha-shetahim ha-`Arviyim Leshe-`avar bi-Medinat Yisrael, 1948–1950]. Sedeh-boker; Beer-Sheva: Ben-Gurion University of the Negev Press, 2001.

"Jewish Settlement of Former Arab Towns and Their Incorporation into the Israeli Urban System (1948–50)". *Israel Affairs* 9, nos 1–2 (2003): 149–64.

Gonen, Amiram, and Shlomo Hasson. "Public Housing as a Geo-Political Instrument in Israeli Towns". *State, Government and International Relations* 18 (1988): 28–37.

Gordon, Avery. *Ghostly Matters: Haunting and the Sociological Imagination*. Minneapolis, MN: University of Minnesota Press, 1997.

Governmental Borders Committee. "Borders Committee Report on the Jurisdiction of Tel Aviv, Ramat Gan, Bne Brak and Givatayim". *Tel-Aviv Municipality Official Gazette [Yediot iriyat Tel Aviv]* 18, no. 5–6 (January 1949): 73–4.

Granovsky, Abraham. *The Land System in Palestine. History and Structure.* Translated by Maurice Simon. London: Eyre & Spottiswoode, 1952.

Greenberg, Rabbi Dr. Shmuel. "Letter to the Tel Aviv Municipal Sub-Committee for Construction and Urban Development", 18 December 1953. ISA/GL/1/6352.

Groag, Shmuel. "On Conservation and Forgetting". *Block*, no. 4 (2007): 33–6.

Guha, Ranajit. *Elementary Aspects of Peasant Insurgency in Colonial India.* Delhi: Oxford University Press, 1983.

Gvati, Haim. *A Hundred Years of Settlement: The Story of Jewish Settlement in the Land of Israel.* Jerusalem: Keter, 1985.

Hacohen, Dvora. *Immigrants in Turmoil: Mass Immigration to Israel and its Repercussions in the 1950s and After.* Syracuse, NY: Syracuse University Press, 2003.

Halamish, Municipal-Governmental Company for Housing in Gush Dan. *It is time to change your apartment!* (leaflet) n.d., likely late 1960s. TAHMA.

"Kfar Shalem Survey. The Construction and Eviction of Development Areas". Survey. Tel Aviv, 1969. TAMHA.

Halodnivicz, Y. "Letter to Tel Aviv Mayor Haim Levanon", 16 May 1955. TAMHA 4/2224.

Hamblin, W. Kenneth. *The Earth's Dynamic Systems: A Textbook in Physical Geology.* Fourth edition. Minneapolis, MN: Burgess, 1985.

Hasson, Shlomo. *Urban Social Movements in Jerusalem: The Protest of the Second Generation.* Albany, NY: State University of New York Press in Cooperation with the Jerusalem Institute for Israel Studies, 1993.

Hatuka, Tali. *Revisionist Moments: Political Violence, Architecture and Urban Space in Tel Aviv [Rig'e tikun: alimut politit, arkhitekturah yeha-merhav ha-'ironi be-Tel Aviv].* Tel Aviv: Resling, 2008.

Helman, Anat. "Cleanliness and Squalor in Inter-War Tel-Aviv". *Urban History* 31 (2004): 72–99.

Herzl, Theodor. *The Jews' State.* Translated by Henk Overberg. Northvale, NJ: Jason Aronson, 1997.

Hetherington, Kevin. *The Badlands of Modernity: Heterotopia and Social Ordering.* London; New York: Routledge, 1997.

Hever, Hannan. *Producing the Modern Hebrew Canon: Nation Building and Minority Discourse.* Translated by Laurence J. Silberstein. New York: New York University Press, 2002.

"A Map of Sand: From Hebrew Literature to Israeli Literature". In *Coloniality and Postcolonial Condition: Implications for Israeli Society [Kolonyaliyut veha-matsav ha-postkolonyali: antologyah shel targum u-makor],* edited by Yehouda Shenhav, 414–37. Jerusalem: The Van Leer Jerusalem Institute; Hakibbutz Hameuchad Publishers, 2004.

Toward the Longed-For Shore: The Sea in Hebrew Culture and Modern Hebrew Literature [El ha-hof ha-mekuyeh: ha-yam ba-tarbut ha-Ivrit uva-sifrut ha-'Ivrit ha-modernit]. Jerusalem: The Van Leer Jerusalem Institute; Hakibbutz Hameuchad Publishers, 2007.

Hever, Hannan, and Yehouda Shenhav. "Arab Jews – A Genealogy of a Term [ha-Yehudim ha-Aravim: gilgulo shel munach]". *Pe'amim: Studies on Jewish Heritage in the East* 125, no. 27 (2011): 56–74.

Hofnung, Menachem. "States of Emergency and Ethnic Conflict in Liberal Democracies: Great Britain and Israel". *Terrorism and Political Violence* 63 (1994): 340–65.

Hofnung, Menaḥem. *Democracy, Law, and National Security in Israel.* Aldershot; Brookfield: Dartmouth, 1996.

Home, Robert K. *Of Planting and Planning: The Making of British Colonial Cities.* London: Spon, 1997.

Ikas, Karin, and Gerhard Wagner, eds. *Communicating in the Third Space.* New York: Routledge, 2009.

"Introduction". *Teoryah Uvikoret [Theory and Criticism]*, 1 (1991).

Israeli Information Administration. "Pitu'ach ha-karka ve' bitchon ha-medina [Land Development and National Security]". Israeli Information Administration, January 1962. 44.0.5.90. Israeli State Archives.

Jabareen, Yosef. "Response to 'Memory and Planning: Uses and Abuses'". The Van Leer Jerusalem Institute, 2006.

Jacobs, Jane M. *Edge of Empire: Postcolonialism and the City.* London: Routledge, 1996.

Jamieson, Robert L. "Taking the Sting Out of Place Names". 21 July 2004. www. seattlepi.com/jamieson/182919_robert21.html.

Janowitz, Anne F. *England's Ruins: Poetic Purpose and the National Landscape.* Cambridge, MA: Blackwell, 1990.

Jewish National Fund Central Bureau. "Salama C Construction Plan", June 1959. CZA KKL5/25149.

Kadman, Noga. *Erased from Space and Consciousness [Be-tside ha-derekh uve-shule ha-toda'ah: deḥiḳat ha-kefarim ha-'Aravim she-hitroḳenu be-1948 meha-śiaḥ ha-Yiśre'eli].* Jerusalem: November Books, 2008.

Kadmon, Naftali. *Toponomasticon: Geographical Gazetteer of Israel.* Jerusalem: Carta, 1994.

Kamp-Bandau, Irmel, Winfried Nerdinger, and Pe'era Goldman. *Tel Aviv Modern Architecture, 1930–1939.* Tubingen: Wasmuth, 1994.

Katriel, Tamar, and Aliza Shenhar. "Tower and Stockade: Dialogic Narration in Israeli Settlement Ethos". *Quarterly Journal of Speech* 76, no. 4 (1990): 359–80.

Kavuri-Bauer, Santhi. "Architecture." In *Encyclopaedia of Islam and the Muslim World*, edited by Richard C. Martin. New York: Macmillan; Thomson/Gale, 2004.

Kedar, Alexander. "Majority Time, Minority Time: Land, Nationality and Adverse Possession Law in Israel". *'Iyunei Mishpat* 21 (1998): 665–746.

Kemp, Adriana. "Border Space and National Identity in Israel." In *Space, Land, Home [Merhav, Adamah, Bayit]*, edited by Yehouda A. Shenhav. Jerusalem; Tel Aviv: The Van Leer Jerusalem Institute; Hakibbutz Hameuchad Publishers, 2003.

Kemp, Adriana, Uri Ram, and David Newman. *Israelis in Conflict: Hegemonies, Identities and Challenges.* Brighton; Portland, OR: Sussex Academic Press, 2004.

"Kfar Salama Mosque". *Tel Aviv – Yafo Centennial Year 1909–2009*. Accessed 7 April 2009. www.tlv100.co.il/HE/CityVisit/buildings/Pages/bezalel_religion_salame.aspx.

Kfar Shalem Council. "Public petition", 17 April 1972. TAMHA 4/25–2130.

Kfar Shalem Neighbourhood Council. "Letter to Tel Aviv Mayor Shlomo Lahat", 9 March 1981. TAMHA 4/25–3132.

Kfar Shalem Residents. "Objection to the Promulgation of 'Renewal Project' ". Kfar Shalem Survey, Appendix 2.5, n.d.

Kfar Shalem Residents' Council. "Letter to Tel-Aviv Mayor Yehoshua Rabinovich", 7 August 1973. TAMHA 4/2520.

"Public Petition", 14 August 1978. TAMHA 4/25–2131.

Khalidi, Rashid. *Palestinian Identity: The Construction of Modern National Consciousness*. New York: Columbia University Press, 1997.

Khalidi, Walid. *All That Remains: The Palestinian Villages Occupied and Depopulated by Israel in 1948*. Washington, DC: Institute for Palestine Studies, 1992.

Kimmerling, Baruch. *Zionism and Territory: The Socio-Territorial Dimensions of Zionist Politics*. Berkeley: Institute of International Studies, University of California, 1983.

Kincaid, Jamaica. *A Small Place*. New York: Farrar Straus Giroux, 1988.

King, Anthony D. "Exporting Planning: The Colonial and Neo-Colonial Experience". In *Shaping an Urban World: Planning in the 20th Century*, edited by Gordon Cherry, 203–26. New York: St. Martin's Press, 1980.

"Actually Existing Postcolonialisms: Colonial Urbanism and Architecture After the Postcolonial Turn". In *Postcolonial Urbanism: Southeast Asian Cities and Global Processes*, edited by Ryan Bishop, John Phillips, and Wei-Wei Yeo, 167–86. New York; London: Routledge, 2003.

Klaff, Vivian Z. "Residence and Integration in Israel: A Mosaic of Segregated Groups". In *Migration, Ethnicity and Community*, edited by Ernest Krausz, 53–73. New Brunswick, NJ: Transaction Books, 1980.

Kletter, Raz. *Just Past?: The Making of Israeli Archaeology*. London; Oakville, CT: Equinox, 2006.

Klinghoffer, Hans. "On Emergency Regulations in Israel". In *Jubilee to Pinchas Rosen [Sefer yovel le-Pinhas Rozen]*, edited by Haim Cohen, 86–121. Jerusalem: Mifal Hasichpul, 1962.

Kunin, Seth. *God's Place in the World: Sacred Space and Sacred Place in Judaism*. London; New York: Cassell, 1998.

Laor, Yitzhak. *Narratives With No Natives: Essays on Israeli Literature [Anu kotvim otakh moledet: masot al sifrut Yiśre'elit]*. Tel Aviv: Hakibbutz Hameuchad Publishers, 1995.

Law Yone, Hubert, and Rachel Kallus. "The Dynamics of Ethnic Segregation in Israel". In *The Power of Planning: Spaces of Control and Transformation*, edited by Oren Yiftachel, 171–88. Geojournal Library, v. 67. Dordrecht: Kluwer Academic, 2001.

Lears, T. J. Jackson. "The Concept of Cultural Hegemony: Problems and Possibilities". *The American Historical Review* 90, no. 3 (June 1985): 567–93.

Lefebvre, Henri. *The Production of Space*. Malden, MA: Blackwell, 2007.

Lentin, Ronit. "The Memory of Dispossession, Dispossessing Memory: Israeli Networks Commemorising the Nakba". In *Performing Global Networks*, edited by Karen Fricker and Ronit Lentin, 206–20. Newcastle: Cambridge Scholars Publishing, 2007.

Leshem, Noam. "Memory Activism: Reclaiming Spatial Histories in Israel". In *The Politics of Cultural Memory*, edited by Lucy Burke, Simon Faulkner, and James Aulich, 158–81. Newcastle: Cambridge Scholars Publishing, 2010.

Lestringant, Frank. *Mapping the Renaissance World: The Geographical Imagination in the Age of Discovery*. Berkeley: University of California Press, 1994.

Levanon, Yitzhak. Memo to the Governmental Names Committee. "Names of Neighbourhoods in Jaffa etc." Memo to the Government Names Committee, 7 May 1953. TAHMA 4/2212.

LeVine, Mark. *Overthrowing Geography: Jaffa, Tel Aviv, and the Struggle for Palestine, 1880–1948*. Berkeley, CA; London: University of California Press, 2005.

Levinger, Esther. "Socialist-Zionist Ideology in Israeli War Memorials of the 1950s". *Journal of Contemporary History* 28, no. 4 (1993): 715–46.

Liebman, Charles, and Eliezer Don-Yiḥya. *Civil Religion in Israel: Traditional Judaism and Political Culture in the Jewish State*. Berkeley: University of California Press, 1983.

Local Sustainability Center. "The Planting of Temporary Groves in Vacated Areas – Tel Aviv-Jaffa", 10 October 2007. www.kayamut.org.il/site/node/31.

Maduel, Aharon. Interview with the author. Audio recording, 5 May 2009.

Maier, Charles S. "Overcoming the Past? Narrative and Negotiation, Remembering and Reparation: Issues at the Interface of History and the Law". In *Politics and the Past: On Repairing Historical Injustices*, edited by John Torpey, 295–304. Lanham, MD: Rowman & Littlefield Publishers, 2002.

Mann, Barbara. *A Place in History: Modernism, Tel Aviv, and the Creation of Jewish Urban Space*. Stanford, CA: Stanford University Press, 2006.

Mann, Itamar. "Think of 'Habima' as a Tragic Landscape Painting". *Haaretz*, 30 June 2007, sec. Culture and Literature. www.haaretz.co.il/hasite/spages/876351.html.

Masalha, Nur. *Catastrophe Remembered: Palestine, Israel and the Internal Refugees*. London: Zed Books, 2005.

Massey, Doreen. *For Space*. London: Sage, 2005.

Mawani, Renisa. *Colonial Proximities: Crossracial Encounters and Juridical Truths in British Columbia, 1871–1921*. Vancouver: UBC Press, 2009.

Mazor, Lea. "Between Bible and Zionism: Introduction and Sources". *Cathedra* 110 (2003): 101–22.

McGarry, John. "'Demographic Engineering': The State-Directed Movement of Ethnic Groups as a Technique of Conflict Regulation". *Ethnic and Racial Studies* 21, no. 4 (1998): 613–38.

Meir, Golda. *My Life*. London: Weidenfeld and Nicolson, 1975.

Meishar, Naama. "Fragile Guardians: Nature Reserves and Forests Facing Arab Villages". In *Constructing a Sense of Place: Architecture and the Zionist Discourse*, edited by Haim Yacobi, 303–25. Design and the Built Environment Series. Aldershot; Burlington, VT: Ashgate, 2004.

Meyer, Michael A. *The Origins of the Modern Jew: Jewish Identity and European Culture in Germany, 1749–1824*. Detroit: Wayne State University Press, 1967.

Miller, Stuart. *"Benevolent Assimilation": The American Conquest of the Philippines, 1899–1903*. New Haven: Yale University Press, 1982.

Mills, Amy. *Streets of Memory: Landscape, Tolerance, and National Identity in Istanbul*. Athens: University of Georgia Press, 2010.

Milshtain, Uri. *The War of Independence [Toldot milhemet ha-atsmaut]*. Vol. 2 (3 vols). Tel Aviv: Zemora-Bitan, n.d.

Mitchell, Don. *The Lie of the Land: Migrant Workers and the California Landscape*. Minneapolis: University of Minnesota Press, 1996.

Mitchell, W. J. Thomas. *Landscape and Power*. University of Chicago Press, 2002.

Monk, Daniel Bertrand. "Autonomy Agreements: Zionism, Modernism and the Myth of 'Bauhaus' Vernacular". *AA Files* 28 (1994): 94–8.

Moore-Gilbert, Bart. "Spivak and Bhabha". In *A Companion to Postcolonial Studies*, edited by Henry Schwarz and Sangeeta Ray, 451–66. Oxford: Basil Blackwell, 2000.

Morahg, Gilead. "Shading the Truth: A.B. Yehoshua's 'Facing the Forests' ". In *History and Literature: New Readings of Jewish Texts in Honor of Arnold J. Band*, edited by David C. Jacobson and William Cutter, 401–18. Brown Judaic Studies, No. 334. Providence, RI: Program in Judaic Studies, Brown University, 2002.

Morris, Benny. *Righteous Victims: A History of the Zionist-Arab Conflict, 1881–1999*. London: J. Murray, 2000.

   Birth of the Palestinian Refugee Problem Revisited. Cambridge: Cambridge University Press, 2004.

Mousa, Eva. "Beer el-Sabe Municipality Refuses to Allow Muslim Residents and Visitors to Pray in the Big Mosque, Due to Concerns over 'Public Safety and Security' ". *Adalah's Newsletter, Vol. 9*, January 2006. www.adalah.org/newsletter/eng/jan05/mesq.pdf.

Murray, Martin. *Taming the Disorderly City: The Spatial Landscape of Johannesburg After Apartheid*. Ithaca: Cornell University Press, 2008.

Myers, David N. *Re-Inventing the Jewish Past: European Jewish Intellectuals and the Zionist Return to History*. Studies in Jewish History. New York: Oxford University Press, 1995.

Nagid, Haim. "Israel". In *The World Encyclopaedia of Contemporary Theatre*, edited by Don Rubin. London: Routledge, 1994. catalogue.bl.uk Library Catalog.

Navaro-Yashin, Yael. *The Make-Believe Space: Affective Geography in a Postwar Polity*. Durham, NC: Duke University Press, 2012.

Neiger, Moti, Eyal Zandberg, and Assam Abu-Ra'iyeh. "Civil or Ethnic Media? An Evaluation of the Coverage of the October 2000 Violent Clashes Between the Police and Israeli Arab Citizens". Jerusalem: Keshev – The Center for the Protection of Democracy in Israel, 2001. www.keshev.org.il/images/stories/PDF/civil_or_ethnic_media_full_text_heb.pdf.

"News and Views: 'Nigger Creeks' Are Gone but There's Still a Lot of Leftover Racism on the Maps of the United States". *The Journal of Blacks in Higher Education* 26 (2000): 67–8.

Nietzsche, Friedrich. *Untimely Meditations*, edited by Daniel Breazeale. Translated by Reginald John Hollingdale. Cambridge: Cambridge University Press, 1997.

Nimni, Ephraim. *The Challenge of Post-Zionism: Alternatives to Israeli Fundamentalist Politics*. London: Zed Books, 2003.

Nitzan-Shiftan, Alona. "Contested Zionism – Alternative Modernism: Erich Mendelson and the Tel Aviv Chug in Mandate Palestine". In *Constructing a Sense of Place: Architecture and the Zionist Discourse*, edited by Haim Yacobi, 147–80. Design and the Built Environment Series. Aldershot; Burlington, VT: Ashgate, 2004.

Nora, Pierre. "Between Memory and History: Les Lieux de Mémoire". *Representations* no. 26 (Spring 1989): 7–24.

North African Synagogue Salama-Tel Aviv. "Letter to the Ministry of Religious Affairs", 7 September 1950. ISA/GL/3/6536.

"Letter to Tel Aviv Municipality Permits Department", 7 September 1950. ISA/GL/3/6536.

Noyes, John K. *Colonial Space: Spatiality in the Discourse of German South West Africa 1884–1915*. Studies in Anthropology and History, v. 4. Chur, Switzerland; Philadelphia: Harwood Academic Publishers, 1992.

Nuriely, Benny. "Strangers in a National Space: Arab-Jews in the Palestinian Ghetto in Lod". *Teoryah Uvikoret [Theory and Criticism]* 29 (2005): 13–42.

Ofrat, Gideon. *Earth, Man, Blood: The Pioneer Myths and the Rituals of the Land in Settlement Plays [Adamah, adam, dam: Mitos he-haluts u-fulhan ha-adamah be-mahazot ha-hityashvut]*. Tel Aviv: Ts'erikover, 1980.

Olick, Jeffrey K., and Joyce Robbins. "Social Memory Studies: From 'Collective Memory' to the Historical Sociology of Mnemonic Practices". *Annual Review of Sociology* 24 (1998): 105–40.

"Operation 'Hametz': The conquering of the Or Yehouda region". *The Alexandroni Brigade*. Accessed 6 February 2009. www.alexandroni.org/site. php?battle=hamez.

Ophir, Adi. "On Sanctifying the Holocaust: An Anti-Theological Treatise". *Tikkun* 2, no. 1 (1987): 61–7.

Ophir, Adi, ed. *50 to 48: Critical Moments in the History of the State of Israel – Essays and Chronicle [Ḥamishim le-arba'im u-shemonah: momenṭim biḳortiyim be-toldot Medinat Yiśra'el; te'ud eru'im – masot u-ma'amarim]*. Jerusalem: The Van Leer Jerusalem Institute; Hakibbutz Hameuchad Publishers, 1999.

Or, Theodore, Hashem Hatib, and Shimon Shamir. "The Official Commission for the Investigation of Clashes Between the Security Forces and Israeli Citizens in October 2000". Jerusalem, August 2003. www.elyon1.court.gov. il/heb/veadot/or/inside_index.htm.

Oza, Rupal. "The Geography of Hindu Right-Wing Violence in India". In *Violent Geographies: Fear, Terror, and Political Violence*, edited by Derek Gregory and Allan Pred, 153–74. New York: Routledge, 2007.

Padan, Yehiam. *Guide to Tel Aviv-Jaffa Streets [Tel-Aviv-Yafo: Madrikh Ha-reḥovot]*. Tel Aviv: The Tel Aviv Municipality; Milo Publishing House, 2003.

Palestine Royal Commission. "Report Presented by the Secretary of State for the Colonies to Parliament by Command of His Majesty, July 1937". London: HMSO, 7 July 1937.

Papastergiadis, Nikos. "The Invasion Complex: The Abject Other and Spaces of Violence". *Geografiska Annaler: Series B, Human Geography* 88, no. 4 (1 December 2006): 429–42. doi:10.1111/j.0435-3684.2006.00231.x.

Pappé, Ilan. "An Uneasy Coexistence: Arabs and Jews in the First Decade of Statehood". In *Israel: The First Decade of Independence*, edited by Ilan S. Troen and Noah Lucas, 617–58. Albany: State University of New York Press, 1995.

The Ethnic Cleansing of Palestine. Oxford: Oneworld, 2006.

Pawley, Martin. *Architecture Versus Housing*. London: Studio Vista, 1971.

Peled, Shimrit. "Mizrahiuot (Mizrahiness), Ashkenaziuot (Ashkenaziness), and Space in the Israeli Novel after the 1967 War". *Teoryah Uvikoret [Theory and Criticism]* 29 (2006): 149–72.

Perera, Nihal. "Indigenising the Colonial City: Late 19th-century Colombo and its Landscape". *Urban Studies* 39 (2002): 1703–21.

"Contesting Visions: Hybridity, Liminality, and Authorship of the Chandigarh Plan". *Planning Perspectives* 19 (April 2004): 175–99.

Piterberg, Gabriel. *The Returns of Zionism: Myths, Politics and Scholarship in Israel*. London; New York: Verso, 2008.

Plaut, Joshua E. *Greek Jewry in the Twentieth Century, 1913–1983: Patterns of Jewish Survival in the Greek Provinces Before and After the Holocaust*. Madison; London; Cranbury, NJ: Fairleigh Dickinson University Press; Associated University Presses, 1996.

Puggioni, Raffaela. "Resisting Sovereign Power: Camps In-Between Exception and Dissent". In *The Politics of Protection: Sites of Insecurity and Political Agency*, edited by Jef Huysmans, Andrew Dobson, and Raia Prokhovnik. First edition, 68–83. Routledge Advances in International Relations and Global Politics 43. London; New York: Routledge, 2006.

Rabasa, José. *Inventing America: Spanish Historiography and the Formation of Eurocentrism*. First edition. Norman, OK: University of Oklahoma Press, 1993.

Rabinowitz, R. "Club on 16 Righteous Street in Kefar Shalem (in the mosque). Letter to Mrs Hannah Zohar", 9 July 1981. TAMHA 4/25–3132.

Ram, Shelomo. "Letter to Jewish National Fund", 7 May 1956. CZA KKL5/23519.

Ram, Uri. *The Globalization of Israel: McWorld in Tel Aviv, Jihad in Jerusalem*. London; New York: Routledge, 2007.

"Ways of Forgetting: Israel and the Obliterated Memory of the Palestinian Nakba". *Journal of Historical Sociology* 22, no. 3 (1 September 2009): 366–95. doi:10.1111/j.1467-6443.2009.01354.x.

Rapoport, Meron. "Suddenly They Are Called 'Squatters'". *Haaretz*, 25 December 2007. www.haaretz.com/hasen/spages/881760.html.

"A Mosque Once Stood Here". *Haaretz*, 16 September 2009. www.haaretz.com/hasen/pages/ShArt.jhtml?itemNo=625854.

Raulff, Ulrich. "Interview with Giorgio Agamben – Life, A Work of Art Without an Author: The State of Exception, the Administration of Disorder and Private Life". *German Law Journal* 5 (1 May 2004): 609–14.

Robin, Ron. "The Necropolitics of Homeland: The Role of Tombs and Village Cemeteries in the Middle East Conflict". In *Homelands: Poetic Power and the*

Politics of Space, edited by Bo Stråth and Ron Robin, 209–19. Bruxelles; New York: P.I.E.-Peter Lang, 2003.

Robinson, Jennifer. *Ordinary Cities: Between Modernity and Development*. London: Routledge, 2006.

Rokach, Yisrael. "On Greater Tel Aviv". *Tel-Aviv Municipality Official Gazette [Yediot iriyat Tel Aviv]* 19, nos 5–6 (December 1949): 73–4.

Rosen-Zvi, Issachar. *Taking Space Seriously: Law, Space, and Society in Contemporary Israel*. Aldershot; Burlington, VT: Ashgate, 2004.

Rotbard, Sharon. *White City, Black City [`Ir levanah, `ir shehorah]*. Tel Aviv: Bavel, 2005.

"Stockade and Tower: The Pattern of Israeli Architecture". *Sedek* 2 (January 2008): 35–49.

Roth, Michael S., Claire L. Lyons, and Charles Merewether, eds. *Irresistible Decay: Ruins Reclaimed*. Bibliographies & Dossiers 2. Los Angeles, CA: The Getty Research Institute for the History of Art and the Humanities, 1997.

Rubin, Yariv, and Ofer Pinkhasov. *License to Live [Rishayon Likhyot]*. Documentary, 2007.

Rutherford, Jonathan. "The Third Space: Interview with Homi Bhabha". In *Identity: Community, Culture, Difference*, 207–21. London: Lawrence and Wishart, 1990.

Ryan, Simon. "Inscribing the Emptiness: Cartography, Exploration and the Construction of Australia". In *De-Scribing Empire: Post Colonialism and Textuality*, edited by Chris Tiffin and Alan Lawson, 115–30. London; New York: Routledge, 1994.

The Cartographic Eye: How Explorers Saw Australia. Cambridge [England]; New York: Cambridge University Press, 1996.

Sa'di, Ahmad H., and Lila Abu-Lughod, eds. *Nakba: Palestine, 1948, and the Claims of Memory*. Cultures of History. New York: Columbia University Press, 2007.

Sahar, Yehezqel. *My Life Story [Sippur Hayyay]*. Tel-Aviv: Israel Ministry of Defence Press, 1992.

Said, Edward. *Orientalism*. New York: Pantheon Books, 1978.

Sanders, Mark. *Complicities: The Intellectual and Apartheid*. Durham, NC: Duke University Press, 2003.

Schein, Richard. "The Place of Landscape: A Conceptual Framework for Interpreting an American Scene". *Annals of the Association of American Geographers* 87, no. 4 (1997): 660–80.

Schmitt, Carl. *The Nomos of the Earth in the International Law of the Jus Publicum Europaeum*. New York: Telos Press, 2003.

Segev, Tom. *1967: Israel, the War, and the Year That Transformed the Middle East*. New York: Metropolitan Books, 2008.

Shafir, Gershon. *Land, Labor and the Origins of the Israeli-Palestinian Conflict, 1882–1914*. Berkeley: University of California Press, 1996.

Shai, Aron. "The Fate of Abandoned Arab Villages in Israel, 1965–1969". *History & Memory* 18, no. 2 (2006): 86–106.

Shamir, Ronen. "Suspended in Space: Bedouins Under the Law of Israel". *Law and Society Review* 30, no. 2 (1996): 231–58.

Shapira, Anita. "Hirbet Hizah: Between Remembrance and Forgetting". *Jewish Social Studies* 7, no. 1 (2000): 1–62.

Land and Power: The Zionist Resort to Force, 1881–1948. Studies in Jewish History. New York: Oxford University Press, 1992.

"The Holocaust: Private Memories, Public Memory". *Jewish Social Studies* 4, no. 2 (1 January 1998): 40–58. doi:10.2307/4467520.

Shapira, Anita, and Derek Jonathan Penslar. *Israeli Historical Revisionism: From Left to Right*. Potland, OR: Frank Cass, 2003.

Shapira, Moshe Haim. "On the Annexation and it Causes". *Tel-Aviv Municipality Official Gazette [Yediot iriyat Tel Aviv]* 19, nos 5–6 (December 1949): 73–4.

"The Annexation of Jaffa – Bond and Bridge Between Past and Future". *Tel-Aviv Municipality Official Gazette [Yediot iriyat Tel Aviv]* 23, nos 1–3 (1950): 1.

Sharon, Arieh. "Planning in Israel". *Town and Planning Review* 23, no. 1 (April 1952): 66–82.

Sharon, Smadar. "Planners, the State, and the Shaping of National Space in the 1950s". *Teoryah Uvikoret [Theory and Criticism]* 29 (Autumn 2006): 31–57.

Shenhav, Yehouda. *The Arab Jews: A Postcolonial Reading of Nationalism, Religion, and Ethnicity*. Stanford, CA: Stanford University Press, 2006.

Shimony, Batya. *On the Threshold of Redemption: The Story of the Ma'abara – First and Second Generation ['Al saf ha-ge'ulah: sipur ha-ma'abarah – dor rishon ye-sheni]*. Or Yehudah: Kinneret, Zmora-Bitan; Dvir, 2008.

Shohat, Ella. "Reflections of an Arab Jew". *Against the Current* 18 (2003): 13–14.

Silberstein, Laurence. *The Postzionism Debates: Knowledge and Power in Israeli Culture*. New York: Routledge, 1999.

Simone, AbdouMaliq. *For the City Yet to Come: Changing African Life in Four Cities*. Durham: Duke University Press, 2004.

Simpson, James. *The Oxford English Literary History: 1350–1547: Reform and Cultural Revolution*. Vol. 2. Oxford: Oxford University Press, 2002.

Sivan, Emmanuel. "To Remember is to Forget: Israel's 1948 War". *Journal of Contemporary History* 28, no. 2 (1 April 1993): 341–59. doi: 10.2307/260714.

Slyomovics, Susan. *The Object of Memory: Arab and Jew Narrate the Palestinian Village*. Philadelphia: University of Pennsylvania Press, 1998.

Soja, Edward. *Postmodern Geographies: The Reassertion of Space in Critical Social Theory*. London; New York: Verso, 1989.

Thirdspace: Journeys to Los Angeles and Other Real-and-Imagined Places. Cambridge, MA: Blackwell, 1996.

"Thirdspace: Toward a New Consciousness of Space and Spatiality". In *Communicating in the Third Space*, edited by Karin Ikas and Gerhard Wagner, 49–61. New York: Routledge, 2008.

Spivak, Gayatri Chakravorty. "Can the Subaltern Speak?" In *Marxism and the Interpretation of Culture*, edited by Cary Nelson and Lawrence Grossberg, 271–313. Urbana, IL: University of Illinois Press, 1988.

State of Israel. *Absentees' Property Law*, 1950.

Amendment no. 40 (2011) to the Budgets Foundations Law (1985) – Reducing Budget or Support for Activity Contrary to the Principles of the State, 2011. www.knesset.gov.il/Laws/Data/law/2286/2286.pdf.

State of Israel Provisional Council. *Abandoned Areas Ordinance*, 1948.

Law and Administration Ordinance, 1948.

Steinberg, Jonny. *Midlands*. Johannesburg; Cape Town: Jonathan Ball Publishers, 2002.

Stewart, Kathleen. *A Space on the Side of the Road: Cultural Poetics in an "Other" America*. Princeton: Princeton University Press, 1996.

"Road Registers". *Cultural Geographies* 21, no. 4 (1 October 2014): 549–63. doi:10.1177/1474474014525053.

Stoler, Ann Laura. "Imperial Debris: Reflections on Ruins and Ruination". *Cultural Anthropology* 23, no. 2 (2008): 191–219.

Along the Archival Grain: Epistemic Anxieties and Colonial Common Sense. Princeton, NJ: Princeton University Press, 2009.

Tal, David. *War in Palestine, 1948: Strategy and Diplomacy*. Cass series – Israeli History, Politics, and Society. London; New York: Routledge, 2004.

Tel Aviv Municipal Council. "Meeting Protocol", 26 December 1982. TAHMA 4/25–3132.

Tel Aviv Municipal Council Forum. "Meeting Protocol", 16 July 2006. www. meitallehavi.com/_Uploads/dbsAttachedFiles/protocol16.pdf.

Tel Aviv Municipal Names Committee. "For the Assignment of Names to Tel Aviv's Streets", 22 March 1942. TAMHA 4/25–2629.

Tel Aviv Regional Governance. "Demarcation of Streets and Houses". Letter to Tel Aviv Mayor, February 1954. TAMHA 4/2212.

"The Black Panthers in Israel Archive". *The Israeli Left Archive*. Accessed 2 July 2009. www.israeli-left-archive.org/?site=localhost&a=p&p=about&c=blackpan&ct=1&qto=3&l=en&w=utf-8.

The Committee for Locating and Preserving Sites in Jerusalem. "Meeting Protocol", 24 February 1963. ISA/GL/2/44889.

The Israeli Labor Movement. "Nir Etzion – Communal Village". The Israeli Labor Movement. Accessed 31 January 2009. www.tnuathaavoda.info/zope/home/100/places/1169114473/.

The Settlement Department. "Monthly Reports for the Haifa Region", May 1949. CZA 15S 9388.

"The Street Names of Israeli Jaffa". *Tel Aviv-Jaffa Municipality Official Gazette [Yediot iriyat Tel Aviv-Yaffo]* 22, nos 1–3 (1954): 25.

Tiffin, Chris, and Allan Lawson, eds. *De-Scribing Empire: Post-colonialism and Textuality*. London; New York: Routledge, 1994.

Till, Karen E. *The New Berlin: Memory, Politics, Place*. Minneapolis: University of Minnesota Press, 2005.

"Wounded Cities: Memory-Work and a Place-Based Ethics of Care". *Political Geography* 31, no. 1 (January 2012): 3–14.

"Towards an Inclusive Archeology in Jerusalem", n.d.

Turner, Frederick. *The Frontier in American History*. New York: Holt, Rinehart and Winston, 1962.

Tzur, Muki, and Sharon Rotbard, eds. *Neither in Jaffa Nor in Tel Aviv: Stories, Testimonies and Documents from Shapira Neighborhood*. Tel Aviv: Bavel, 2009.

"US Board on Geographic Names (BGN)". Accessed 17 September 2009. www. geonames.usgs.gov/index.html.

United Nations. *Resolution 181, Session 1 – Future Government of Palestine.* A/RES/181(II)(A+B), 1947.

"Unsigned Logbook Entry", 2 May 1948. Hagana Archives 105/94.

"Unsigned Memo to Mordechai Vershuvski", n.d. TAMHA 4/25–2130.

Virshuvski, Mordechai. "Internal Memo to Mayor Rabinowitz", 14 June 1972. TAMHA 4/25–2130.

Vital, David. *The Origins of Zionism.* Oxford: Clarendon, 1980.

Vladislavic, Ivan. *Portrait with Keys: The City of Johannesburg Unlocked.* London: Portobello, 2006.

Weingrod, Alex. "Changing Israeli Landscapes: Buildings and the Uses of the Past". *Cultural Anthropology* 8, no. 3 (1993): 370–87.

Weiss, Yfaat. *A Confiscated Memory: Wadi Salib and Haifa's Lost Heritage.* New York: Columbia University Press, 2011.

Welter, Volker. *Biopolis: Patrick Geddes and the City of Life.* Cambridge, MA: MIT Press, 2002.

Werbner, Pnina. "Global Pathways. Working Class Cosmopolitans and the Creation of Transnational Ethnic Worlds". *Social Anthropology* 7, no. 1 (1999): 17–35. doi: 10.1017/S0964028299000026.

Winograd, Eliyahu, Yaacov Zemach, and Avigdor Mishaeli. "The Committee for the Examination of Events in Kefar Shalem". Investigation Commission. Jerusalem: State of Israel, 14 March 1983. TAMHA 25–3132.

Yacobi, Haim. "The Daily Life in Lod: On Power, Identity and Spatial Protest in the Mixed City of Lod". *Jamaa* (2003): 69–109.

 "'The Third Place': Architecture, Nationalism and Postcolonialism", *Teoryah Uvikoret [Theory and Criticism]* 30 (Spring 2007): 63–88.

 "Architecture, Orientalism and Identity: The Politics of the Israeli-Built Environment". *Israel Studies* 13, no. 1 (2008): 94–118.

 "From State-Imposed Urban Planning to Israeli Diasporic Place: The Case of Netivot and the Grave of Baba Sali". In *Jewish Topographies: Visions of Space, Traditions of Place,* edited by Julia Brauch, Anna Lipphardt, and Alexandra Nocke, 63–80. Aldershot; Burlington VT: Ashgate, 2008.

 The Jewish-Arab City: Spatio-Politics in a Mixed Community. London; New York: Routledge, 2009.

Yahav, Dan. *Yaffo, Bride of the Sea: From Central City to a Slum, a Model of Spatial Inequality [Yafo, kalat ha-yam: me-'ir rioshah li-shekhunot 'oni, degem le-i-shiyyon merhavi].* Tel Aviv: Tamuz, 2004.

Yakira, Elhanan. *Post-Zionism, Post-Holocaust: Three Essays on Denial, Repression, and Relegitimation of Israel [Post-Tsiyonut, Post-Sho'ah: Sheloshah Perakim "al Hakhashah, Hashkahah U-Shelilat Yiśra"el].* Tel Aviv: Am Oved, 2006.

Yehoshua, A. B. *The Continuing Silence of a Poet: The Collected Stories of A.B. Yehoshua.* London: Flamingo, 1990.

Yeoh, Brenda. *Contesting Space: Power Relations and the Urban Built Environment in Colonial Singapore.* Kuala Lumpur; New York: Oxford University Press, 1996.

Yerushalmi, Yosef Haim. *Zakhor: Jewish History and Jewish Memory.* Seattle: University of Washington Press, 1982.

Yiftachel, Oren. "The Internal Frontier: Territorial Control and Ethnic Relations in Israel". In *Ethnic Frontiers and Peripheries: Landscapes of Development and*

Inequality in Israel, edited by Avinoam Meir and Oren Yiftachel, 39–68. Boulder, CO; Oxford: Westview, 1998.

Ethnocracy: Land and Identity Politics in Israel Palestine. Philadelphia: University of Pennsylvania Press, 2006.

Yiftachel, Oren, and Erez Tzfadia. "Between Periphery and 'Third Space': Identity of Mizrahim in Israel's Development Towns". In *Israelis in Conflict: Hegemonies, Identities and Challenges*, edited by Adriana Kemp, David Newman, Uri Ram, and Oren Yiftachel, 203–35. Brighton [England]; Portland, OR: Sussex Academic Press, 2004.

Yizhar, S. "The Story of Hirbet Hiz'ah". In *Caravan; a Jewish Quarterly Omnibus*, edited by Jacob Sonntag and Stefan Zweig. New York: Yoseloff, 1962.

Young, James E. *The Texture of Memory: Holocaust Memorials and Meaning*. New Haven: Yale University Press, 1993.

Zakim, Eric. *To Build and Be Built: Landscape, Literature, and the Construction of Zionist Identity*. Philadelphia: University of Pennsylvania Press, 2006.

Zamir, Yitzhak. "Human Rights and National Security". *Israel Law Review* 23, nos 2–3 (1989): 375–406.

Zeeligman, Isaac Leo. "Signs of Changes and Editorial Alterations in the Massorah and the Septuagint". In *Studies in Biblical Literature [Mehkarim besifrut mikra'it]*, edited by Avi Horowitz, Emanuel Tov, and Sarah Yefet. Jerusalem: The Hebrew University Magnes Press, 1992.

Zertal, Idith. *Israel's Holocaust and the Politics of Nationhood*. Cambridge; New York: Cambridge University Press, 2005.

Zerubavel, Yael. *Recovered Roots: Collective Memory and the Making of Israeli National Tradition*. Chicago: University of Chicago Press, 1995.

"The Forest as a National Icon: Literature, Politics, and the Archaeology of Memory". *Israel Studies* 1, no. 1 (1996): 60–99.

Zohar, Hannah. "Letter to Tel Aviv Mayor Shlomo Lahat", 10 June 1981. TAHMA 4/25–3132.

Index

Abu Kabir, 3
Agamben, Georgio, 79–80, 84n31, 85
Agnon, S.Y., 51
agricultural lands, 68n85, 86, 137, 148
agricultural settlement, 49, 53, 54
Ahad Ha'am, 49–51, 52
ambivalence, 23, 56, 60, 69, 89, 112, 119–20,
    155, 164, 168–9
Amwas, 68
Anielewicz, Mordechai, 169–71, 170f6.2,
    See also monuments
antagonism and conflict, 27, 28, 152–3
    disillusionment, 84, 93, 96–7, 132, 139, 148
    protest against house demolition, 73–4,
        194, 206
    spatial manifestations, 68
Appadurai, Arjun, 65
Arab property, 42, 83n25, 97, 175n44
    "invasion", 14, 60, 67, 73, 84–5, 92, 97,
        98, 99, 102
    expropriation, 22, 55, 79, 82, 83, 92, 100,
        101–2, 180, 207
    settling Jews in, 10, 16, 83–4, 85
Arab space
    and political dissent, 28, 74, 137, 191
    as backward, 61, 128, 141
    as empty, 41, 52, 53, 54, 58, 128, 210–11
    as third space, 25
    legal status, 35, 81–3, 100
    political transformation, 11, 27–8, 35–6,
        113, 164, 182
    resilience, 16–17, 35, 128, 129, 141, 186,
        190, 198, 212
Arab-Jews, 89, 130, 154
    spatial dimensions, 23, 24–5, 88–9, 204
    theorisation, 23–4, 199, 201–2
archaeology, 57, 58, 61, 63
archaeology of the surface, 70
archive, 29–30, 41, 48, 52, 64, 68
    and ruins, 70
    spatial, 39, 75, 191

art, 10, 69, 189n86
Azaryahu, Maoz, 107, 109, 114, 123,
    123n61
Azoulay, Ariella, 100n76, 105, 208

Balasi, Dudu, 40–1, 71
Ballas, Shimon, 88–90
Bat Yam, 2, 4
Bauhaus, 134n7, 166
Bedouin, 95, 97n71, 98n74, 139, 206
Beersheba, 65, 195n101
Beit Govrin, 65
Beit Nuba, 68
Ben Gurion, David, 5, 55, 57–8, 67, 85, 86
Benjamin, Shlomit, 23, 24, 25, 175n44
Benjamin, Walter, 101
Benvenisti, Meron, 52
Ben-Yishai, A.Z., 112
Berger, Tamar, 22–3
Bethlehem, Louise, 26, 207n15
Bhabha, Homi, 23, 25, 26, 64n69, 129, 130,
    155–6, 157, *See also* third-space
biblical Israel, 49, 50, 114, 115
Bir'em, 68
Black Panthers, 152–3, *See also* antagonism
    and conflict
Brenner, Yossef Haim, 49, 51, 52, 60
Busi Dudu, 125

Carter, Paul, 14, 21–2, 29, 31, 111, 191,
    See also spatial history
cartography, 32, 51, *See also* maps
cemeteries and graves, 5, 41, 172, 180–1,
    185, 188, 193, *See also* religious sites
Chakrabarty, Dipesh, 137n17
Chatterjee, Partha, 156
civilising mission, 117, 118, 119, 134
clean slate, 46, 126, 133
collective memory, 25, 33, 64, 73, 86, 106–
    7, 118, 192, 209–10, 213–14, *See also*
    commemoration

Other Books in the Series